FIX-IT and FORGET-IT®

Lazy AND Slow COOKBOOK

FIX-IT and FORGET-IT®
Lazy AND Slow
COOKBOOK

365 Days of Slow Cooker Recipes

HOPE COMERFORD
PHOTOGRAPHS BY BONNIE MATTHEWS

Good Books

New York, New York

Good Books books may be purchased in bulk at special discounts for sales promotion, corporate gifts, fund-raising, or educational purposes. Special editions can also be created to specifications. For details, contact the Special Sales Department, Good Books, 307 West 36th Street, 11th Floor, New York, NY 10018 or info@skyhorsepublishing.com.

Good Books is an imprint of Skyhorse Publishing, Inc.®, a Delaware corporation.

Visit our website at www.goodbooks.com.

10 9 8 7 6 5 4 3 2 1

Library of Congress Cataloging-in-Publication Data is available on file.

Cover design by Laura Klynstra
Cover photo courtesy of istockphoto.com

Print ISBN: 978-1-68099-174-1
Ebook ISBN: 978-1-68099-175-8

Printed in China

Table of Contents

Acknowledgments

I would like to extend a tremendous thank-you to the Fix-It and Forget-It community for welcoming me to this "family" and making my transition here such a positive one. I would also like to thank my husband, children, family, and friends who encouraged me every step of the way with their love and support. I am beyond grateful for each and every one of you!

Welcome to Fix-It and Forget-It Lazy and Slow!

Let's be honest: we all love our slow cookers! We are able to keep our house cool on hot days, keep our family fed on busy days, feed our friends on the go, and feed ourselves on lazy days! We know slow cookers aren't just for using in the winter. This book was designed to feed your family a delicious, home-cooked meal *every* day of the year, week by week, Sunday through Saturday. Yup! All 365 days. All 52 weeks. I've also done my best to include recipes for most of the major holidays. To make your lives even easier, I've included weekly shopping lists.

Let's talk about how this book works . . .

This book is divided into four seasons; Spring, Summer, Fall, Winter. Each season has thirteen weeks' worth of recipes. Each week begins on a Sunday and ends on a Saturday. You'll have a shopping list at the beginning of each week to make your trip to the grocery store a breeze. I've designed each week so you can eat a variety of recipes, all while using the leftovers from your previous meals. So often, we let all this good food we prepare go bad in the fridge! By using our leftovers to make another meal or two, you should hopefully have a bit less waste.

I encourage you to read through the entire week's worth of recipes before hitting the grocery store along with the shopping list. Personalize it! Change your protein, veggie, etc. if there is something else you prefer instead. If you prefer to serve your meal with pasta instead of rice, or quinoa instead of pasta, go for it! Just be sure to make these notes on your weekly shopping lists so you come home from the grocery store with the ingredients you need.

Each shopping list is divided into categories to make your grocery store trip efficient. The lists include a section called "Do You Have These On Hand?" for common ingredients you might already have in your home, but you may find you already have things from other categories as well. For example, "½ cup butter" may be listed in the "Dairy and Refrigerated" section. You may already have this. In this case, just cross it off your list. However, there may be "4 Granny Smith apples" listed under "Produce" and you may only have two apples. Just change the quantity on the list for yourself.

Sometimes you'll see "optional" next to certain ingredients on the weekly shopping list. This means it may be a topping or optional ingredient in a recipe for the week. This is another reason I encourage you to read through the whole week's worth of recipes before you shop for the week. You might want the optional lettuce on your tacos, but not the avocado. Or, you may like pepperoncini on your tacos, but not lettuce. You get the idea. Like I said, change up your shopping list if something doesn't work for you.

Since most holidays change days of the week from year to year, you may need to rearrange your week a bit for the recipes to fit exactly with the holiday.

A Few Things You Should Know . . .

Not all slow cookers are created equal . . . or work equally as well for everyone!

Those of us who use slow cookers frequently know we have our own preferences when it comes to which slow cooker we choose to use. For instance, I *love* my programmable slow cooker, but there are many programmable slow cookers I've tried that I've strongly disliked. Why? Because some go by increments of 15 or 30 minutes and some go by 4, 6, 8, or 10 hours. I dislike those restrictions, but I have family and friends who don't mind them at all! I am also pretty brand loyal when it comes to my manual slow cookers because I've had great success with those and have had unsuccessful moments with slow cookers of other brands. So, which slow cooker(s) is/are best for your household?

It really depends on how many people you're feeding and if you're gone for long periods of time. Here are my recommendations:

For 2–3 person household	3–5 quart slow cooker
For 4–5 person household	5–6 quart slow cooker
For a 6+ person household	6½–7 quart slow cooker

Large slow cooker advantages/disadvantages:

Advantages:

- You can fit a loaf pan or a baking dish into a 6- or 7-quart, depending on the shape of your cooker. That allows you to make bread or cakes, or even smaller quantities of main dishes. (Take your favorite baking dish and loaf pan along when you shop for a cooker to make sure they'll fit inside.)

- You can feed large groups of people, or make larger quantities of food, allowing for leftovers, or meals, to freeze.

Disadvantages:

- They take up more storage room.

- They don't fit as neatly into a dishwasher.

- If your crock isn't ⅔–¾ full, you may burn your food.

Small slow cooker advantages/disadvantages:

Advantages:

- They're great for lots of appetizers, for serving hot drinks, for baking cakes straight in the crock, and for dorm rooms or apartments.

- Great option for making recipes of smaller quantities.

Disadvantages:

- Food in smaller quantities tends to cook more quickly than larger amounts. So keep an eye on it.

- Chances are, you won't have many leftovers. So, if you like to have leftovers, a smaller slow cooker may not be a good option for you.

My recommendation:

Have at least two slow cookers; one around 3 to 4 quarts and one 6 quarts or larger. A third would be a huge bonus (and a great advantage to your cooking repertoire!). The advantage of having at least a couple is you can make a larger variety of recipes. Also, you can make at least two or three dishes at once for a whole meal.

Manual vs. programmable

If you are gone for only six to eight hours a day, a manual slow cooker might be just fine for you. If you are gone for more than eight hours during the day, I would highly recommend purchasing a programmable slow cooker that will switch to warm when the cook time you set is up. It will allow you to cook a wider variety of recipes.

The two I use most frequently are my 4-quart manual slow cooker and my 6½-quart programmable slow cooker. I like that I can make smaller portions in my 4-quart slow cooker on days I don't need or want leftovers, but I also love how my 6½-quart slow cooker can accommodate whole chickens, turkey breasts, hams, or big batches of soups. I use them both often.

Get to know your slow cooker . . .

Plan a little time to get acquainted with your slow cooker. Each slow cooker has its own personality—just like your oven (and your car). Plus, many new slow cookers cook hotter and faster than earlier models. I think that with all of the concern for food safety, the slow cooker manufacturers have amped up their settings so that "High," "Low," and "Warm" are all higher temperatures than in the older models. That means they cook hotter—and therefore, faster—than the first slow cookers. The beauty of these little machines is that they're supposed to cook low and slow. We count on that when we flip the switch in the morning before we leave the house for ten hours or so. So, because none of us knows what kind of temperament our slow cooker has until we try it out, nor how hot it cooks—don't assume anything. Save yourself a disappointment and make the first recipe in your new slow cooker on a day when you're at home. Cook it for the shortest amount of time the recipe calls for. Then, check the food to see if it's done. Or if you start smelling food that seems to be finished, turn off the cooker and rescue your food.

Also, all slow cookers seem to have a "hot spot," which is of great importance to know, especially when baking with your slow cooker. This spot may tend to burn food in that area if you're not careful. If you're baking directly in your slow cooker, I recommend covering the "hot spot" with some foil.

Take notes . . .

Don't be afraid to make notes in your cookbook. It's yours! Chances are, it will eventually get passed down to someone in your family and they will love and appreciate all of your musings. Take note of which slow cooker you used and exactly how long it took to cook the recipe. The next time you make it, you won't need to try to remember. Apply what you learned to the next recipes you make in your cooker. If another recipe says it needs to cook 7–9 hours, and you've discovered your slow cooker cooks on the faster side, cook that recipe for 6–6½ hours and then check it. You can always cook a recipe longer—but you can't reverse things if it's overdone.

Get creative . . .

If you know your morning is going to be hectic, prepare everything the night before, take it out so the crock warms up to room temperature when you first get up in the morning, then plug it in and turn it on as you're leaving the house.

If you want to make something that has a short cook time and you're going to be gone longer than that, cook it the night before and refrigerate it for the next day. Warm it up when you get home. Or, cook those recipes on the weekend when you know you'll be home and eat them later in the week.

Slow Cooking Tips and Tricks and Other Things You May Not Know

- Slow cookers tend to work best when they're ⅔ to ¾ of the way full. You may need to increase the cooking time if you've exceeded that amount, or reduce it if you've put in less than that. If you're going to exceed that limit, it would be best to reduce the recipe, or split it between two slow cookers. (Remember how I suggested owning at least two or three slow cookers?)

- Keep your veggies on the bottom. That puts them in more direct contact with the heat. The fuller your slow cooker, the longer it will take its contents to cook. Also, the more densely packed the cooker's contents are, the longer they will take to cook. And finally, the larger the chunks of meat or vegetables, the more time they will need to cook.

- Keep the lid on! Every time you take a peek, you lose 20 minutes of cooking time. Please take this into consideration each time you lift the lid! I know, some of you can't help yourself and are going to lift anyway. Just don't forget to tack on 20 minutes to your cook time for each time you peeked!

- Sometimes it's beneficial to remove the lid. If you'd like your dish to thicken a bit, take the lid off during the last half hour to hour of cooking time.

- If you have a big slow cooker (7- to 8-quart), you can cook a small batch in it by putting the recipe ingredients into an oven-safe baking dish or baking pan and then placing that into the cooker's crock. First, put a trivet or some metal jar rings on the bottom of the crock, and then set your dish or pan on top of them. Or a loaf pan may "hook onto" the top ridges of the crock belonging to a large oval cooker and hang there straight and securely, "baking" a cake or quick bread. Cover the cooker and flip it on.

- The outside of your slow cooker will be hot! Please remember to keep it out of reach of children and keep that in mind for yourself as well!

- Get yourself a quick-read meat thermometer and use it! This helps remove the question of whether or not your meat is fully cooked, and helps prevent you from overcooking your meat as well.

- Internal Cooking Temperatures:
  - Beef—125–130°F (rare); 140–145°F (medium); 160°F (well-done)
  - Pork—140–145°F (rare); 145–150°F (medium); 160°F (well-done)
  - Turkey and Chicken—165°F

- Frozen meat: The basic rule of thumb is, don't put frozen meat into the slow cooker. The meat does not reach the proper internal temperature in time. This especially applies to thick cuts of meat! Proceed with caution!

- Add fresh herbs 10 minutes before the end of the cooking time to maximize their flavor.
- If your recipe calls for cooked pasta, add it 10 minutes before the end of the cooking time if the cooker is on High; 30 minutes before the end of the cooking time if it's on Low. Then the pasta won't get mushy.
- If your recipe calls for sour cream or cream, stir it in 5 minutes before the end of the cooking time. You want it to heat but not boil or simmer.
- Approximate Slow Cooker Temperatures (Remember, each slow cooker is different):
  - High—212°F–300°F
  - Low—170°F–200°F
  - Simmer—185°F
  - Warm—165°F
- Cooked beans freeze well. Store them in freezer bags (squeeze the air out first) or freezer boxes. Cooked and dried bean measurements:
  - 16-oz. can, drained = about 1¾ cups beans
  - 19-oz. can, drained = about 2 cups beans
  - 1 lb. dried beans (about 2½ cups) = 5 cups cooked beans

SPRING

Week 1

THIS WEEK'S
Menu

Sunday: Orchard Ham
Monday: Split Pea Soup
Tuesday: Ham 'n' Apple Cheese Pie
Wednesday: Baked Lamb Shanks
Thursday: Lamb Rice
Friday: Easy Creamy Chicken
Saturday: Comforting Chicken and Stuffing

Recommended Side Dish: Green Bean Casserole
Special Dessert: Hot Fudge Cake

Shopping List

PROTEIN

5–6 lb. bone-in ham

5 lamb shanks

10 boneless skinless
   chicken thighs

FROZEN

2 lb. bag frozen green beans

DAIRY and REFRIGERATED

4 cups apple cider or apple
   juice

2¾ sticks butter

6–8 slices mild cheese of
   your choice

½ cup shredded cheese of
   your choice

2 cups reduced-fat
   sour cream

2 eggs

½ cup milk

PRODUCE

1 cup diced or thinly sliced
   carrots

2 small carrots

2 cups chopped celery

1 rib celery

1 medium onion

1 small onion

2–3 tart apples

CANNED/DRY GOODS

2 10¾-oz. cans cream of
   chicken soup

8-oz. can tomato sauce

1¼ cups golden seedless raisins

3 cups dried split peas

1 cup pinenuts

2 cups long-grain basmati
   rice, uncooked

2 envelopes dry onion soup
   mix

Download this shopping list to your
smartphone!
(x.co/ShopList)

12 cups day-old bread cubes	poultry seasoning
	4 cloves garlic
DO YOU HAVE THESE ON HAND?	flour
	sugar
dry mustard	2¾ cups brown sugar
ground cloves	unsweetened cocoa powder
garlic powder	baking powder
dried oregano	vanilla extract
salt	1½ cups chocolate chips
pepper	4 cups chicken stock
dried thyme	2½ cups chicken broth
bay leaves	
allspice	**SPIRITS**
dried parsley flakes	½ cup dry white wine
rubbed sage	

Orchard Ham

Phyllis Good, Lancaster, PA

Makes 6–8 servings

Prep. Time: 20 minutes
Cooking Time: 8½–10½ hours
Ideal slow-cooker size: 4- or 5-qt.

5–6-lb. bone-in ham (or
    larger; whatever fits your
    slow cooker)
4 cups cider, or apple juice
1 cup brown sugar
2 tsp. dry mustard
1 tsp. ground cloves
1¼ cups golden seedless
    raisins

1. Place ham in slow cooker. Pour cider over meat.
2. Cover. Cook on Low 8–10 hours.
3. While the ham is cooking, make a paste by mixing brown sugar, dry mustard, cloves, and a few tablespoons of hot cider from the cooker in a bowl. Set aside.
4. At the end of the cooking time, remove ham from cider and place in a 9×13-inch baking pan, or one that's big enough to hold the ham.
5. Brush paste over ham. Then pour a cup of juice from the slow cooker into the baking pan. (Don't pour it over the ham; you don't want to wash off the paste.) Stir raisins into the cider in the baking pan.
6. Bake at 375° for 20–30 minutes, or until the paste has turned into a glaze.
7. Let the ham stand for 10–15 minutes, and then slice and serve. Top the slices with the cider-raisin mixture.

Split Pea Soup

Phyllis Good, Lancaster, PA

Makes 8–10 servings

Prep. Time: 20 minutes
Cooking Time: 4–8 hours
Ideal slow-cooker size: 6-qt.

3 cups dried split peas (a little
    over 1 pound)
3 qts. water
½ tsp. garlic powder
½ tsp. dried oregano
1 cup diced or thinly sliced
    carrots
1 cup chopped celery
1 tsp. salt
¼–½ tsp. pepper (coarsely
    ground is great)
leftover meaty hambone

1. Put all ingredients into slow cooker, except the hambone. Stir well.
2. Settle hambone into mixture.

5. Layer ⅓ of bread mixture into crock.

6. Cover with half of cooked chicken.

7. Cover with half of remaining bread mixture.

8. Top with remaining chicken.

9. Cover with remaining bread mixture.

10. Cover. Cook on Low 3–4 hours. If you like a crusty finish on stuffing, take lid off during last 45 minutes of cooking.

Green Bean Casserole

Beverly Hummel, Fleetwood, PA

Makes 6 servings

Prep. Time: 20 minutes
Cooking Time: 2–3 hours
Ideal slow-cooker size: 3-qt.

2 Tbsp. butter, melted
2 Tbsp. flour
1 tsp. sugar
1 cup sour cream
2 lbs. frozen green beans, cooked and drained
½ cup shredded cheddar cheese
1 cup french-fried onions

1. In a saucepan, melt butter. Whisk in flour until smooth. Add sugar and sour cream. Stir over low heat until thick and hot.

2. Combine green beans with sour cream sauce. Place in slow cooker.

3. Sprinkle green bean mixture with cheese and onion rings.

4. Cover and cook on Low 2–3 hours.

Hot Fudge Cake

Lucille Hollinger, Richland, PA

Makes 8 servings

Prep. Time: 20 minutes
Cooking Time: 2–3 hours
Ideal slow-cooker size: 3-qt.

1¾ cups brown sugar, *divided*
1 cup flour
6 Tbsp. unsweetened cocoa powder, *divided*
2 tsp. baking powder
½ tsp. salt
½ cup milk
2 Tbsp. butter, melted
½ tsp. vanilla extract
1½ cups chocolate chips
1¾ cups boiling water

1. In a small bowl, combine 1 cup brown sugar, flour, 3 Tbsp. cocoa, baking powder, and salt.

2. In another bowl, combine milk, butter, and vanilla. Stir wet into dry ingredients just until combined.

3. Spread batter into greased slow cooker. Sprinkle with chocolate chips.

4. In another bowl, combine the remaining ¾ cup brown sugar and 3 Tbsp. cocoa.

5. Stir in boiling water. Pour over batter, and do not stir.

6. Cover and cook on High for 2–3 hours, or until a toothpick inserted near center of cake comes out clean.

SPRING

Week 2

THIS WEEK'S
Menu

Sunday: Leg of Lamb with Rosemary and Garlic
Monday: Herbed Lamb Stew
Tuesday: White Bean Fennel Soup
Wednesday: Glazed Holiday Ham
Thursday: Creamy Ham and Red Beans over Rice
Friday: Tasty Ranch Chicken
Saturday: Ranch Chicken Avocado Wraps

Recommended Side Dish: Scalloped Potatoes
Special Dessert: Bread Pudding

Shopping List

PROTEIN

4–5 lb. leg of lamb (have butcher cut off shank end if too large to fit in your crock)

4–5 lb. bone-in ham

8 boneless, skinless chicken thighs

FROZEN

10-oz. pkg. frozen peas

DAIRY and REFRIGERATED

½ cup apple juice

½ cup orange juice

1 Tbsp. lime juice

1½ cups shredded sharp cheddar cheese

1⅓ cups grated Parmesan cheese

½ cup plain Greek yogurt

2¾ cups milk

4 eggs

6 Tbsp. butter or margarine

PRODUCE

1 Tbsp. fresh chopped rosemary

2 tsp. fresh minced parsley

1 small fennel bulb

3 medium onions

2 cups diced onions

1 large onion

1½–2 cups diced celery

1 cup diced green bell pepper

3 cups chopped spinach

4 lbs. potatoes

2 ripe avocados

Download this shopping list to your smartphone!
(x.co/ShopList)

CANNED/DRY GOODS

15-oz. can white kidney or cannellini beans

14½-oz. can diced tomatoes

10-oz. can cheddar cheese soup

1 lb. dry red-skinned kidney beans

3 cups rice

½ cup ranch dressing

4–6 sandwich wraps

8 slices bread (raisin bread recommended)

DO YOU HAVE THESE ON HAND?

salt

pepper

celery seed

marjoram

thyme

dry mustard

cinnamon

creole seasoning

5 bay leaves

12 cloves garlic

olive oil

canola oil

Dijon mustard

apple cider vinegar

4 cups beef broth

5 cups fat-free chicken broth

flour

vanilla extract

sugar

½ cup brown sugar

½ cup honey

¼–½ cup raisins

SPIRITS

½ cup white wine

Leg of Lamb with Rosemary and Garlic

Hope Comerford,
Clinton Township, MI

Makes 6–8 servings

Prep. Time: 5 minutes
Cooking Time: 7–8 hours
Ideal slow-cooker size: 7-qt.

1 tsp. olive oil
4–5 lb. leg of lamb
6 cloves garlic, crushed
3 Tbsp. Dijon mustard
1 Tbsp. fresh chopped rosemary
1 tsp. salt
1 tsp. black pepper
½ cup white wine

1. Coat the bottom of your crock with olive oil.
2. Pat the leg of lamb dry with a paper towel.
3. Mix together the garlic, Dijon mustard, rosemary, salt, and pepper. Rub this mixture all over the leg of lamb. Place the leg of lamb in the slow cooker.
4. Pour the wine into the crock around the leg of lamb.
5. Cover and cook on Low 7–8 hours.

Herbed Lamb Stew

Jan Mast, Lancaster, PA

Makes 6 servings

Prep. Time: 20–30 minutes
Cooking Time: 6¼ hours
Ideal slow-cooker size: 6-qt.

leftover lamb, chopped
2 medium onions, chopped
4 cups beef broth
3–4 medium potatoes, peeled and thinly sliced
½–1 tsp. salt, according to your taste preferences
¼ tsp. pepper
¼ tsp. celery seed
¼ tsp. marjoram
¼ tsp. thyme
10-oz. pkg. frozen peas
6 Tbsp. flour
½ cup cold water

1. Add all ingredients to slow cooker except the peas, flour, and water.
2. Cover. Cook on Low 6 hours, or until potatoes are tender.
3. Stir in peas.
4. In a small bowl, dissolve flour in water. When smooth, stir into pot.
5. Cover. Turn cooker to High and cook an additional 15 to 20 minutes, or until broth thickens.

White Bean Fennel Soup

Janie Steele, Moore, OK

Makes 6 servings

Prep. Time: 20–30 minutes
Cooking Time: 1–3 hours
Ideal slow-cooker size: 5-qt.

1 Tbsp. olive or canola oil
1 large onion, chopped
1 small fennel bulb, sliced thin
5 cups fat-free chicken broth
15-oz. can white kidney or
  cannellini beans, rinsed and
  drained
14½-oz. can diced tomatoes,
  undrained
1 tsp. dried thyme
¼ tsp. black pepper
1 bay leaf
3 cups chopped fresh spinach

1. Sauté onion and fennel in oil in skillet until brown.
2. Combine onion, fennel, broth, beans, tomatoes, thyme, pepper, and bay leaf.
3. Cook on Low 2–3 hours, or on High 1 hour, until fennel and onions are tender.
4. Remove bay leaf.
5. Add spinach about 10 minutes before serving.

Glazed Holiday Ham

Jennifer Archer, Kalona, IA

Makes 8–10 servings

Prep. Time: 5 minutes
Cooking Time: 6–8 hours
Ideal slow-cooker size: 6- or 7-qt.
  oval

4–5 lb. bone-in, cured ham
½ cup apple juice
½ cup orange juice
½ cup brown sugar
½ cup honey

1. Grease interior of slow-cooker crock.
2. Place ham in crock.
3. In a bowl, mix remaining ingredients until combined.
4. Pour over ham.
5. Cover. Cook on Low 4–5 hours, or until instant-read meat thermometer registers 100°F when stuck into center of ham (but not against bone).
6. If you're home and available, baste ham with glaze every hour or so.
7. Using two sturdy metal spatulas, lift cooked ham onto cutting board. Cover and keep warm for 15 minutes, so it can gather its juices.
8. Cut into slices or chunks. Spoon glaze over top.
9. Pass additional glaze in a bowl to diners to add more to their individual servings.

Creamy Ham and Red Beans over Rice

Phyllis Good, Lancaster, PA

Makes 6 servings

Prep. Time: 20 minutes
Cooking Time: 5–11 hours
Standing Time: 1 hour
Ideal slow-cooker size: 6-qt.

1 lb. dried red-skinned kidney beans
2 Tbsp. oil
2 cups diced onions
1½–2 cups diced celery
1 cup diced green bell pepper
4 large cloves garlic, minced
1 Tbsp. creole seasoning
4 bay leaves
1 tsp. dried thyme
2 qts. water
leftover meaty ham bone
salt and pepper, *optional*
6 cups cooked rice

1. Place dried beans in stockpot. Cover with water by 3 inches.
2. Bring to a boil and cook 2 minutes.
3. Cover. Remove from heat and let stand 1 hour. Drain.
4. Grease interior of slow cooker.
5. Pour beans into slow cooker.
6. Stir in oil, diced vegetables, garlic, creole seasoning, bay leaves, and thyme. Add water.
7. Submerge ham bone in mixture.
8. Cover. Cook on Low 9–11 hours or on High 5–7 hours, or until beans are tender and meat is falling off the bone.
9. Using tongs or a slotted spoon, remove ham bone from cooker. Fish out bay leaves, too.
10. Allow meat to cool enough to pull or cut into bite-sized pieces.
11. Stir meat chunks back into bean mixture. Heat 15 minutes.
12. Place 1 cup or so cooked rice in each individual serving bowl. Top with creamy ham and beans.

Tasty Ranch Chicken

Kathleen A. Rogge, Alexandria, IN

Makes 6–8 servings

Prep. Time: 15 minutes
Cooking Time: 4–5 hours
Ideal slow-cooker size: 4- or 5-qt.

½ cup ranch salad dressing
1 Tbsp. flour
8 boneless, skinless chicken thighs
½ cup shredded cheddar cheese
⅓ cup grated Parmesan cheese

1. Grease interior of slow-cooker crock.
2. Mix salad dressing and flour in a shallow bowl.
3. Coat each thigh with dressing/flour mixture. Place in slow cooker. If you need to make a second layer, stagger the pieces so they don't fully overlap each other.
4. Mix cheeses together in a small bowl. Sprinkle over chicken. Lift pieces on the second layer to sprinkle cheese over pieces in first layer.
5. Cover. Cook on Low for 4 hours, or until instant-read meat thermometer registers 160°–165°F when inserted in thickest part of thighs.
6. If you wish, place chicken on rimmed baking sheet and run under the broiler to brown the cheese and chicken. But watch carefully so it doesn't burn.

Ranch Chicken Avocado Wraps

Hope Comerford, Clinton Township, MI

Makes 4–6 wraps

Prep. Time: 10 minutes

leftover chicken, cut into slices
4–6 sandwich wraps
1 avocado, sliced

Avocado Ranch Aioli:
1 large avocado, pit removed, sliced
½ cup plain Greek yogurt
¼ cup milk
1 tsp. apple cider vinegar
2 cloves garlic, minced
2 tsp. fresh minced parsley
1 Tbsp. lime juice
¼ tsp. salt

1. These are good with either warm or cold chicken, but if you choose to use

warm chicken, warm it while you make the aioli.

2. In a food processor, place all of the avocado ranch aioli ingredients. Blend until smooth and well-mixed, scraping the sides when necessary.

3. On each sandwich wrap, lay out the chicken and a couple slices of avocado. Drizzle the garlic ranch aioli over each sandwich.

Scalloped Potatoes

Betty Moore, Avon Park, FL

Makes 8 servings

Prep. Time: 15 minutes
Cooking Time: 3–4 hours
Ideal slow-cooker size: 4-qt.

3 lbs. sliced potatoes
1 medium onion, chopped
1 cup shredded sharp
   cheddar cheese
salt and pepper, to taste
½ cup milk
10-oz. can cheddar cheese
   soup
1 tsp. dry mustard
½ cup grated Parmesan cheese

1. Layer potatoes, onion, and cheddar cheese in greased slow cooker, adding salt and pepper to each layer.

2. Separately, mix milk, cheese soup, and dry mustard. Pour over layers in slow cooker.

3. Sprinkle with Parmesan.

4. Cover and cook on High 3–4 hours, until potatoes are tender.

Bread Pudding

Winifred Ewy, Newton, KS
Helen King, Fairbank, IA
Elaine Patton,
West Middletown, PA

Makes 6 servings

Prep. Time: 20 minutes
Cooking Time: 3–4 hours
Ideal slow-cooker size: 4-qt.

8 slices bread (raisin bread is
   especially good), cubed
4 eggs
2 cups milk
¼ cup sugar
4 Tbsp. butter, melted, or
   margarine
½ cup raisins (use only ¼ cup
   if using raisin bread)
½ tsp. cinnamon
Sauce:
2 Tbsp. butter or margarine
2 Tbsp. flour

1 cup water
¾ cup sugar
1 tsp. vanilla extract

1. Place bread cubes in greased slow cooker.

2. Beat together eggs and milk. Stir in sugar, butter, raisins, and cinnamon. Pour over bread and stir.

3. Cover and cook on High 1 hour. Reduce heat to Low and cook 3–4 hours, or until thermometer reaches 160°F.

4. Make sauce just before pudding is done baking. Begin by melting butter in saucepan. Stir in flour until smooth. Gradually add water, sugar, and vanilla. Bring to boil. Cook, stirring constantly for 2 minutes, or until thickened.

Serving Suggestion: Serve sauce over warm bread pudding.

SPRING

Week 3

THIS WEEK'S

Menu

Sunday: Our Favorite Ribs
Monday: Classic Beef Chili
Tuesday: Come-Back-For-More Barbecued Chicken
Wednesday: Baked Potatoes with Chili
Thursday: BBQ Pork Rib Soup
Friday: Barbecued Chicken Pizza
Saturday: Herby Fish on a Bed of Vegetables

Recommended Side Dish: Garden Vegetables
Special Dessert: Chocolate Soufflé

Shopping List

PROTEIN
4 lbs. pork spare ribs

1½ lbs. extra-lean ground beef

6 chicken breast halves

4 to 6, 4 to 6–oz. white fish
  filets (flounder, cod, or
  haddock recommended)

cooked and crumbled
  bacon, *optional*

FROZEN
16-oz. pkg. frozen mixed
  vegetables

DAIRY and REFRIGERATED
8–12 oz. pkg. prepared pizza
  dough

2 cups shredded mozzarella
  cheese

1–2 cups shredded Swiss or
  mozzarella cheese

2⅓ cups sour cream

4 eggs

PRODUCE
2 medium onions

½ cup chopped onion

¼–½ cup diced red or white
  onion

¼ cup red onion, sliced or
  diced, *optional*

1 cup chopped green bell
  pepper

chopped chives, *optional*

2–3 leeks

1 rib celery

1 jalapeño pepper

4–6 russet potatoes

8–12 little new potatoes

8–12 plum tomatoes, or canned

fresh oregano sprigs, for
  garnish

Download this shopping list to your
smartphone!

(x.co/ShopList)

CANNED/DRY GOODS

28-oz. can crushed tomatoes

15-oz. can red kidney beans

15-oz. can great northern
  beans

15-oz. can cannellini beans

15½-oz. can diced tomatoes,
  or fresh

2 8-oz. cans crushed
  pineapple

20-oz. can pineapple bits,
  optional

4-oz. can diced green chilies

10¾-oz. can cream of
  mushroom soup

6-oz. can french-fried onions

18¾-oz. pkg. chocolate cake
  mix

3-oz. box instant chocolate
  pudding mix

DO YOU HAVE THESE ON HAND?

chili powder

ground cumin

salt

sea salt

pepper

dried dill

dried basil

10 cloves garlic

olive oil

vegetable oil

6 cups chicken or beef broth

1 cup barbecue sauce,
  teriyaki flavored, or your
  choice of flavors

2 Tbsp. tomato paste

brown sugar

ketchup

1½ cups vinegar of your
  choice

cornstarch

soy sauce

Worcestershire sauce

1 cup chocolate chips,
  optional

Our Favorite Ribs

Phyllis Good, Lancaster, PA

Makes 8 servings

Prep. Time: 20 minutes
Cooking Time: 3½–4½ hours
Ideal slow-cooker size: 4- or 5-qt.

4 Tbsp. oil
4 lbs. pork spareribs, cut in pieces
½ cup chopped onion
½ cup chopped green bell pepper
2 8 oz. cans crushed pineapple, undrained
1½ cups vinegar of your choice
¾ cups water, *divided*
4 Tbsp. ketchup
1 cup brown sugar
4 Tbsp. soy sauce
2 tsp. Worcestershire sauce
4 cloves garlic, sliced thinly
4 Tbsp. cornstarch

1. Brown spareribs in oil in large skillet. Remove meat and place in slow cooker.
2. Pour off all but 2 Tbsp. drippings from the skillet.
3. Add onion and green pepper and cook until tender. Stir in pineapple, vinegar, ½ cup water, ketchup, brown sugar, soy sauce, Worcestershire sauce, and garlic. Bring to boil.
4. Pour hot sauce over spareribs in slow cooker.
5. Cover and cook on Low for 3–4 hours, until ribs are falling-off-the-bone tender.
6. Whisk together the remaining ¼ cup water with the cornstarch. Whisk into sauce and ribs in slow cooker. Cover and cook on Low for an additional 10–20 minutes, until thickened.

Classic Beef Chili

Esther S. Martin, Ephrata, PA

Makes 6–8 servings

Prep. Time: 20 minutes
Cooking Time: 2–3 hours
Ideal slow-cooker size: 4-qt.

1½ lb. extra-lean ground beef
2 cloves garlic, chopped fine

2 Tbsp. chili powder
1 tsp. ground cumin
28-oz. can crushed tomatoes
15-oz. can red kidney beans,
  rinsed and drained
1 medium onion, chopped
4-oz. can diced green chilies,
  undrained
2 Tbsp. tomato paste
fresh oregano sprigs, for
  garnish

1. In large nonstick skillet, brown beef and garlic over medium heat. Stir to break up meat. Add chili powder and cumin. Stir to combine.

2. Mix together tomatoes, beans, onion, chilies, and tomato paste in slow cooker. Add beef mixture and mix thoroughly.

3. Cook on High 2–3 hours, or until flavors are well blended.

4. Garnish with oregano to serve.

Come-Back-For-More Barbecued Chicken

Leesa DeMartyn, Enola, PA

Makes 6–8 servings

Prep. Time: 10 minutes
Cooking Time: 6–8 hours
Ideal slow-cooker size: 5-qt.

6 chicken breast halves
1 cup ketchup
⅓ cup Worcestershire sauce
½ cup brown sugar
1 tsp. chili powder
½ cup water

1. Place chicken in slow cooker.

2. Whisk remaining ingredients in a large bowl. Pour sauce mixture over chicken.

3. Cover and cook on Low for 6–8 hours, or until chicken is tender but not overcooked.

Baked Potatoes with Chili

Hope Comerford,
Clinton Township, MI

Makes 4–6 servings

Prep. Time: 10 minutes
Cooking Time: 8 hours
Ideal slow-cooker size: 4-qt.

4–6 russet potatoes, scrubbed
  and rinsed
olive oil
sea salt
pepper
leftover chili
Additional toppings, optional:
sour cream
chopped chives
cooked and crumbled bacon
shredded cheese of your
  choice

1. Lay out one piece of foil for each potato and place the potato on each. Prick each potato several times with a knife or fork. This prevents them from exploding.

2. Drizzle olive oil over each potato, then rub it in.

3. Sprinkle sea salt and pepper over each potato and wrap up the foil on each potato.

4. Place the potatoes into the slow cooker. You can add more potatoes, but be aware your slow cooker should not be more than ¾ of the way full, so you may need a larger slow cooker.

5. Cook on Low for 8 hours.

6. Warm up leftover chili.

7. To serve, cut each potato in half and top with chili and any other additional toppings you choose.

BBQ Pork Rib Soup

Hope Comerford,
Clinton Township, MI

Makes 6 servings

Prep. Time: 15 minutes
Cooking Time: 4–6 hours
Ideal slow-cooker size: 4- to 5-qt.

leftover rib meat, cut off the
 bone, chopped
1 medium onion, chopped
15-oz. can great northern
 beans, drained and rinsed
15-oz. can cannellini beans,
 drained and rinsed
1 jalapeño pepper, seeded,
 diced
1 rib celery, diced
4 cloves garlic, minced
6 cups chicken or beef broth

1. Place all ingredients into
the slow cooker.
2. Cook on Low for 4–6
hours.

Barbecued Chicken Pizza

Susan Roth, Salem, OR

Makes 4–6 servings

Prep. Time: 20–25 minutes
Cooking Time: 2½–3 hours
*Standing Time: 2 hours before you
 begin*
Ideal slow-cooker size: 6-qt.

8- or 12-oz. pkg. prepared
 pizza dough, depending
 how thick you like your
 pizza crust
1 cup barbecue sauce,
 teriyaki flavored, or your
 choice of flavors
leftover chicken, chopped
20-oz. can pineapple tidbits,
 drained, *optional*
½ cup green bell pepper,
 chopped, *optional*
¼ cup red onion, sliced or
 diced, *optional*
2 cups shredded mozzarella
 cheese

1. If the dough's been
refrigerated, allow it to stand
at room temperature for 2
hours.
2. Grease interior of slow-
cooker crock.
3. Stretch the dough into
a large circle so that it fits
into the crock, covering the
bottom and reaching up the
sides by an inch or so the whole
way around. (If the dough
is larger than the bottom of
the cooker, fold it in half and
stretch it to fit the bottom and
an inch up the sides. This will
make a thicker crust.)
4. Bake crust, uncovered,
on High, 1 hour.
5. Spread barbecue sauce
over hot crust.
6. Drop chopped chicken
evenly over sauce.
7. If you wish, spoon
pineapple, chopped peppers,
and onion over chicken.
8. Sprinkle evenly with
cheese.
9. Cover. Cook on High for
about 2 hours, or until the
crust begins to brown around
the edges.
10. Uncover, being careful
not to let the condensation on
the lid drip onto the pizza.
11. Let stand for 10 minutes.
Cut into wedges and serve.

Herby Fish on a Bed of Vegetables

Phyllis Good, Lancaster, PA

Makes 4–5 servings

Prep. Time: 20–30 minutes
Cooking Time: 4¼–5¼ hours
Ideal slow-cooker size: 4- or 5-qt.

8–12 little new potatoes,
 peeled or not
4 Tbsp. olive oil, *divided*
salt, to taste
pepper, to taste
2–3 leeks
8–12 plum tomatoes, sliced in
 half, or 15½-oz. can diced
 tomatoes, undrained
¼–½ cup diced red or white
 onion
2 tsp. dried dill
2 tsp. dried basil
4 to 6 4-oz. to 6-oz. white
 fish fillets (flounder, cod, or
 haddock work well)

1. Grease the interior of the
crock.
2. Wash the potatoes well.
Slice them thin. (Bring out
your mandoline if you have
one. If you don't, get one.
You'll make this dish more
often.)
3. Layer the slices into the
slow cooker. Drizzle each
layer with oil, using about
2 Tbsp. total. Salt and pepper
each layer as you go.

4. Cut the dark green tops off each leek. Split each leak from top to bottom into quarters. Hold each quarter under running water to wash out any sand and dirt.

5. Chop leeks into ½-inch-wide slices. Layer into slow cooker on top of the potatoes. Salt and pepper these layers, too.

6. Scatter tomatoes over top.

7. Cover. Cook on Low 4–5 hours, or until potatoes and leeks are as soft as you like them.

8. Meanwhile, put the diced onion in a microwave-safe bowl. Cover and cook on High 1 minute, or just until onions are softened.

9. Add the remaining 2 Tbsp. oil to onions. Stir in dill and basil, too.

10. When the veggies are as tender as you want, lay the fish fillets on top of the vegetables. Lay the thicker ends of the fillets around the outside of the crock first; that's where the heat source is. Put the thinner fillets in the middle.

11. Spread the red onion-herb mixture over the tops of the fish.

12. Cover. Turn cooker to High and cook for 15 minutes. Using a fork, test the thicker parts of the fillets to see if they're flaky. If not, cook 5 minutes more and test again.

13. When the fish is flaky, use a fish spatula to lift the fish onto a plate. Tent with foil to keep warm.

14. Using a slotted spoon, lift out the layers of vegetables and put them on a platter or serving dish with low sides. Lay the fish over top and serve.

Garden Vegetables

Esther Gingerich, Parnell, IA
Judy A. and Sharon Wantland,
Menomonee Falls, WI

Makes 6 servings

Prep. Time: 15 minutes
Cooking Time: 2½–4 hours
Ideal slow-cooker size: 3-qt.

16-oz. pkg. frozen vegetables, thawed (combination of broccoli, carrots, cauliflower, etc.)
10¾-oz. can cream of mushroom soup
half a soup can water
⅓ cup sour cream
1–2 cups shredded Swiss or mozzarella cheese, *divided*
6-oz. can french-fried onions, *divided*

1. In slow cooker, combine thawed vegetables, soup, water, sour cream, half the cheese, and half the onions.
2. Cover and cook on Low 2½–4 hours, or until vegetables are as soft as you like them.
3. Fifteen minutes before the end of the cooking time, sprinkle remaining cheese and onions on top.

Chocolate Soufflé

Rachel Yoder, Middlebury, IN

Makes 10–12 servings

Prep. Time: 5 minutes
Cooking Time: 6 hours
Ideal slow-cooker size: 6-qt.

18¼-oz. pkg. chocolate cake mix
½ cup vegetable oil
2 cups sour cream
4 eggs, beaten
3-oz. box instant chocolate pudding mix
1 cup chocolate chips, *optional*

1. Combine all ingredients in a large mixing bowl.
2. Spray interior of slow cooker with nonstick cooking spray. Pour soufflé mixture into cooker.
3. Cover and cook on Low for 6 hours. (Do not lift the lid until the end of the cooking time!)
4. Insert toothpick into center of cake to see if it comes out clean. If it does, the soufflé is finished. If it doesn't, continue cooking another 15 minutes. Check again. Repeat until it's finished cooking.
5. Serve warm from the cooker with ice cream or frozen yogurt.

SPRING

Week 4

THIS WEEK'S
Menu

Sunday: Slurping Good Sausages
Monday: Creamy Ziti in the Crock
Tuesday: Savory Turkey and Mushrooms
Wednesday: Sweet Pepper and Sausage Burritos
Thursday: Magical Turkey Pie
Friday: California Tacos
Saturday: Hamburger Lentil Soup

Recommended Side Dish: Risi Bisi (Peas and Rice)
Special Dessert: Apple Peanut Crumble

Shopping List

PROTEIN

4 lbs. sweet Italian sausage

3 lbs. boneless skinless turkey thighs

1½ lbs. ground beef

FROZEN

½ lb. frozen green beans, or fresh

1 cup frozen corn, or fresh, or canned

½ cup frozen baby peas

DAIRY and REFRIGERATED

¾ cup or so of grated Parmesan cheese

11 oz. cream cheese

1 cup mozzarella cheese

1½ cups shredded cheddar cheese

1 stick butter, plus 2 Tbsp. butter

1 9-inch piecrust

PRODUCE

6 green, yellow, or red bell peppers

3 large onions

3 medium onions

3 cups fresh mushrooms

1 cup sliced potatoes

1 cup sliced carrots

2 carrots

1½ ribs celery

2 Tbsp. chopped fresh parsley, or dried

4–5 cooking apples

CANNED/DRY GOODS

24-oz. jar of your favorite pasta sauce

Download this shopping list to your smartphone!

(x.co/ShopList)

5 cups spaghetti or marinara sauce	**DO YOU HAVE THESE ON HAND?**
6-oz. can tomato paste	dried parsley, or fresh
14½-oz. can diced tomatoes	dried basil
10¾-oz. can cream of celery soup	pepper
	salt
15½-oz. can pinto beans	ground cumin
½-qt. tomato juice	garlic powder
4 cups uncooked ziti pasta	marjoram
¾ cup raw brown rice	Italian seasoning
1 cup dry lentils	cinnamon
1½ cups converted long-grain white rice, uncooked	nutmeg
	2–3 cloves garlic
2 cups salsa	1 cup beef broth
salsa, *optional*	29 oz. chicken broth
6 6-inch whole wheat tortillas	cornstarch
	flour
taco shells	brown sugar
1 envelope dry taco seasoning	soy sauce
	½ cup quick-cooking oats
	2 Tbsp. peanut butter

Slurping Good Sausages

Phyllis Good, Lancaster, PA

Makes 10–12 servings

Prep. Time: 20 minutes
Cooking Time: 6 hours
Ideal slow-cooker size: 4-qt.

4 lbs. sweet Italian sausage, cut into 5-inch lengths
24-oz. jar of your favorite pasta sauce
6-oz. can tomato paste
1 large green, yellow, or red bell pepper, chopped
1 large onion, sliced thin
1 Tbsp. grated Parmesan cheese, plus a little more
1 cup water
2 Tbsp. chopped fresh parsley, or 2 tsp. dried parsley

1. Place sausage pieces in skillet. Add water to cover. Simmer 10 minutes. Drain. (This cooks off some of the fat from the sausage.)
2. Combine pasta sauce, tomato paste, chopped green pepper, sliced onion, 1 Tbsp. grated cheese, and water in slow cooker. Stir in sausage pieces.
3. Cover. Cook on Low 6 hours.
4. Just before serving, stir in parsley.

Serving Suggestion: Serve in buns, or cut sausage into bite-sized pieces and serve over cooked pasta. Sprinkle with more Parmesan cheese.

Creamy Ziti in the Crock

Judi Manos, West Islip, NY

Makes 8 servings

Prep. Time: 20 minutes
Cooking Time: 2–3 hours
Ideal slow-cooker size: 5- to 6-qt.

5 cups spaghetti or marinara sauce, *divided*
8-oz. pkg. cream cheese, cubed, room temperature
¾ cup chopped leftover sausage
1 tsp. dried basil
⅛ tsp. pepper
14½-oz. can diced tomatoes, undrained
4 cups uncooked ziti pasta, *divided*
1 cup mozzarella cheese, *divided*
⅓ cup grated Parmesan cheese

1. Grease interior of slow-cooker crock.

2. Heat 1–2 cups spaghetti sauce in saucepan or microwave. Add cream cheese cubes and stir until melted.

3. Add remaining spaghetti sauce, leftover sausage, basil, pepper, and diced tomatoes to warmed creamy sauce.

4. Put ⅓ of tomato sauce mixture in bottom of crock.

5. Add 2 cups ziti, topped with ½ cup mozzarella.

6. Add half of remaining tomato mixture.

7. Layer in final 2 cups of ziti and ½ cup mozzarella.

8. Spoon on remaining tomato mixture. Sprinkle with Parmesan.

9. Cover. Cook on High for 2–3 hours, until pasta is al dente and sauce is bubbling at edges.

Variations: Add some spinach leaves, sliced black olives, chopped kielbasa, or sliced mushrooms as you make layers. Just keep the sauce and pasta proportions the same so there is enough liquid for the pasta.

Savory Turkey and Mushrooms

Clara Newswanger,
Gordonville, PA

Makes 6–8 servings

Prep. Time: 20 minutes
Cooking Time: 4–4½ hours
Ideal slow-cooker size: 5-qt.

1 medium onion, chopped
½ stick (4 Tbsp.) butter
3 cups fresh mushrooms, sliced
4 Tbsp. cornstarch
1 cup beef broth
2 Tbsp. soy sauce
3 lbs. boneless, skinless turkey thighs, cut in 4-inch cubes
salt and pepper, *optional*

1. Sauté chopped onion in butter in saucepan.

2. Stir in mushrooms and cornstarch until well mixed.

3. Stir in beef broth and soy sauce. Bring to a boil, stirring continuously so mixture thickens but doesn't stick.

4. Grease interior of slow-cooker crock.

5. Place cut-up turkey evenly over bottom of crock. Pour sauce over meat.

6. Cover. Cook on Low 4–4½ hours, or until turkey is tender when pierced with a fork.

7. Taste broth and season with salt and pepper if you wish.

8. Serve over cooked rice or noodles.

Sweet Pepper and Sausage Burritos

Anita King, Bellefontaine, OH

Makes 6 servings

Prep. Time: 35 minutes
Cooking Time: 2 hours
Standing Time: 5 minutes
Ideal slow-cooker size: 5-qt.

¾ cup raw brown rice
1¼ cups water
leftover sausages, sliced
1 medium onion, chopped
2 tsp. ground cumin
½ tsp. black pepper
5 medium sweet red, yellow, or green bell peppers, diced
1½ cups shredded cheddar cheese
3-oz. pkg. cream cheese, cubed
6 whole wheat tortillas, about 6 inches in diameter
salsa, as mild or hot as you like, *optional*

1. Grease interior of slow-cooker crock.

2. Place raw brown rice, water, leftover sausage slices, onion, cumin, and black pepper in crock. Stir until well mixed.

3. Cover. Cook on High for 1¾ hours, or until rice is nearly tender.

4. Stir in peppers at the end of cooking time, along with cheddar and cream cheeses.

5. Cover. Continue cooking on High 30 more minutes, or until rice and peppers are as tender as you like them.

6. Spoon ⅔ cup rice-pepper-cheese mixture onto lower half of each tortilla. Fold in the sides. Then bring up the bottom and roll up.

7. Place each burrito, seam side down, in greased 9x13-inch baking pan.

8. Cover. Bake at 425°F 10–15 minutes.

9. Let stand 4 minutes. Serve with salsa if you wish.

Magical Turkey Pie

Marilyn Kurtz, Willow Street, PA

Makes 4–5 servings

Prep. Time: ½ hour
Cooking Time: 4–5 hours
Ideal slow-cooker size: 5-qt.

½ lb. frozen or fresh green beans (thawed if frozen)
1 cup sliced potatoes, peeled or not
1 cup sliced carrots
1 cup frozen (and thawed), or fresh, or canned corn
⅓ cup chopped onion
leftover chicken, chopped
¼ tsp. salt
10¾-oz. can cream of celery soup
¼ soup can water
1 9-inch piecrust

1. Grease interior of slow-cooker crock.
2. Put green beans, potatoes, carrots, corn, onion, and chicken cubes in crock in the order given.
3. In a bowl, blend together salt, soup, and water. When well mixed, pour over other ingredients in crock.
4. Cover. Cook on Low for 4–5 hours of until veggies are as tender as you like.
5. Serve. Or, if you're looking for a special touch, stir all ingredients together well. Then transfer to a greased 11x13-inch baking dish.
6. Top "pie" with baked piecrust hearts, made ahead. Then serve.

7. To make hearts: Use recipe for one 9-inch piecrust, rolled out and cut into heart shapes.
8. Put hearts on baking sheet and prick each with a fork.
9. Bake at 400°F for about 10–12 minutes until lightly browned. Store in tightly covered container until ready to use.

California Tacos

Mary June Hershberger, Lynchburg, VA

Makes 6–8 servings

Prep. Time: 20 minutes
Cooking Time: 3 hours
Ideal slow-cooker size: 2-qt.

1½ lb. ground beef
1 medium onion, chopped
1 green bell pepper, chopped
1 envelope, or 4 Tbsp., dry taco seasoning
2 cups salsa, your choice of heat
15½-oz. can pinto beans, rinsed and drained
salt and pepper to taste
taco shells

1. Grease interior of slow-cooker crock.
2. If you have time, brown beef in skillet. Drain off drippings and place meat in crock.
3. If you don't have time, crumble beef over bottom of crock.
4. Stir in onion and bell pepper, taco seasoning, salsa, and pinto beans.
5. Cover. Cook on Low for 3 hours.
6. Serve in taco shells.

Hamburger Lentil Soup (page 43)

Hamburger Lentil Soup

Juanita Marner,
Shipshewana, IN

Makes 6 servings

Prep. Time: 20 minutes
Cooking Time: 4–10 hours
Ideal slow-cooker size: 5-qt.

leftover beef
½ cup chopped onions
2 carrots, diced
1½ ribs celery, diced
1 garlic clove, minced, or 1
   tsp. garlic powder
½ qt. tomato juice
1½ tsp. salt
1 cups dry lentils, washed,
   with stones removed
6 cups water
¼ tsp. dried marjoram
1½ tsp. brown sugar

1. Combine all ingredients in slow cooker.
2. Cover. Cook on Low 8–10 hours, or High 4–6 hours.

Risi Bisi (Peas and Rice)

Cyndie Marrara,
Port Matilda, PA

Makes 6 servings

Prep. Time: 10–15 minutes
Cooking Time: 2½–3½ hours
Ideal slow-cooker size: 4-qt.

1½ cups converted long-grain
   white rice, uncooked
¾ cup chopped onions
2 cloves garlic, minced

2 14½-oz. cans reduced-
   sodium chicken broth
⅓ cup water
¾ tsp. Italian seasoning
½ tsp. dried basil leaves
½ cup frozen baby peas,
   thawed
¼ cup grated Parmesan
   cheese

1. Combine rice, onions, and garlic in slow cooker.
2. In saucepan, mix together chicken broth and water. Bring to boil. Add Italian seasoning and basil leaves. Stir into rice mixture.
3. Cover. Cook on Low 2–3 hours, or until liquid is absorbed.
4. Stir in peas. Cover. Cook 30 minutes. Stir in cheese.

Apple Peanut Crumble

Phyllis Attig, Reynolds, IL
Joan Becker, Dodge City, KS
Pam Hochstedler, Kalona, IA

Makes 4–5 servings

Prep. Time: 10 minutes
Cooking Time: 5–6 hours
Ideal slow-cooker size: 4-qt.

4–5 cooking apples, peeled
   and sliced
⅔ cup packed brown sugar
½ cup flour
½ cup quick-cooking oats
½ tsp. cinnamon
¼–½ tsp. nutmeg
5⅓ Tbsp. (⅓ cup) butter,
   softened
2 Tbsp. peanut butter

1. Place apple slices in slow cooker.
2. Combine brown sugar, flour, oats, cinnamon, and nutmeg.
3. Cut in butter and peanut butter. Sprinkle over apples.
4. Cover cooker and cook on Low 5–6 hours.

Week 5

THIS WEEK'S
Menu

Sunday: Pita Burgers
Monday: Pork Chops Pierre
Tuesday: Ohio Chili
Wednesday: Slow-Cooked Pork Stew
Thursday: Israeli Couscous with Vegetables
Friday: Kona Chicken
Saturday: Szechwan-Style Chicken and Broccoli

Recommended Side Dish: Baked Lima Beans
Special Dessert: Fruit-Filled Cake (also known as Dump Cake!)

Shopping List

PROTEIN
2 lbs. lean ground chuck

3–4 lbs. (6–8) ½-inch thick
  bone-in pork chops

8 good-sized boneless
  skinless chicken thighs

½ lb. bacon

DAIRY and REFRIGERATED
1 egg

1 stick, plus 2 Tbsp. butter

PRODUCE
1 small onion

5 medium onions

2 large onions

⅓ cup chopped scallions

4 ribs celery

¾ cup chopped celery

3 large green bell peppers

1 medium green bell pepper

1 medium red bell pepper

¼ lb. baby carrots

½ cup shredded carrots

1½ large potatoes

1 parsnip

5 mushrooms

2 cups broccoli florets

fresh ginger

CANNED/DRY GOODS
14-oz. can no-salt-added
  stewed tomatoes

2 15-oz. cans tomato sauce

2 15-oz. cans diced
  tomatoes

2 15-oz. cans dark red
  kidney beans

15-oz. can pinto beans

15-oz. can ranch beans

4-oz. can green chilies

Download this shopping list to your
smartphone!
(x.co/ShopList)

21-oz. can blueberry or
  cherry pie filling

20-oz. can pineapple chunks

20-oz. can crushed
  pineapple

3 cups low-sodium canned
  vegetable juice

14½-oz. can chicken broth

½ cup picante sauce

1½ cups tomato juice

12-slice pkg. pita bread

18½-oz. pkg. yellow cake mix

1 lb. dry lima beans

1 cup uncooked Israeli
  couscous

**DO YOU HAVE THESE ON
HAND?**

dry mustard

salt

pepper

ground cumin

chili powder

cinnamon

bay leaves

dried thyme

hot red pepper flakes

dried dill weed

ground ginger

9 cloves garlic

1½ cups vegetable stock

1 beef bouillon cube

cornstarch

unsweetened cocoa powder

½ Tbsp. plus 2 tsp. quick-
  cooking tapioca

white rice

sugar

brown sugar

dark brown sugar

olive oil

apple cider vinegar

¾ cup mild molasses (not
  blackstrap)

Worcestershire sauce

soy sauce

1 cup ketchup

1 Tbsp. lemon juice

prepared mustard

1 cup dry oatmeal

1 cup chopped nuts

SPIRITS

½ cup white wine

Pita Burgers

Phyllis Good, Lancaster, PA

Makes 12 servings

Prep. Time: 15–20 minutes
Cooking Time: 4–6 hours
Ideal slow-cooker size: 4-qt.

2 lbs. lean ground chuck
1 cup dry oatmeal
1 egg
1 medium onion, finely
   chopped
15-oz. can tomato sauce
2 Tbsp. brown sugar
½ tsp. salt
2 Tbsp. apple cider vinegar
1 Tbsp. Worcestershire sauce
1 Tbsp. soy sauce
12-slice pkg. pita bread

1. Combine the ground chuck, dry oatmeal, egg, and chopped onion in a mixing bowl. Shape the mixture into 12 burgers.
2. In a medium-sized bowl, combine the tomato sauce, brown sugar, salt, vinegar, Worcestershire sauce, and soy sauce.
3. Dip each burger in the sauce, and then stack them into your slow cooker. Pour any remaining sauce over the burgers in the cooker.
4. Cover. Cook on Low 4–6 hours, or until the burgers are as cooked as you like them.
5. Invite everyone who's eating to lift a burger out of the cooker with tongs and put it into a pita pocket with some dribbles of sauce.

Pork Chops Pierre

Genelle Taylor, Perrysburg, OH

Makes 6 servings

Prep. Time: 30–40 minutes
Cooking Time: 4½–6½ hours
Ideal slow-cooker size: 3-qt.

6–8 bone-in, lean pork chops, each ½-inch thick, totaling 3–4 lbs.
½ tsp. salt, *optional*
⅛ tsp. pepper
2 medium onions, chopped
2 ribs celery, chopped
1 large green bell pepper, sliced
14-oz. can no-salt-added stewed tomatoes
½ cup ketchup
2 Tbsp. apple cider vinegar
2 Tbsp. brown sugar
2 Tbsp. Worcestershire sauce
1 Tbsp. lemon juice
1 beef bouillon cube
2 Tbsp. cornstarch
2 Tbsp. water

1. Place chops in slow cooker. Sprinkle with salt and pepper.
2. Spoon onions, celery, green pepper, and tomatoes over chops.
3. In a small bowl, combine ketchup, apple cider vinegar, sugar, Worcestershire sauce, lemon juice, and bouillon cube. Pour over vegetables.
4. Cover. Cook on Low 4–6 hours, just until chops are tender but not dry.
5. Remove chops to a platter and keep warm.
6. In a small bowl, mix together cornstarch and water until smooth. Stir into liquid in slow cooker.
7. Cover. Cook on High 30 minutes or until sauce thickens. Serve over chops.

Ohio Chili

Bob Coffey, New Windsor, NY

Makes 15 servings

Prep. Time: 25 minutes
Cooking Time: 8 hours
Ideal slow-cooker size: 5½-qt.

2 large onions, chopped
3 cloves garlic, smashed and
chopped
2 large green bell peppers,
chopped
2 ribs celery, chopped
2 15-oz. cans dark red kidney
beans, rinsed and drained
15-oz. can pinto beans, rinsed
and drained
15-oz. can ranch beans,
undrained
2 15-oz. cans diced tomatoes,
undrained
4-oz. can chopped green chilies
15-oz. can tomato sauce
½ tsp. ground cumin
2 tsp. chili powder
1 Tbsp. unsweetened cocoa
powder
1 tsp. ground cinnamon
2 bay leaves
4 leftover burgers, crumbled
into bite-sized pieces

1. Place all ingredients in
slow cooker.
2. Cover and cook for 8
hours on Low.

Slow-Cooked Pork Stew

Virginia Graybill, Hershey, PA

Makes 4 servings

Prep. Time: 20–30 minutes
Cooking Time: 3–6 hours
Ideal slow-cooker size: 5-qt.

leftover pork chops, chopped
¼ lb. baby carrots
1½ large potatoes, cut into
1-inch cubes
1 parsnip, cut into 1-inch
cubes
1 medium onion, cut into
wedges, slices, or chopped
coarsely
2 cloves garlic, minced
1 tsp. ground black pepper,
depending on your taste
preferences
½ tsp. dried thyme
½ tsp. salt
3 cups low-sodium canned
vegetable juice
1 Tbsp. brown sugar
1½ tsp. prepared mustard
2 tsp. quick-cooking tapioca

1. Place pork, carrots,
potatoes, parsnips, onion,
garlic, pepper, thyme, and salt
in crock. Mix together well.
2. In a medium bowl,
combine vegetable juice,
brown sugar, mustard, and
tapioca. Pour over meat and
vegetables.
3. Cover. Cook on Low 6
hours or on High 3 hours.

Israeli Couscous with Vegetables

Barbara Hershey, Lititz, PA

Makes 2–4 servings

Prep. Time: 10 minutes
Cooking Time: 10 minutes
Standing Time: 30 minutes

1½ cups vegetable stock
dash of hot red pepper flakes
1 cup uncooked Israeli
couscous
2 Tbsp. butter
1 tsp. dried dill weed
1 clove garlic, minced
5 mushrooms, sliced thinly
⅓ cup chopped scallions, tops
included
½ cup coarsely shredded carrots

1. In medium saucepan,
combine stock and red pepper.
Bring to boil and add couscous.
2. Turn heat off. Cover. Let
stand 30 minutes.
3. In large skillet melt butter
and add dill, garlic, mushrooms,
scallions, and carrots. Sauté 5–6
minutes or until soft.
4. Add couscous to
vegetable mixture. Stir gently.
Serve immediately.

Kona Chicken

Jean Harris Robinson,
Pemberton, NJ

Makes 6 servings

Prep. Time: 30 minutes
Cooking Time: 5 hours
Ideal slow-cooker size: 5-qt.

8 good-sized boneless,
    skinless chicken thighs
2 Tbsp. olive oil
½ cup white wine
14½-oz. can, or 1¾ cups
    homemade, chicken broth
20-oz. can pineapple chunks
2 Tbsp. packed dark brown
    sugar
1 Tbsp. soy sauce
1 minced clove garlic
1 medium green bell pepper,
    chopped
1 Tbsp. grated fresh ginger
3 Tbsp. cornstarch
3 Tbsp. cold water

1. Grease interior of slow-cooker crock.
2. Brown chicken briefly in large skillet in olive oil. Do it in batches over high heat so the pieces brown and don't just steam in each other's juices. Lay browned thighs in crock as they finish in skillet.
3. Deglaze pan with wine.
4. Combine wine and pan drippings, broth, pineapple chunks and their juice, brown sugar, soy sauce, garlic, green pepper, and fresh ginger in a bowl. Pour over chicken.
5. Cover. Cook on Low 4 hours, or until instant-read meat thermometer registers 160°–165°F when stuck in center of thighs.
6. Lift cooked thighs onto platter, cover, and keep warm.
7. In a small bowl, stir together cornstarch and water until smooth.
8. Stir into sauce in crock until smooth.
9. Cover. Cook on High 10 minutes, or until thickened.
10. Serve chicken, on deep platter, covered with sauce.

Szechwan-Style Chicken and Broccoli

Jane Meiser, Harrisonburg, VA

Makes 4 servings

Prep. Time: 20 minutes
Cooking Time: 1–3 hours
Ideal slow-cooker size: 4-qt.

Leftover chicken, chopped
½ cup picante sauce
2 Tbsp. soy sauce
½ tsp. sugar
½ Tbsp. quick-cooking
    tapioca
1 medium onion, chopped
2 cloves garlic, minced
½ tsp. ground ginger
2 cups broccoli florets
1 medium red bell pepper, cut
    into pieces
cooked rice

1. Place all ingredients except the rice into the slow cooker. Stir.
2. Cover. Cook on High 1–1½ hours or Low for 2–3 hours.
3. Serve over cooked rice.

Baked Lima Beans

Phyllis Good, Lancaster, PA

Makes 10–12 servings

Prep. Time: 5 minutes
*Soaking Time: 8 hours, or
    overnight*
Cooking Time: 11–13 hours
Ideal slow-cooker size: 4-qt.

1 lb. dry lima beans
2½ cups water
½ cup minced onion
¾ cup chopped celery
¾ cup mild molasses (not
    blackstrap)
½ cup brown sugar
½ cup ketchup
1½ tsp. dry mustard
1½ tsp. salt
1½ cups tomato juice
1½ Tbsp. Worcestershire
    sauce
¼ tsp. pepper
½ lb. bacon

1. Wash beans, making sure you get rid of any hulls or stones. Pour them into your slow cooker. Cover them with water that comes at least 2 inches above the beans. Cover the cooker and soak the beans for 8 hours or overnight.
2. Pour off the soaking water. Add 2½ cups fresh water.
3. Stir in all of the ingredients except the bacon.
4. Cover. Cook on Low 11–13 hours, or until the beans are tender.
5. While the bean mixture is cooking, fry the bacon until crisp. Remove from

the drippings and place on a paper-towel–covered plate to drain. Then break the bacon into pieces. Set aside until nearly the end of the cooking time.

6. Fifteen minutes before the beans finish cooking, stir in the bacon pieces.

Fruit-Filled Cake (also known as Dump Cake!)

Phyllis Good, Lancaster, PA

Makes 8–10 servings

Prep. Time: 15 minutes
Cooking Time: 2–3 hours
Ideal slow-cooker size: 4-qt.

21-oz. can blueberry or cherry pie filling
20-oz. can crushed pineapple
18½-oz. pkg. yellow cake mix
cinnamon
1 stick butter, straight out of the refrigerator
1 cup chopped nuts, *optional*

1. Grease the inside, bottom, and sides of your slow cooker with cooking spray.

2. Use a safety can opener to open the blueberry, or cherry, pie filling and the crushed pineapple. Using a rubber spatula, scrape the pie filling into the greased slow cooker.

3. Scrape the crushed pineapple on top of the pie filling. Be careful not to mix the layers.

4. Sprinkle the dry cake mix on top of the pineapple. Do not mix the layers. Sprinkle the top of the cake mix with cinnamon.

5. Using a kitchen shears, carefully snip the butter into small pieces. Sprinkle these pieces on top of the cinnamon-covered cake mix.

6. Top the cake with nuts if you wish. Do not stir!

7. Cover your slow cooker. Cook on High for 2–3 hours.

8. After 2 hours, use a potholder to remove the slow cooker lid. Carefully stick a toothpick into the center of the cake topping and pull it out. If the toothpick looks wet, the cake needs to keep cooking. If it has some dry crumbs on it, it's finished cooking.

9. If the cake needs to cook longer, test it with a toothpick every 15 minutes until it's done.

10. Let the cake cool until it's either warm or room temperature. Then it's ready to eat.

SPRING

Week 6

THIS WEEK'S
Menu

Sunday: Melt-In-Your-Mouth Sausages

Monday: Chicken Ginger

Tuesday: Zuppa Toscana (Better Than Olive Garden)

Wednesday: Dad's Spicy Chicken Curry

Thursday: Machacha Beef

Friday: Creamy Spirals with Beef

Saturday: Tuna Salad Casserole

Recommended Side Dish: Creamy Red Potatoes

Special Dessert: Creamy Orange Cheesecake

Shopping List

PROTEIN

3 lbs. sweet Italian sausage

8 chicken breast halves

2 lb. beef roast

FROZEN

5-oz. pkg. frozen chopped spinach

¼ cup frozen orange juice concentrate

DAIRY and REFRIGERATED

1 Tbsp. grated Parmesan cheese

2–4 cups shredded cheddar cheese

1 cup heavy whipping cream

2 cups half-and-half

8-oz. pkg. cream cheese

2 8-oz. pkgs. fat-free cream cheese

3 hard-boiled eggs

3 eggs

6 Tbsp. butter

3 Tbsp. light soft tub margarine

½ cup plain low-fat yogurt

PRODUCE

1 large green bell pepper

3 large onions

2 medium onions

1 cup diced carrots

2 cups broccoli florets

1 cup cauliflower florets

1 cup chopped kale or Swiss chard

2 lbs. small red potatoes, plus 2 more red potatoes

4–6 potatoes

Download this shopping list to your smartphone!

(x.co/ShopList)

½–1½ cups diced celery	ground ginger
1 tsp. orange zest	salt
	pepper
CANNED/DRY GOODS	garlic powder
48-oz. jar spaghetti sauce	cumin
6-oz. can tomato paste	ground coriander
4-oz. can chopped green	ground cloves
chilies	ground cardamom
10¾-oz. can cheddar cheese	cinnamon
soup	chili powder
10¾-oz. can cream of celery	red pepper flakes
soup	turmeric
10¾-oz. can cream of potato	dry mustard
soup	seasoning salt
2 7-oz. cans tuna	3–4 cloves garlic
1 cup salsa	sesame oil
1 lb. uncooked spiral pasta	32-oz. carton chicken broth
6 oz. potato chips	2 beef bouillon cubes
1 envelope dry ranch	flour
dressing mix	sugar
¾ cup graham cracker crumbs	¼ cup sesame seeds
	½ cup low-sodium soy sauce
DO YOU HAVE THESE ON	¼ cup rice vinegar
HAND?	vanilla extract
dried parsley, or fresh	½ cup mayonnaise

Melt-In-Your-Mouth Sausages

Ruth Ann Gingrich,
New Holland, PA
Ruth Hershey, Paradise, PA
Carol Sherwood, Batavia, NY
Nancy Zimmerman,
Loysville, PA

Makes 6–8 servings

Prep. Time: 15 minutes
Cooking Time: 6 hours
Ideal slow-cooker size: 4-qt.

3 lbs. sweet Italian sausage,
  cut into 5-inch lengths
48-oz. jar spaghetti sauce
6-oz. can tomato paste
1 large green bell pepper,
  thinly sliced
1 large onion, thinly sliced
1 Tbsp. grated Parmesan
  cheese
1 tsp. dried parsley, or 1 Tbsp.
  chopped fresh parsley
1 cup water

1. Place sausage in skillet.
Cover with water. Simmer 10
minutes. Drain.

2. Combine remaining
ingredients in slow cooker.
Add sausage.

3. Cover. Cook on Low 6
hours.

Serving Suggestion: Serve
in buns, or cut sausage into
bite-sized pieces and serve
over cooked spaghetti.
Sprinkle with more Parmesan
cheese and garnish with
parsley, if desired.

Chicken Ginger

Dianna R. Milhizer, Brighton, MI

Makes 6–8 servings

Prep. Time: 30 minutes
Cooking Time: 4–6 hours
Ideal slow-cooker size: 6-qt.

8 uncooked chicken breast
  halves, cut up
1 cup diced carrots
½ cup minced onion
½ cup low-sodium soy sauce
¼ cup rice vinegar
¼ cup sesame seeds
1 Tbsp. ground ginger, or ¼
  cup grated fresh ginger
¾ tsp. salt
1 tsp. sesame oil
2 cups broccoli florets
1 cup cauliflower florets

1. Combine all ingredients except broccoli and cauliflower in slow cooker.

2. Cover. Cook on Low 3–5 hours. Stir in broccoli and cauliflower and cook an additional hour.

Serving Suggestion: Serve over brown rice.

Zuppa Toscana (Better Than Olive Garden)

Shelia Heil, Lancaster, PA

Makes 8 servings

Prep. Time: 30 minutes
Cooking Time: 3½–6½ hours
Ideal slow-cooker size: 6-qt.

4–6 potatoes, chopped
1 large onion, chopped
3–4 cloves garlic, minced
32-oz. carton chicken broth
leftover Italian sausage, sliced
2 Tbsp. flour
1 cup heavy whipping cream, room temperature
1 cup chopped kale or Swiss chard
salt and pepper, to taste

1. Add potatoes, onion, garlic, and broth to cooker. Add just enough water to cover vegetables.

2. Cover and cook on High 3–4 hours or Low 5–6 hours, until potatoes are tender. Add in the leftover sausage the last hour of cooking.

3. Separately, whisk together flour and cream until smooth.

4. Thirty minutes before serving, add cream/flour mixture to cooker. Stir. Add kale.

5. Cook on High for 30 minutes, until broth thickens slightly. Taste for salt and pepper, and adjust as needed.

Variations: If you prefer to prepare without milk products, skip the cream and flour mixture. It is delicious either way.

Dad's Spicy Chicken Curry

Tom and Sue Ruth, Lancaster, PA

Makes 4 servings

Prep. Time: 25 minutes
Cooking Time: 6–8 hours
Ideal slow-cooker size: 4- or 5-qt.

water
1 medium onion, diced
5-oz. pkg. frozen chopped spinach, thawed and squeezed dry
½ cup plain low-fat yogurt
2 diced red potatoes
½ tsp. salt
½ tsp. garlic powder
½ tsp. ground ginger
½ tsp. ground cumin
½ tsp. ground coriander
½ tsp. pepper
½ tsp. ground cloves
½ tsp. ground cardamom
½ tsp. ground cinnamon
¼ tsp. chili powder
½ tsp. red pepper flakes

1½ tsp. turmeric
leftover chicken, chopped

1. Place all ingredients into the slow cooker except the leftover chicken.

2. Cover. Cook on Low 4–6 hours, or until potatoes are tender. Stir in the leftover chicken the last hour of cooking.

Machacha Beef

Jeanne Allen, Rye, CO

Makes 8–10 servings

Prep. Time: 15 minutes
Cooking Time: 10–12 hours
Ideal slow-cooker size: 4-qt.

2 lb. beef roast
1 large onion, sliced
4-oz. can chopped green chilies
2 beef bouillon cubes
1½ tsp. dry mustard
½ tsp. garlic powder
1 tsp. seasoning salt
½ tsp. pepper
1 cup salsa

1. Combine all ingredients except salsa in slow cooker. Add just enough water to cover.

2. Cover cooker and cook on Low 10–12 hours, or until beef is tender. Drain and reserve liquid.

3. Shred beef using two forks to pull it apart.

4. Combine beef, salsa, and enough of the reserved liquid to make desired consistency.

5. Use this filling for burritos, chalupas, quesadillas, or tacos.

Creamy Spirals with Beef

Janet Oberholtzer, Ephrata, PA
Renee Baum, Chambersburg, PA

Makes 10–12 servings

Prep. Time: 30 minutes
Cooking Time: 2–2½ hours
Ideal slow-cooker size: 4- to 5-qt.

1 lb. uncooked spiral pasta
¾ stick (6 Tbsp.) butter
2 cups half-and-half
10¾-oz. can cheddar cheese soup
1½ cups leftover shredded beef
2–4 cups shredded cheddar cheese, depending upon how creamy you'd like the dish to be

1. Cook pasta according to package directions, being careful not to overcook it. Drain.
2. Return pasta to saucepan. Stir in butter until it melts.
3. Combine half-and-half and soup in slow cooker, blending well.
4. Stir pasta, leftover shredded beef, and shredded cheese into mixture in cooker.
5. Cover and cook on Low 2–2½ hours, or until heated through and until cheese melts. (If you're home, stir the dish at the end of the first hour of cooking.)

Tuna Salad Casserole

Charlotte Fry, St. Charles, MO
Esther Becker, Gordonville, PA

Makes 4 servings

Prep. Time: 10 minutes
Cooking Time: 5–8 hours
Ideal slow-cooker size: 4-qt.

2 7-oz. cans tuna
10¾-oz. can cream of celery soup
3 hard-boiled eggs, chopped
½–1½ cups diced celery
½ cup diced onions
½ cup mayonnaise
¼ tsp. ground pepper
1½ cups crushed potato chips, *divided*

1. Combine all ingredients except ¼ cup potato chips in slow cooker. Top with remaining chips.
2. Cover. Cook on Low 5–8 hours.

Creamy Red Potatoes (page 59)

Creamy Red Potatoes

Mrs. J. E. Barthold,
Bethlehem, PA

Makes 4–6 servings

Prep. Time: 10 minutes
Cooking Time: 8 hours
Ideal slow-cooker size: 4-qt.

2 lbs. small red potatoes,
  quartered
8-oz. pkg. cream cheese,
  softened
10¾-oz. can cream of potato
  soup
1 envelope dry ranch salad
  dressing mix

1. Place potatoes in slow
cooker.
2. Beat together cream
cheese, soup, and salad
dressing mix. Stir into
potatoes.
3. Cover. Cook on Low 8
hours, or until potatoes are
tender.

Creamy Orange Cheesecake

Jeanette Oberholtzer,
Manheim, PA

Makes 10 servings

Prep. Time: 35 minutes
Cooking Time: 2½–3 hours
Cooling Time: 4 or more hours
Chilling Time: 4 or more hours
Ideal slow-cooker size: 5- or 6-qt.

Crust:
¾ cup graham cracker
  crumbs

2 Tbsp. sugar
3 Tbsp. melted, light, soft tub
  margarine

Filling:
2 8-oz. pkgs. fat-free
  cream cheese, at room
  temperature
⅔ cup sugar
2 eggs
1 egg yolk
¼ cup frozen orange juice
  concentrate
1 tsp. orange zest
1 Tbsp. flour
½ tsp. vanilla extract

1. Combine crust
ingredients. Pat into 7- or
9-inch springform pan,
whichever size fits into your
slow cooker.
2. Cream together cream
cheese and sugar. Add eggs
and yolk. Beat for 3 minutes.
3. Beat in juice, zest, flour,
and vanilla. Beat 2 minutes.
4. Pour batter into crust.
Place on rack in slow cooker.
5. Cover. Cook on High
2½–3 hours. Turn off and
leave stand for 1–2 hours, or
until cool enough to remove
from cooker.
6. Cool completely before
removing sides of pan. Chill
in refrigerator at least 4 hours
before serving.

SPRING

Week 7

THIS WEEK'S
Menu

Sunday: Turkey Loaf
Monday: Turkey Burgers
Tuesday: Glazed Ham in a Bag
Wednesday: Cheddar and Ham Soup
Thursday: Creamy Lasagna
Friday: Sweet Potato Chowder
Saturday: Easy Stuffed Shells

Recommended Side Dish: Country French Vegetables
Special Dessert: Apple Coconut Pudding

Shopping List

PROTEIN

2 lbs. ground turkey

5-lb. cooked bone-in ham

FROZEN

1 cup frozen peas

20-oz. bag frozen stuffed
  shells

DAIRY and REFRIGERATED

4 eggs

3 Tbsp. orange juice

¼ cup lemon juice

3 cups milk

1 stick plus 5 Tbsp. butter

2 cups shredded cheddar
  cheese

1½ cups cottage cheese

8 oz. sour cream

cheese slices, *optional*

PRODUCE

3 medium onions

¾ cup chopped onion

2 carrots

½ cup chopped carrots

1 rib celery

⅔ cup finely chopped celery

4 green onions

1 parsnip

1 turnip or rutabaga

½ lb. mushrooms

2 cups diced potatoes

3 potatoes

2 medium red potatoes

1 medium sweet potato

1 Tbsp. minced fresh
  rosemary, or dried

1 Tbsp. minced fresh thyme,
  or dried

⅓ cup chopped parsley

6–7 apples

Download this shopping list to your
smartphone!
(x.co/ShopList)

CANNED/DRY GOODS

16-oz. can evaporated milk

15-oz. can marinara or
 spaghetti sauce

15-oz. can green beans

18-oz. butter recipe golden
 cake mix

14½-oz. can chicken broth

¾ cup dry bread crumbs

3–4 uncooked lasagna
 noodles

hamburger buns

1 cup shredded coconut

pickles, *optional*

relish, *optional*

DO YOU HAVE THESE ON HAND?

salt

black pepper

sesame seeds

garlic powder, or fresh
 minced

seasoning salt

dried oregano

parsley flakes

crushed red pepper

1 clove garlic, or powder

1 tsp. chicken bouillon
 granules

extra-virgin olive oil

Worcestershire sauce

ketchup

Dijon mustard

prepared mustard, *optional*

mayonnaise, *optional*

flour

½ cup chopped walnuts

Turkey Loaf

Dottie Schmidt,
Kansas City, MO

Makes 10–12 servings

Prep. Time: 15 minutes
Cooking Time: 3–4 hours
Ideal slow-cooker size: 4- or 5-qt.

2 lbs. ground turkey
¾ cup dry bread crumbs
⅔ cup finely chopped celery
2 eggs, beaten
4 green onions, finely
  chopped
½ tsp. salt
¼ tsp. black pepper
2 Tbsp. Worcestershire sauce
2 Tbsp. ketchup
1–2 Tbsp. sesame seeds

1. Grease interior of slow-cooker crock.

2. Make a tinfoil sling for your slow cooker so you can lift the cooked Turkey Loaf out easily. Begin by folding a strip of tinfoil accordion-fashion so that it's about 1½–2 inches wide, and long enough to fit from the top edge of the crock, down inside, and up the other side, plus a 2-inch overhang on each side of the cooker. Make a second strip exactly like the first.

3. Place the one strip in the crock, running from end to end. Place the second strip in the crock, running from side to side. The two strips should form a cross in the bottom of the crock.

4. Combine all ingredients except ketchup and sesame seeds in bowl, mixing together gently but well.

Once well mixed, set aside half of the mixture and refrigerate for turkey burgers later this week.

5. Form the remaining turkey mixture into a 6-inch-long loaf and place in crock, centering loaf where foil strips cross.

6. Spread ketchup over top of loaf. Sprinkle with sesame seeds.

7. Cover. Cook on Low for 3–4 hours, or until instant-read meat thermometer registers 150°–155°F when stuck in center of loaf.

8. Using foil handles, lift loaf out of crock and onto cutting board. Cover and keep warm for 10 minutes. Then slice and serve.

2. Cover with marinara sauce.

3. Pour green beans in center.

4. Cover. Cook on Low 8 hours, or on High 3 hours.

Country French Vegetables

Phyllis Good, Lancaster, PA

Makes 4–5 servings

Prep. Time: 10 minutes
Cooking Time: 3–6 hours
Ideal slow-cooker size: 5-qt.

3 Tbsp. extra-virgin olive oil, *divided*

3 potatoes, unpeeled, cut in 1-inch pieces

2 carrots, unpeeled, cut in 1-inch pieces

1 parsnip, peeled, cut in 1-inch pieces

1 turnip or rutabaga, peeled, cut in 1-inch pieces

2 medium onions, cut in wedges

½ lb. fresh mushrooms, halved

1 Tbsp. minced fresh, or ½ tsp. dried, rosemary

1 Tbsp. minced fresh, or ½ tsp. dried, thyme

⅓ cup chopped fresh parsley

¾ tsp. salt

¼ tsp. freshly ground black pepper

1. Lightly grease slow cooker with 1 Tbsp. olive oil.

2. Combine all ingredients with remaining 2 Tbsp. olive oil in slow cooker

3. Cover and cook on Low for 3–6 hours, depending how tender you want the vegetables or how long you want to be away from home.

Apple Coconut Pudding

Phyllis Good, Lancaster, PA

Makes 4–6 servings

Prep. Time: 15 minutes
Cooking Time: 2 hours
Standing Time: 30 minutes
Ideal slow-cooker size: 5-qt.

18-oz. butter recipe golden cake mix

1 cup shredded coconut

1 stick butter, at room temperature

6 cups peeled, sliced, firm baking apples, approximately 6–7 apples

½ cup chopped walnuts

1 cup water

¼ cup lemon juice

1. Combine dry cake mix and coconut in a large bowl. Cut in butter with pastry cutter.

2. Place sliced apples in lightly greased slow cooker. Sprinkle with walnuts.

3. Sprinkle crumb mixture evenly over apples and walnuts.

4. In a small bowl combine water and lemon juice and pour over top of apples and crumbs.

5. Cover and cook on High for 2 hours, until set and apples are soft.

6. Allow to sit for 30 minutes in the turned-off cooker before spooning out into dessert dishes. Lovely with ice cream or whipped cream.

SPRING

Week 8

THIS WEEK'S Menu

Sunday: Tempting Tortilla Casserole
Monday: Hamburger Vegetable Soup
Tuesday: Old-Fashioned Stewed Chicken
Wednesday: Chicken Gumbo
Thursday: Chicken Pasta
Friday: Cedric's Casserole
Saturday: Pizza in a Bowl

Recommended Side Dish: Maple-Nut Cornbread with Country Bacon
Special Dessert: Blueberry Crisp

Shopping List

PROTEIN
2¾ lbs. ground beef
6 lb. whole chicken
4 oz. sliced pepperoni
6 strips double-smoked bacon

DAIRY and REFRIGERATED
1½ cups grated cheese, your
   choice
1½ cups shredded
   mozzarella cheese
8 oz. smoked Gouda cheese
9 Tbsp. butter
½ cup buttermilk
2 eggs
vanilla yogurt, *optional*

PRODUCE
1 small onion
2 medium onions
1½ cups chopped onion
1 rib celery
½ cup chopped celery
1 carrot
½ cup chopped carrots
½ green bell pepper
1 cup chopped bell peppers
1 cup okra
1 large tomato
1 cup chopped tomatoes
1 large zucchini
3 cups shredded cabbage
1½ cups fresh mushrooms
1 Tbsp. chopped parsley, or
   dried
1 Tbsp. chopped thyme, or
   dried
1 Tbsp. chopped rosemary,
   or dried
4 cups blueberries
½ tsp. grated lemon peel

Download this shopping list to your
smartphone!
(x.co/ShopList)

CANNED/DRY GOODS

1 envelope dry taco seasoning

16-oz. can fat-free refried beans

16-oz. can chopped tomatoes

14½-oz. can low-sodium diced tomatoes

26-oz. jar fat-free, low-sodium marinara sauce

10¾-oz. can tomato soup

bag of tortilla chips

¼ cup barley

1 envelope chicken gravy mix

macaroni

2 Tbsp. evaporated milk, or cream

DO YOU HAVE THESE ON HAND?

bay leaf

seasoned salt

salt

pepper

Old Bay Seasoning

Italian seasoning

cinnamon

3–4 cloves garlic

2 tsp. beef bouillon granules

3 cups chicken broth

1 cup yellow cornmeal

baking soda

baking powder

flour

½ cup whole wheat flour

sugar

½ cup brown sugar

vegetable oil

¾ cup dry rolled oats

¼ cup maple syrup

½ cup pecans

2 Tbsp. quick-cooking tapioca

2 Tbsp. lemon juice

¼ cup ketchup

Tempting Tortilla Casserole

Phyllis Good, Lancaster, PA

Makes 4 servings

Prep. Time: 20 minutes
Cooking Time: 3–4 hours
Ideal slow-cooker size: 3-qt.

2¾ lb. ground beef
1 envelope dry taco
   seasoning
1½ cups (6 oz.) grated
   cheese of your choice,
   divided
16-oz. can fat-free refried
   beans
bag of tortilla chips (for
   topping the casserole)

1. Brown the ground beef. Reserve 1¾ lb. of it for later this week in your refrigerator.

2. Add the remaining browned ground beef and the taco seasoning to your slow cooker and mix well.

3. Sprinkle 1 cup of cheese over top of the meat.

4. Use a rubber spatula to scrape the refried beans on top of the cheese. Spread the beans out in an even layer. Be careful not to disturb the grated cheese while you do it.

5. Sprinkle the remaining cheese on top of the beans.

6. Cover your slow cooker. Cook on Low for 3–4 hours.

7. Top the casserole with tortilla chips just before serving.

Hamburger Vegetable Soup

Judy Buller, Bluffton, OH

Makes 5–6 servings

Prep. Time: 20 minutes
Cooking Time: 4–8 hours
Ideal slow-cooker size: 4- to 5-qt.

¾ lb. leftover browned ground
   beef
½ cup chopped onion
½ cup chopped celery
½ cup chopped carrots
3 cups water
2 tsp. beef bouillon granules
1 bay leaf
¼ cup barley
16-oz. can chopped tomatoes
¼ cup ketchup
1 tsp. seasoned salt
salt and pepper, to taste

1. Place all ingredients into your slow cooker.

2. Cover and cook 4 hours on High or 6–8 hours on Low.

Old-Fashioned Stewed Chicken

Bonnie Goering, Bridgewater, VA

Makes 6–8 servings

Prep. Time: 20 minutes
Cooking Time: 8¼ hours
Ideal slow-cooker size: 5-qt.

6-lb. chicken, cut up
1 small onion, cut into wedges
1 rib celery, sliced
1 carrot, sliced
1 Tbsp. chopped fresh parsley, or 1 tsp. dried parsley
1 Tbsp. chopped fresh thyme, or 1 tsp. dried thyme
1 Tbsp. chopped fresh rosemary, or 1 tsp. dried rosemary
3 tsp. salt
¼ tsp. pepper
3–4 cups hot water
⅓ cup flour

1. Place chicken in slow cooker. Scatter vegetables, herbs, and seasonings around it and over top. Pour water down along interior wall of cooker so as not to disturb the other ingredients.

2. Cover. Cook on Low 8 hours.

3. Remove chicken from cooker. When cool enough to handle, debone. Set aside and keep warm.

4. In small bowl, stir ⅓ cup flour into 1 cup chicken broth from slow cooker.

5. When smooth, stir back into slow cooker. Continue cooking on Low until broth thickens, stirring occasionally to prevent lumps from forming. When gravy is bubbly and thickened it is ready.

6. Spoon the gravy over the chicken when serving.

Chicken Gumbo

Virginia Bender, Dover, DE

Makes 4 servings

Prep. Time: 25 minutes
Cooking Time: 3–4 hours
Ideal slow-cooker size: 3-qt.

1 medium onion, chopped
3–4 cloves garlic, minced
½ green bell pepper, diced
1 cup okra, sliced
1 cup chopped tomatoes
3 cups chicken broth
1 tsp. Old Bay Seasoning
2 cups chopped leftover chicken

1. Combine all ingredients in slow cooker, except the leftover chicken.

2. Cover. Cook on Low 3–4 hours. The last hour of cooking, add the leftover chicken. Stir.

Serving Suggestion: Serve over rice.

Chicken Pasta

Evelyn L. Ward, Greeley, CO

Makes 4 servings

Prep. Time: 25–30 minutes
Cooking Time: 4 hours and 20 minutes
Ideal slow-cooker size: 4-qt.

remaining leftover chicken, diced
1 large zucchini, diced
1 envelope chicken gravy mix
2 Tbsp. water
2 Tbsp. evaporated milk, or cream
1 large tomato, chopped
4 cups cooked macaroni
8 oz. smoked Gouda cheese, grated

1. Place the chicken, zucchini, gravy mix, and water into the slow cooker and stir together.

2. Cover. Cook on Low 4 hours.

3. Add milk and tomato. Cook an additional 20 minutes.

4. Stir in pasta. Top with cheese. Serve immediately.

Cedric's Casserole

Kathy Purcell, Dublin, OH

Makes 4–6 servings

Prep. Time: 30 minutes
Cooking Time: 3–4 hours
Ideal slow-cooker size: 3-qt.

1 medium onion, chopped
3 Tbsp. butter
remaining 1 lb. browned
    ground beef
½–¾ tsp. salt
¼ tsp. pepper
3 cups shredded cabbage,
    divided
10¾-oz. can tomato soup

1. Sauté onion in skillet in butter.
2. Add ground beef, and onions.
3. Season the meat and onions with salt and pepper.
4. Layer half of cabbage in slow cooker, followed by half of meat mixture.
5. Repeat layers again.
6. Pour soup over top.
7. Cover. Cook on Low 3–4 hours.

Pizza in a Bowl

Phyllis Good, Lancaster, PA

Makes 6 servings

Prep. Time: 10 minutes
Cooking Time: 5–6 hours
Ideal slow-cooker size: 3½-qt.

14½-oz. can low-sodium
    diced tomatoes
26-oz. jar fat-free, low-sodium
    marinara sauce
4 oz. sliced pepperoni
1 cup chopped bell peppers
1 cup chopped onions
1 cup water
1 Tbsp. Italian seasoning
1 cup uncooked macaroni
1½ cups fresh mushrooms,
    sliced, *optional*
1½ cups shredded mozzarella
    cheese

1. Pour the tomatoes, marinara sauce, pepperoni, chopped peppers and onions, water, Italian seasoning, dry macaroni, and mushrooms if you wish into your slow cooker.
2. Cover your slow cooker. Cook the pasta mixture on Low for 5–6 hours.
3. After the pasta has cooked, use a potholder to take the lid off of your slow cooker.
4. Carefully spoon the hot pasta mixture among 6 bowls.
5. Sprinkle each with mozzarella cheese.

Maple-Nut Cornbread with Country Bacon

Phyllis Good, Lancaster, PA

Makes 1 loaf

Prep. Time: 20 minutes
Cooking Time: 2 hours
Ideal slow-cooker size: 3-qt.

6 strips double-smoked
    bacon, or regular if you can't
    find this high-octane kind
1 cup yellow cornmeal
½ cup all-purpose flour
1 tsp. baking soda
1 tsp. baking powder
1 tsp. salt
¼ cup maple syrup
½ cup buttermilk
¼ cup vegetable oil
2 eggs
½ cup pecans, coarsely
    chopped
vanilla yogurt, or maple syrup
    for topping, *optional*

1. Fry the bacon over medium heat in a skillet. When the bacon is crisp, reserve the drippings and remove the bacon to drain on a paper towel. Then crumble the bacon into chunks.
2. Combine the cornmeal, flour, baking soda, baking powder, and salt in a good-sized bowl.
3. In a separate bowl, beat together the maple syrup, buttermilk, oil, and eggs.
4. Stir the liquid mixture into the dry ingredients. Mix well.
5. Combine the pecans with the crumbled bacon. Stir them into the batter.
6. Pour just enough reserved bacon drippings into your greased slow cooker to coat the bottom with a thin film. Then pour the batter into the cooker.
7. Cover. Cook the bread on High for 2 hours, or until a toothpick inserted in center of loaf comes out clean.
8. Serve warm. Vanilla yogurt or maple syrup makes a good topping.

Blueberry Crisp

Phyllis Good, Lancaster, PA

Makes 6–8 servings

Prep. Time: 15–20 minutes
Cooking Time: 2 hours
Ideal slow-cooker size: 4-qt.

½ cup brown sugar
¾ cup dry rolled oats
½ cup whole wheat flour, or
   all-purpose flour
½ tsp. cinnamon
salt
6 Tbsp. butter, at room
   temperature

4 cups blueberries, fresh or
   frozen
2–4 Tbsp. sugar, depending
   on how sweet you like
   things
2 Tbsp. quick-cooking tapioca
2 Tbsp. lemon juice
½ tsp. grated lemon peel

1. In a large bowl, combine brown sugar, oats, flour, cinnamon, and salt. Cut in butter using a pastry cutter or two knives to make crumbs. Set aside.

2. In a separate bowl, stir together blueberries, sugar, tapioca, lemon juice, and lemon peel.

3. Spoon blueberry mixture into greased slow cooker. Sprinkle crumbs over blueberries.

4. Cover and cook on High for 1½ hours. Remove lid and cook an additional 30 minutes on High.

SPRING

Week 9

THIS WEEK'S
Menu

Sunday: Spiced Pot Roast
Monday: Applesauce Meatballs
Tuesday: Lotsa Tomatoes Beef Stew
Wednesday: Homemade Spaghetti Sauce
Thursday: Chicken Delicious
Friday: Downright Flavorful Macaroni and Cheese
Saturday: Wild Rice with Chicken

Recommended Side Dish: Red Bliss Potato Salad
Special Dessert: Rustic Apple Squares

Shopping List

PROTEIN
2-lb. boneless beef top
   round roast
1 lb. ground beef
¾ lb. ground pork
8 boneless skinless chicken
   breast halves

DAIRY and REFRIGERATED
2 cups apple juice
3 eggs
2 hard-boiled eggs
¼ cup grated Parmesan
   cheese
3 cups shredded sharp
   cheddar or Swiss cheese
1½ cups plus 6 Tbsp. milk
1 stick butter

PRODUCE
2 small onions
1 medium onion
1 large onion
¼ cup chopped onion
5–6 carrots
6 ribs celery
¼ cup chopped celery
6 medium tomatoes
4 qts. cherry tomatoes
3–4 potatoes
12 medium red bliss
   potatoes
¼ lb. mushrooms
1 Tbsp. fresh parsley
6 cups sliced, firm red
   apples

CANNED/DRY GOODS
16-oz. can tomato sauce
2 10¾-oz. cans cream of
   celery soup
12-oz. can evaporated milk

Download this shopping list to your
smartphone!
(x.co/ShopList)

1 cup soft bread crumbs

spaghetti

8 oz. dry elbow macaroni

1 cup uncooked wild rice

¾ cup unsweetened
  applesauce

**DO YOU HAVE THESE ON
HAND?**

salt

ground ginger, or fresh

cinnamon

nutmeg

dried basil

dried oregano

2 bay leaves

pepper

dried rosemary

dried thyme

Italian herb seasoning

dry mustard

minced onion

garlic powder

dried sage

celery seed

white pepper

1 whole clove, or ground
  cloves

2 cloves garlic

olive oil

oil of your choice

white vinegar

3 cups chicken stock

1 Tbsp. Old English mustard

baking powder

2 cups all-purpose flour

1 tsp. lemon juice

sugar

¼ cup ketchup

cornstarch

¼ cup mayonnaise

½ cup quick-cooking tapioca

¼ cup slivered almonds

SPIRITS

⅓ cup sherry or white wine,
  optional

Spiced Pot Roast

Janie Steele, Moore, OK

Makes 10 servings

Prep. Time: 30 minutes
Cooking Time: 3–4 hours
Ideal slow-cooker size: 6-qt.

2-lb. boneless beef top round roast
1 Tbsp. olive oil
2 cups apple juice
16-oz. can tomato sauce
2 small onions, chopped
3 Tbsp. white vinegar
1 Tbsp. salt
¾ tsp. ground ginger, or 1 Tbsp. fresh ginger, minced
2–3 tsp. ground cinnamon
¼ cup cornstarch
1 cup water

1. Brown roast in olive oil on all sides in a skillet. Then place in slow cooker.
2. Combine juice, tomato sauce, onions, vinegar, salt, ginger, and cinnamon. Pour over roast.
3. Cook on High 2–3 hours.
4. Mix cornstarch and water until smooth. Remove roast from cooker and keep warm on a platter. Stir cornstarch water into juices in cooker.
5. Return roast to cooker and continue cooking 1 hour on High, or until meat is done and gravy thickens.

Applesauce Meatballs

Mary E. Wheatley, Mashpee, MA

Makes 8–10 servings

Prep. Time: 40 minutes
Cooking Time: 4–6 hours
Ideal slow-cooker size: 3-qt.

1 lb. ground beef
¾ lb. ground pork
1 egg
1 cup soft bread crumbs
¾ cup unsweetened applesauce
¾ tsp. salt
¼ tsp. pepper
oil of your choice
¼ cup ketchup
¼ cup water

1. Combine beef, pork, egg, bread crumbs, applesauce, salt, and pepper in bowl. Form into 1½-inch balls.
2. Brown in oil in batches in skillet. Transfer meat to slow cooker as a batch browns, reserving drippings.
3. Combine ketchup and water in skillet. Stir up browned drippings and mix together well. Spoon over meatballs, making sure that all are covered.
4. Cover. Cook on Low 4–6 hours.

Lotsa Tomatoes Beef Stew

Bernice A. Esau,
North Newton, KS

Makes 6 servings

Prep. Time: 20–25 minutes
Cooking Time: 4–6 hours
Ideal slow-cooker size: 6- or 7-qt.

5–6 carrots, cut in 1-inch
  pieces
1 large onion, cut in chunks
3 ribs celery, sliced
6 medium tomatoes, cut up
  and gently mashed
½ cup quick-cooking tapioca
1 whole clove, or ¼–½ tsp.
  ground cloves
1 tsp. dried basil
½ tsp. dried oregano
2 bay leaves
2 tsp. salt
½ tsp. black pepper
3–4 potatoes, cubed
leftover beef, chopped

1. Place all ingredients in slow cooker except the beef. Mix together well.

2. Cover. Cook on Low 4–6 hours. The last hour of cooking, add the beef and continue cooking until it is warmed through.

Homemade Spaghetti Sauce

Beverly Hummel, Fleetwood, PA

Makes 12 cups

Prep. Time: 20 minutes
Cooking Time: 4–5 hours
Ideal slow-cooker size: 6-qt.

4 qts. cherry tomatoes
1 medium onion, minced
2 cloves garlic, minced
1 Tbsp. oil of your choice
3 tsp. sugar
1 tsp. dried rosemary
2 tsp. dried thyme
2 tsp. Italian herb seasoning
1 tsp. salt
½ tsp. pepper
leftover meatballs
hot cooked spaghetti

1. Stem tomatoes, leaving the skins on. Blend until smooth in blender.

2. In a skillet, sauté onions and garlic in oil.

3. Add sauté to slow cooker. Add tomatoes, sugar, rosemary, thyme, Italian seasoning, salt, and pepper.

4. Add in the leftover meatballs.

5. Simmer on Low in slow cooker until thickened, about 4–5 hours. Remove the lid for the final 30–60 minutes of cooking time if you'd like a thicker sauce.

6. Serve over spaghetti.

Chicken Delicious

Orpha Herr, Andover, NY

Makes 8 servings

Prep. Time: 15–20 minutes
Cooking Time: 4–10 hours
Ideal slow-cooker size: 5-qt.

8 boneless, skinless chicken
  breast halves
1 tsp. fresh lemon juice
salt and pepper, to taste
2 10¾-oz. cans cream of
  celery soup
⅓ cup sherry or wine, *optional*
¼ cup grated Parmesan
  cheese

1. Rinse chicken breasts and pat dry. Place chicken in slow cooker in layers. Season each layer with a sprinkling of lemon juice, salt, and pepper.

2. In a medium bowl, mix soups with sherry or wine if you wish. Pour mixture over chicken. Sprinkle with Parmesan cheese.

3. Cover and cook on Low 8–10 hours, or on High 4–5 hours, or until chicken is tender but not dry or mushy.

Downright Flavorful Macaroni and Cheese

Phyllis Good, Lancaster, PA

Makes 6 servings

Prep. Time: 15 minutes
Cooking Time: 3–4½ hours
Ideal slow-cooker size: 4-qt.

8 oz. elbow macaroni, uncooked
3 cups shredded sharp cheddar or Swiss cheese, *divided*
12-oz. can evaporated milk
1½ cups milk (can be skim, whole, or somewhere in between)
2 eggs
1 tsp. salt
¼ tsp. black pepper
½ tsp. dry mustard, *optional*
2 Tbsp. dry minced onion, *optional*

1. Combine all ingredients, except 1 cup cheese, in greased slow cooker. Sprinkle reserved cup of cheese over top.
2. Cover. Cook on Low 3–4 hours. Do not remove the lid or stir until the mixture has finished cooking.
3. If you'd like a bit of a crusty top, uncover the cooker and cook another 15 minutes.

Wild Rice with Chicken

Phyllis Good, Lancaster, PA

Makes 4–5 servings

Prep. Time: 20 minutes
Cooking Time: 4–8 hours
Ideal slow-cooker size: 4-qt.

1 cup wild rice, uncooked
¼ cup chopped onion
¼ cup chopped celery
leftover chicken, chopped
3 cups chicken stock
¼–½ tsp. salt, depending how salty your stock is
⅛ tsp. pepper
¼ tsp. garlic powder
½ tsp. dried sage
¼ lb. fresh mushrooms, sliced
¼ cup slivered almonds
1 Tbsp. fresh parsley

1. Wash and drain rice.
2. Combine all ingredients, except mushrooms, almonds, and parsley, in greased slow cooker. Mix well.
3. Cover. Cook on Low 4–8 hours, or until rice is tender. Don't lift the lid to check on things until the rice has cooked at least 4 hours.
4. Ten minutes before the end of the cooking time, stir in the mushrooms. Cover and continue cooking.

5. Just before serving, stir in slivered almonds. Garnish with fresh parsley.

Red Bliss Potato Salad

Tim Smith, Wynnewood, PA

Makes 6 servings

Prep. Time: 15 minutes
Cooking Time: 20–25 minutes
Chilling Time: 2½ hours

12 medium red bliss potatoes
3 ribs celery, diced
2 hard-boiled eggs, diced
¼ cup mayonnaise
2 Tbsp. white vinegar
1 Tbsp. Old English, or your choice of dry mustard
1 tsp. celery seed
1 tsp. white pepper
1 tsp. black pepper
salt, to taste

1. Cook whole potatoes until medium soft, but still firm. Drain. Allow to cool, then dice.
2. Put diced potatoes in large bowl. Add rest of ingredients and stir gently.
3. Chill in refrigerator for 2 hours before serving.

Rustic Apple Squares

Phyllis Good, Lancaster, PA

Makes 12 servings

Prep. Time: 25 minutes
Cooking Time: 4 hours
Ideal slow-cooker size: 6-qt. oval

2 cups all-purpose flour
3 tsp. baking powder
½ tsp. salt
1 stick cold butter
6 Tbsp. milk
6 cups sliced firm red apples, peeled
1 tsp. cinnamon
pinch nutmeg
½–1 cup sugar, depending on how sweet your apples are
1 cup boiling water

1. In a large mixing bowl, stir together flour, baking powder, and salt.
2. Cut in butter until crumbly. Stir in milk and blend well to make a soft dough. Really, what you are making is biscuit dough.
3. Divide dough in half. Roll each piece into an oval the size of your slow cooker crock.
4. Grease slow cooker. Place one piece of dough in bottom of the inner crock.
5. Spread the apples over the bottom crust. Sprinkle with cinnamon and nutmeg.
6. Place second pastry crust lightly on top of apples.
7. Use a silicone or plastic knife to cut down through all the layers, making one long cut down the middle and at least 6 cuts side to side.
8. Separately, stir together sugar and boiling water. Pour evenly over dough and apples.
9. Cover and cook on Low for 4 hours until apples are tender.

SPRING

Week 10

Menu

Sunday: Middle Eastern Sandwiches

Monday: Middle Eastern Beef Lettuce Boats

Tuesday: Sunny Chicken

Wednesday: Apple Chicken Salad

Thursday: Garden Vegetable Bake

Friday: Shredded Taco Beef

Saturday: Tostadas

Recommended Side Dish: The Best Broccoli Salad

Special Dessert: Lemon Pudding Cake

Shopping List

PROTEIN
2 4-lb. boneless beef chuck
   roasts
6-lb. whole chicken
10 slices bacon

DAIRY and REFRIGERATED
plain yogurt, *optional*
½ cup plain nonfat Greek
   yogurt
1 cup Miracle Whip dressing
5 Tbsp. butter
3 eggs
1½ cups milk
¾ cup grated sharp cheese
½ cup plus 2 Tbsp. lemon
   juice

PRODUCE
1 large onion
2 medium onions
1 small onion
2¼ cups diced onion
2 Tbsp. minced garlic
1 head romaine lettuce
2–3 tomatoes
1 English cucumber
2 ribs celery
1 bell pepper
2 bunches broccoli
1 cup green beans
2–3 ears of corn
2 Tbsp. horseradish
1 zucchini
9 rosemary sprigs
1 Tbsp. fresh chopped dill
3 lemons
1½ tsp. lemon zest
3 limes
3 oranges
1 green apple
1 red apple

CANNED/DRY GOODS

6-oz. can tomato paste

8-oz. can tomato sauce

1 can refried beans

1¼ cups canned diced green
  chili peppers

10–16 pita breads

1 cup cubed bread

½ cup chipotle salsa

1 envelope dry taco
  seasoning mix

10 tostada shells

⅓ cup dried cranberries

1 cup golden raisins

1 cup chopped cashews

DO YOU HAVE THESE ON HAND?

dried oregano

dried rosemary

salt

pepper

chili powder

dried basil

garlic powder

3 cloves garlic

6 Tbsp. cooking oil

apple cider vinegar

vinegar of your choice

Dijon mustard

½ cup mayonnaise or salad
  dressing

cornstarch

¼ cup hot pepper sauce

prepared mustard

sugar

flour

SPIRITS

1 cup dry red wine

Middle Eastern Sandwiches

Phyllis Good, Lancaster, PA

Makes 10–16 sandwiches

Prep. Time: 50 minutes
Cooking Time: 5–10 hours
Ideal slow-cooker size: 5-qt.

4-lb. boneless beef chuck roast, cut into 1½-inch cubes
4 Tbsp. cooking oil, *divided*
2 cups chopped onions
2 cloves garlic, minced
1 cup dry red wine
6-oz. can tomato paste
1 tsp. dried oregano
1 tsp. dried basil
½ tsp. dried rosemary
2 tsp. salt
dash of pepper
¼ cup cornstarch
¼ cup cold water
10–16 pita breads
lettuce, tomato, cucumber, and plain yogurt, *optional*, for serving

1. Brown meat, 1 lb. at a time, in skillet in 1 Tbsp. oil. As each pound finishes browning, remove the meat with a slotted spoon and transfer it into the slow cooker. Add more oil as needed with each new pound of beef. Reserve drippings in the skillet.

2. Sauté the chopped onions and garlic in drippings until tender.

3. Add wine, tomato paste, oregano, basil, rosemary, salt, and pepper to the onions. Stir, and then spoon over the meat in the cooker.

4. Cover. Cook on Low 8–10 hours, or on High 5–6, or until meat is falling-apart tender, but not dry.

5. Turn cooker to High. Combine cornstarch and water in small bowl until smooth. Stir into meat mixture. Cook until bubbly and thickened, 15–30 minutes, stirring occasionally.

6. Open pita breads. Fill each with the meat mixture, and then lettuce, tomato, cucumber, and yogurt, as desired.

Middle Eastern Beef Lettuce Boats

Hope Comerford, Clinton Township, MI

Makes 4–8 servings

Prep. Time: 20 minutes
Chilling Time: 30 minutes
Cooking Time: 3–4 minutes

1 head romaine, washed, dried
leftover beef, warmed

Tzatziki Sauce:
½ cup plain nonfat Greek yogurt

½ cup diced English cucumber
1 clove garlic, minced
½ tsp. lemon zest
1½ tsp. lemon juice
1 Tbsp. fresh chopped dill
¼ tsp. salt
⅛ tsp. pepper

1. Wash and dry the lettuce.
2. Warm the leftover beef.
3. Mix up all of the ingredients for the tzatziki sauce.
4. To serve, spoon some of the beef into each boat and drizzle with tzatziki sauce.

Serving Suggestion: garnish with chopped tomatoes.

Sunny Chicken

Phyllis Good, Lancaster, PA

Makes 6–8 servings

Prep. Time: 20–30 minutes
Cooking Time: 4–6 hours
Ideal slow-cooker size: 6-qt.

1 large onion, sliced into thin rings, *divided*
3 sweet, juicy oranges, each cut into thin slices, *divided*
3 lemons, thinly sliced, *divided*
3 limes, thinly sliced, *divided*
9 fresh rosemary sprigs, *divided*
2 Tbsp. minced garlic, *divided*
6-lb. chicken
salt and pepper, to taste

1. Layer ⅓ of the onion slices, 1 sliced orange, 1 sliced lemon, and 1 sliced lime into your slow cooker. Top with 3 rosemary sprigs and ⅓ of the minced garlic.
2. Stuff with half the remaining onion slices, 1 sliced orange, 1 sliced lemon, and 1 sliced lime, half the remaining garlic, and 3 rosemary sprigs. Place the stuffed chicken—upside down—in your slow cooker. (That helps to keep the breast meat from drying out.)
3. Sprinkle with plenty of salt and pepper. Spread the rest of the onion, orange, lemon, and lime slices, and the remaining garlic and rosemary sprigs around the chicken and on top of it.
4. Cover. Cook on Low 4–6 hours, or until meat is tender but not dry.
5. Remove chicken from cooker and place right-side up on rimmed baking sheet. Place under broiler until top is nicely browned, only a minute or so, watching closely.
6. Cover chicken with foil for 15 minutes. Then carve, put the pieces on a platter, and spoon the citrus and onion slices over top before serving.

Apple Chicken Salad

Marlene Fonken, Upland, CA

Makes 6 servings

Prep. Time: 30–40 minutes
Chilling Time: 2–12 hours

Dressing:
½ cup mayonnaise, or salad dressing
2 Tbsp. apple cider vinegar
2 Tbsp. lemon juice
2–3 Tbsp. Dijon mustard
2 cups chopped leftover chicken
2 ribs celery, chopped
¼ cup diced onion
1 green apple, chopped
1 red apple, chopped
⅓ cup dried cranberries
salt and pepper, to taste

1. Whisk together mayonnaise, apple cider vinegar, lemon juice, and mustard. Set aside.
2. Mix together chicken, celery, onion, apples, cranberries, salt, and pepper.
3. Pour on dressing and toss to mix. Refrigerate until serving. Flavor develops with longer chilling.

Tips: 1. Break up and soften a handful of rice sticks; drain and add to the finished salad. This salad is gluten-free!
2. If you're starting with raw chicken, chop it into bite-sized pieces. In a saucepan, cover the chicken pieces with water or chicken broth. Cover and cook on medium heat until the chicken pieces are white through, 10–20 minutes.

Drain. This can be done ahead of time.
3. You can substitute 12½-oz. can chicken, drained and broken up, for the leftover chicken in this salad.

Garden Vegetable Bake

Phyllis Good, Lancaster, PA

Makes 4–6 servings

Prep. Time: 20 minutes
Cooking Time: 2½–3 hours
Ideal slow-cooker size: 4- or 5-qt.

1 cup green beans, trimmed and halved
1 zucchini, sliced
2–3 ears corn, kernels cut off
1 medium onion, sliced in rings
1 bell pepper, sliced in rings
2 tomatoes, sliced
salt and pepper, to taste
¾ cup grated sharp cheese
2 Tbsp. butter
1 cup cubed bread

1. In lightly greased slow cooker, layer the vegetables in the order listed, starting with green beans and ending with tomatoes, adding a sprinkle of salt and pepper every other layer.
2. Sprinkle with cheese.
3. Cover and cook on High for 2–2½ hours, until green beans are as tender as you like them.
4. In a skillet, melt butter and add cubed bread. Stir occasionally until bread cubes are toasted.

5. Sprinkle toasted bread cubes on top of bake, pressing down lightly. Continue cooking, uncovered, until bread warms but remains crisp.

Shredded Taco Beef

Phyllis Good, Lancaster, PA

Makes 8–10 servings

Prep. Time: 15 minutes
Cooking Time: 8–10 hours
Ideal slow-cooker size: 4-qt.

4-lb. boneless beef chuck roast
2 Tbsp. oil
1 tsp. salt
1 tsp. pepper
1 medium onion, chopped
1 tsp. chili powder
1 tsp. garlic powder
1¼ cups canned diced green chili peppers
½ cup chipotle salsa
¼ cup hot pepper sauce, or less if you wish
water
flour, *optional*

1. Sear roast on all sides in oil in skillet until well browned. Place in slow cooker. Season on all sides with salt and pepper.
2. Mix together the remaining ingredients, except water and flour, in a bowl. Spoon over the meat.
3. Pour the water in along the side of the roast so you don't wash off the topping,

until the bottom ⅓ of the roast is covered.

4. Cover. Cook on High 5–6 hours. Reduce to Low and cook 2–4 hours more, just until meat falls apart.

5. If you want a thickened sauce, lift the meat onto a platter using a slotted spoon. Then remove 2 cups broth from the cooker. Stir ¼ cup flour into the hot broth until smooth. Pour the broth back into the cooker, stirring until blended in. Return the meat to the cooker and stir the chunks of meat and sauce together.

Tostadas

Elizabeth L. Richards,
Rapid City, SD

Makes 6–10 servings

Prep. Time: 15 minutes
Cooking Time: 6 hours
Ideal slow-cooker size: 3- to 4-qt.

leftover shredded beef
1 can refried beans
1 envelope dry taco
   seasoning mix
8-oz. can tomato sauce
½ cup water
10 tostada shells

1. Combine beef, refried beans, taco seasoning mix, tomato sauce, and water in slow cooker.

2. Cover. Cook on Low 6 hours.

3. Crisp tostada shells according to package directions.

4. Divide the beef mixture evenly among the tostada shells.

The Best Broccoli Salad

Sandra Haverstraw,
Hummelstown, PA

Makes 10–12 servings

Prep. Time: 20–25 minutes
Chilling Time: 8–12 hours

2 bunches fresh broccoli, cut
   or broken into florets (save
   stems for another use)
1 cup golden raisins
1 small onion, chopped
10 slices bacon, fried and
   chopped
1 cup chopped cashews

Dressing:
½ cup sugar
2 Tbsp. vinegar
1 cup Miracle Whip dressing
2 Tbsp. horseradish
¼ tsp. salt
½ tsp. prepared mustard

1. Mix broccoli florets, raisins, chopped onion, and bacon.

2. Prepare dressing by blending sugar, vinegar, Miracle Whip, horseradish, salt, and mustard until smooth.

3. Pour dressing over broccoli mix and toss gently until evenly coated.

4. Cover and refrigerate 8–12 hours. Add cashews just before serving.

Lemon Pudding Cake

Jean Butzer, Batavia, NY

Makes 5–6 servings

Prep. Time: 15 minutes
Cooking Time: 2–3 hours
Ideal slow-cooker size: 3- to 4-qt.

3 eggs, separated
1 tsp. grated lemon peel
¼ cup lemon juice
3 Tbsp. butter, melted
1½ cups milk
¾ cup sugar
¼ cup flour
⅛ tsp. salt

1. Beat egg whites until stiff peaks form. Set aside.

2. Beat egg yolks. Blend in lemon peel, lemon juice, butter, and milk.

3. In separate bowl, combine sugar, flour, and salt. Add to egg-lemon mixture, beating until smooth.

4. Fold into beaten egg whites.

5. Spoon into slow cooker.

6. Cover and cook on High 2–3 hours.

SPRING

Week 11

THIS WEEK'S
Menu

Sunday: Frances's Roast Chicken
Monday: Garlic and Tomato Italian Sausage Bites
Tuesday: Lentil Rice Salad Bowl
Wednesday: Mexican Egg Rolls
Thursday: Pasta Vanessa
Friday: Apricot-Glazed Pork Roast
Saturday: Pork, Apricot, and Almond Salad

Recommended Side Dish: Crunchy Romaine Toss
Special Dessert: Chocolate Éclair Dessert

Shopping List

PROTEIN

4–5 lb. whole fryer chicken

2 lbs. Italian sausage

3½–4 lb. boneless pork loin

FROZEN

1 cup frozen corn

8 oz. frozen whipped topping

DAIRY and REFRIGERATED

½ cup crumbled feta cheese

1½ cups shredded Mexican-blend cheese

goat cheese

¾ cup heavy whipping cream

2½ cups plus 7 Tbsp. milk

8 oz. cream cheese

1¾ sticks butter

4 eggs

PRODUCE

1 large onion

4½ medium onions

12 spring onions (green onions)

1 rib celery

2 cups fresh diced tomatoes

2 medium tomatoes

2 Tbsp. fresh minced basil

⅓ cup fresh basil

¼ cup minced fresh cilantro

2 Tbsp. chopped fresh parsley

2 small cucumbers

1 yellow bell pepper

1 orange bell pepper

4 cups chopped lettuce

1 small head romaine lettuce

4 cups baby spinach

¼ cup shredded red cabbage

Download this shopping list to your smartphone!
(x.co/ShopList)

1½ cups chopped broccoli
1 tsp. grated lime peel
½ tsp. grated lemon peel
2 Tbsp. fresh lemon juice

CANNED/DRY GOODS

10¾-oz. can tomato puree
3 6-oz. cans tomato sauce
6-oz. can tomato paste
1 cup canned black beans
10½-oz. canned condensed
   chicken broth
8-oz. jar apricot preserves
2 tsp. apricot marmalade or
   preserves
3-oz. pkg. ramen noodles
7-oz. pkg. instant vanilla
   pudding mix
rice or quinoa
1 cup brown lentils
1 cup brown long-grain rice
16-oz. pkg. egg roll wrappers
1 lb. whole wheat rotini
   pasta
dried apricots
Craisins®

DO YOU HAVE THESE ON HAND?

salt
pepper
poultry seasoning
dried basil
bay leaf
ground cumin
cayenne pepper
Italian seasoning
fennel seeds
11 cloves garlic
3½ cups stock, water, or
   combination
olive oil
vegetable oil
balsamic vinegar
apple cider vinegar
sugar
honey
Dijon mustard
soy sauce
1 cup flour
6 oz. chocolate chips
2 cups confectioners' sugar
½ cup chopped walnuts
slivered almonds
oil for deep-fat frying

Frances's Roast Chicken

Frances Schrag, Newton, KS

Makes 6–8 servings

Prep. Time: 5–10 minutes
Cooking Time: 4–10 hours
Ideal slow-cooker size: 4- to 5-qt.

4–5-lb. whole frying chicken
salt, to taste
pepper, to taste
½ tsp. poultry seasoning
½ medium onion, chopped
1 rib celery, chopped
¼ tsp. dried basil

1. Sprinkle chicken cavity with salt, pepper, and poultry seasoning. Put onion and celery inside cavity. Put chicken in slow cooker. Sprinkle with basil.
2. Cover. Cook on Low 8–10 hours, or on High 4–6 hours.

Garlic and Tomato Italian Sausage Bites

Hope Comerford,
Clinton Township, MI

Makes 4–8 servings

Prep. Time: 10 minutes
Cooking Time: 4–5 hours
Ideal slow-cooker size: 3-qt.

2 lbs. Italian sausage, cut into
    1-inch pieces
2 cups fresh diced tomatoes
1 medium onion, cut in half,
    then sliced into strips
8 cloves garlic, minced

⅓ cup balsamic vinegar
2 Tbsp. minced fresh basil
cooked rice or quinoa

1. Place the Italian sausage into the slow cooker.
Top with the remaining ingredients except rice or quinoa.
2. Cover. Cook on Low for 4–5 hours.
3. Serve over cooked rice or quinoa.

Lentil Rice Salad Bowl

Phyllis Good, Lancaster, PA

Makes 4–6 servings

Prep. Time: 20 minutes
Cooking Time: 3–4 hours
Ideal slow-cooker size: 5-qt.

1 cup brown lentils, rinsed
1 cup brown long-grain rice,
    uncooked

1 medium onion, chopped
3½ cups water, stock, or
   combination
1 tsp. salt, or less if you used
   salted stock
¼ tsp. freshly ground pepper
1 bay leaf
½ tsp. ground cumin

Salad Topping:
2 Tbsp. fresh lemon juice
½ tsp. grated lemon peel
2 Tbsp. olive oil
½ tsp. salt
2 small cucumbers, diced
2 medium tomatoes, diced
3 spring onions, sliced
⅓ cup chopped fresh basil
½ cup crumbled feta cheese

1. Combine lentils, rice, onion, water/stock, salt, pepper, bay leaf, and cumin in slow cooker.

2. Cook on High for 3–4 hours, until lentils and rice are tender but not mushy.

3. Remove bay leaf. Keep rice mixture in slow cooker while you prepare the salad topping. The salad will wilt if it sits in its dressing too long.

4. In a medium bowl, combine lemon juice, peel, olive oil, and salt. Whisk well.

5. Place the rest of the topping ingredients in the bowl and mix gently.

6. To serve, place a scoop of the lentil rice mixture in a soup bowl. Top with a scoop of the salad. Enjoy outside with a tall iced tea!

Mexican Egg Rolls

Brittany Miller, Millersburg, OH

Makes 18 egg rolls

Prep. Time: 35–40 minutes
*Cooking Time: 5 minutes/batch;
   about 20 minutes total*

2½ cups leftover chicken,
   diced or shredded
1½ cups (6-oz.) shredded
   Mexican-blend cheese
1 cup frozen corn, thawed
1 cup canned black beans,
   rinsed and drained
5 green onions, chopped
¼ cup minced fresh cilantro
1 tsp. salt
1 tsp. ground cumin
1 tsp. grated lime peel
¼ tsp. cayenne pepper
16-oz. pkg. egg roll wrappers
oil for deep-fat frying

1. In large bowl, combine chicken, cheese, corn, beans, green onions, cilantro, salt, cumin, lime peel, and pepper.

2. Place ¼ cup of mixture in center of one egg roll wrapper. Keep remaining wrappers covered with damp paper towel until ready to use.

3. Fold bottom corner over filling. Fold sides toward the center over filling. Moisten remaining corner with water. Roll up tightly to seal. Repeat with each wrapper.

4. In electric skillet or deep-fat fryer, heat oil to 375°. Fry egg rolls, a few at a time, for 2 minutes on each side or until golden brown.

5. Drain on paper towels.

Pasta Vanessa

Phyllis Good, Lancaster, PA

Makes 6 servings

Prep. Time: 30 minutes
Cooking Time: 4–6 hours
Ideal slow-cooker size: 5-qt.

2 medium onions, chopped
1 yellow bell pepper, chopped
1 orange bell pepper, chopped
10¾-oz. can tomato puree
3 6-oz. cans tomato sauce
6-oz. can tomato paste
1 cup water
salt, to taste
pepper, to taste
1½ tsp. Italian seasoning
¼ tsp. fennel seeds
3 cloves garlic, chopped fine
2 Tbsp. honey
leftover Italian sausage
¾ cup heavy whipping cream
1 lb. whole wheat rotini pasta
2 Tbsp. chopped fresh parsley

1. In the slow cooker, place the onions, peppers, tomato puree, sauce, paste, and water. Blend well.
2. Cook on Low 4–6 hours.
3. Season with salt, pepper, Italian seasoning, fennel, and garlic. Then stir in honey. Add in the leftover Italian sausage.
4. Cook on Low 30–60 additional minutes, or until the sausage is warmed through.
5. Bring a pot of water to boil for the pasta.
6. Separately, warm the heavy whipping cream in the microwave or a small saucepan until steaming hot. Just before serving, add whipping cream to tomato mixture. Now that the two are combined, turn off the slow cooker and do not allow the sauce to boil.
7. Serve sauce over cooked rotini. Sprinkle with fresh parsley.

Apricot-Glazed Pork Roast

Jean Butzer, Batavia, NY
Virginia Blish, Akron, NY

Makes 10–12 servings

Prep. Time: 10 minutes
Cooking Time: 3–6 hours
Ideal slow-cooker size: 5- to 6-qt.

10½-oz. can condensed chicken broth
8-oz. jar apricot preserves
1 large onion, chopped
2 Tbsp. Dijon mustard
3½–4-lb. boneless pork loin

1. Mix broth, preserves, onion, and mustard in a bowl.
2. Cut roast to fit, if necessary, and place in cooker. Pour glaze over meat.
3. Cover and cook on Low 4–6 hours, or on High 3 hours, or until tender.

Pork, Apricot, and Almond Salad

Hope Comerford, Clinton Township, MI

Makes 4–6 servings

Prep. Time: 15 minutes

leftover pork
4 cups chopped lettuce
4 cups baby spinach
¼ cup shredded red cabbage

Dressing:
¼ cup balsamic vinegar
¼ cup olive oil
½ tsp. salt
⅛ tsp. pepper
2 tsp. apricot marmalade or preserves

Toppings:
slivered almonds
goat cheese
dried apricots
Craisins®

1. Warm the leftover pork.
2. Mix together the lettuce, spinach, and cabbage. Divide the lettuce mixture up among plates or bowls. Place a serving of pork on each salad.
3. Mix together dressing ingredients.
4. Add desired toppings to each salad.
5. Drizzle dressing over each salad.

Crunchy Romaine Toss

Jolene Schrock, Millersburg, OH
Jamie Mowry, Arlington, TX
Lucille Hollinger, Richland, PA

Makes 4–6 servings

Prep. Time: 20–30 minutes
Cooking Time: 10 minutes

Dressing:
½ cup sugar
½ cup vegetable oil
¼ cup apple cider vinegar
2 tsp. soy sauce

salt and pepper, to taste
3-oz. pkg. ramen noodles, broken up, seasoning packet discarded
2 Tbsp. butter
1½ cups chopped broccoli
1 small head romaine lettuce, torn up
4 green onions, chopped
½ cup chopped walnuts

1. In the blender, combine sugar, oil, vinegar, soy sauce, salt, and pepper. Blend until sugar is dissolved.
2. In a skillet, sauté ramen noodles in butter until golden brown.
3. In a large bowl, combine broccoli, lettuce, green onions, and noodles.
4. Just before serving, toss with nuts and dressing.

Chocolate Éclair Dessert

Rhonda Freed, Croghan, NY

Makes 10 servings

Prep. Time: 25 minutes
Cooking/Baking Time: 50 minutes
Cooling Time: 30 minutes

1 cup water
1 stick butter
1 cup flour
¼ tsp. salt
4 eggs
7-oz. pkg. instant vanilla pudding mix
2½ cups milk
8 oz. cream cheese, softened
8 oz. frozen whipped topping, thawed

Topping:
6 oz. chocolate chips
½ stick (4 Tbsp.) butter
2 cups confectioners' sugar
7 Tbsp. milk

1. Heat water and butter just until boiling.
2. Remove from heat and add flour and salt. Beat until a ball forms.
3. Add eggs one at a time, beating after each one.
4. Spread in an ungreased 15×10-inch jelly roll pan.
5. Bake at 400°F for 35 minutes.
6. Remove from oven and immediately punch down flat. Cool at least 30 minutes.
7. Mix pudding mix and 2½ cups milk for 2 minutes.
8. Add cream cheese and mix until smooth.
9. Spread over cooled crust. Top with whipped topping.
10. Make chocolate topping by melting chocolate chips and butter in microwave for 1–2 minutes.
11. Add confectioners' sugar and milk and mix until smooth.
12. Drizzle on top. Refrigerate.

SPRING

Week 12

THIS WEEK'S
Menu

Sunday: Garlic Lime Chicken
Monday: Chicken Pasta Salad
Tuesday: Super Beef Barbecue
Wednesday: Sausage and Sauerkraut Supper
Thursday: Slow Cooker Pizza
Friday: Beef Barbecue Street Tacos
Saturday: Cabbage Roll Casserole

Recommended Side Dish: Extra Good Mashed Potatoes
Special Dessert: Slow Cooker Crème Brûlée

Shopping List

PROTEIN
8–10 skinless chicken thighs
3–4 lb. rump roast
2-lb. pkg. smoked sausage
  links
cooked hamburger, *optional*
chipped ham, *optional*
smoked turkey, *optional*

FROZEN
½ cup frozen whipped
  topping

DAIRY and REFRIGERATED
4 hard-boiled eggs
5 egg yolks
½ cup sour cream
1½ cups fat-free sour cream
2 cups milk
2 cups heavy cream
8-oz. fat-free cream cheese

1–2 cups shredded
  mozzarella cheese
½ cup queso fresco
2 Tbsp. butter
32-oz. bag refrigerated
  sauerkraut, or canned

PRODUCE
2 cups diced celery
2 medium onions
¾ cup shredded red cabbage
1 medium head cabbage
½ cup fresh cilantro
1 cup fresh parsley
5 lbs. potatoes
broccoli florets, *optional*
sliced mushrooms, *optional*
1 apple
2 limes
4 cups seedless grapes
fresh berries, for garnish

Download this shopping list to your
smartphone!
(x.co/ShopList)

CANNED/DRY GOODS

15-oz. can pineapple tidbits

14½-oz. can diced garlic and
  onion tomatoes

18-oz. bottle barbecue sauce

16-oz. jar whole dill pickles

1½ cups pizza sauce

1½ cups brown rice

20 (or so) white corn tortillas

1½ cups buttermilk baking
  mix

1 cup dry small pasta

sandwich rolls

DO YOU HAVE THESE ON HAND?

dry mustard

pepper

salt

garlic powder

onion salt or garlic salt

3 cloves garlic

¼–⅓ cup lime juice

¼ cup plus 1 Tbsp. lemon
  juice

sugar

brown sugar

¼ cup superfine sugar

1 Tbsp. high-quality vanilla
  extract

½ cup soy sauce

1 cup mayonnaise

Worcestershire sauce

1 cup ketchup

olive oil

½ cup cashew pieces

Garlic Lime Chicken

Loretta Krahn,
Mountain Lake, MN

Makes 8 servings

Prep. Time: 10 minutes
Cooking Time: 4 hours
Ideal slow-cooker size: 5-qt.

8–10 skinless chicken thighs
½ cup soy sauce
¼–⅓ cup lime juice, according
    to your taste preference
1 Tbsp. Worcestershire sauce
2 cloves garlic, minced, or 1
    tsp. garlic powder
½ tsp. dry mustard
½ tsp. ground pepper

1. Grease interior of slow-cooker crock.
2. Place chicken in slow cooker.
3. Combine remaining ingredients in a bowl. Pour over chicken.
4. Cover. Cook on Low 4 hours, or until instant-read thermometer registers 160°–165°F when stuck in thighs, but not against bone.

Chicken Pasta Salad

Esther Gingerich, Kalona, IA

Makes 12 servings

Prep. Time: 15 minutes
Cooking Time for pasta: 15 minutes

leftover chicken, diced
2 cups cooked small pasta, or
    macaroni (1 cup dry)
2 cups diced celery
2 cups seedless grape halves
4 hard-boiled eggs, diced
15-oz. can pineapple tidbits,
    drained

Dressing:
1 cup mayonnaise
½ cup sour cream
½ cup frozen whipped
    topping, thawed
1 Tbsp. lemon juice
1 Tbsp. sugar
½ tsp. salt
½ cup cashew pieces

1. In a large bowl, combine chicken, macaroni, celery, grapes, eggs, and pineapple.
2. Whisk dressing ingredients until smooth. Pour dressing over salad; toss to coat.
3. Chill at least one hour. Just before serving, fold in cashews.

Super Beef Barbecue

Linda E. Wilcox, Blythewood, SC

Makes 10–12 servings

Prep. Time: 15 minutes
Cooking Time: 9–10 hours
Ideal slow-cooker size: 6-qt.

3–4-lb. rump roast
1 clove garlic, minced, or ¼
   cup finely chopped onion
18-oz. bottle barbecue sauce
1 cup ketchup
16-oz. jar whole dill pickles,
   undrained
sandwich rolls

1. Cut roast into quarters and place in slow cooker.
2. In a bowl, stir together garlic, barbecue sauce, and ketchup. When well blended, fold in pickles and their juice. Pour over meat.
3. Cover and cook on Low 8–9 hours, or until meat begins to fall apart.
4. Remove the pickles and discard them.
5. Lift the meat out onto a platter and shred by pulling it apart with 2 forks.
6. Return meat to sauce and heat thoroughly on Low, about 1 hour.
7. Serve in sandwich rolls.

Sausage and Sauerkraut Supper

Bonnie Goering, Bridgewater, VA

Makes 8 servings

Prep. Time: 10 minutes
Cooking Time: 6–10 hours
Ideal slow-cooker size: 4- to 5-qt.

2-lb. pkg. smoked sausage
   links, cut into 2-inch pieces
32-oz. bag refrigerated, or
   canned, sauerkraut, drained
½ medium onion, chopped
1 apple, cored and chopped
2–3 Tbsp. brown sugar
water

1. Combine all ingredients in slow cooker, with water covering half the contents.
2. Cover and cook on Low 6–10 hours, or until vegetables are as tender as you like them.

Serving Suggestion: **Serve with mashed potatoes.**

Slow Cooker Pizza

Phyllis Good, Lancaster, PA

Makes 4–6 servings

Prep. Time: 40 minutes
Cooking Time: 2 hours
Ideal slow-cooker size: 5- or 6-qt.

1 Tbsp. olive oil
1½ cups buttermilk baking mix (like Bisquick)
⅓ cup very hot water
1½ cups pizza sauce, *divided*
your choice of pizza toppings—cooked hamburger, chipped ham or smoked turkey, broccoli florets, sautéed onions, sliced mushrooms, for example
1–2 cups shredded mozzarella cheese

1. Drizzle olive oil on the bottom of your slow cooker. Using a paper towel, wipe it around the sides, too.
2. Mix the baking mix and hot water together in a bowl until it forms a smooth ball.
3. Using your fingers, or a rolling pin, stretch the ball until it's about 4 inches bigger around than the bottom of your cooker. Put the dough into the cooker, spreading it out so that it reaches up the sides of the cooker by an inch or so the whole way around.
4. Pour 1 cup sauce on top of the crust. Spread it out so that it covers the crust evenly.
5. Scatter pizza toppings evenly over the sauce.
6. Spoon another cup of sauce over the toppings.
7. Sprinkle evenly with cheese.
8. Cover. Cook on High for about 2 hours, or until the crust begins to brown around the edges.
9. Uncover, being careful not to let the condensation on the lid drip onto the pizza. Let stand for 15 minutes. Cut into wedges and serve.

Beef Barbecue Street Tacos

Hope Comerford,
Clinton Township, MI

Makes 6 servings

Prep. Time: 10 minutes
Cooking Time: 5 minutes

leftover beef
20 (or so) white corn tortillas
¾ cup shredded red cabbage
½ cup queso fresco
½ cup onions, diced
½ cup fresh cilantro, chopped
2 limes, chopped into wedges

1. Warm the leftover beef.
2. Warm the tortillas in a skillet or on a griddle.
3. To serve, spoon some of the beef into the warmed tortilla. Top with some red cabbage, queso fresco, onions, and fresh cilantro. Squeeze some fresh lime juice over the top.

Cabbage Roll Casserole

Hope Comerford,
Clinton Township, MI

Makes 8–10 servings

Prep. Time: 15 minutes
Cooking Time: 4–6 hours
Ideal slow-cooker size: 6-qt.

1 medium head cabbage, chopped
2 tsp. garlic powder
¼ cup lemon juice, *divided*
1 onion, chopped
14½-oz. can diced garlic and onion tomatoes
1 cup fresh parsley, chopped
1½ cups brown rice
1 tsp. salt
1 tsp. pepper
3–4 cups water
leftover sausage, cut into bite-sized pieces

1. Place the chopped cabbage in the crock. Pour ½ of the lemon juice over it.
2. In a bowl, mix the onion, diced tomatoes, parsley, rice, remaining lemon juice, garlic powder, salt, and pepper.
3. Pour the rice/tomato/onion/parsley mixture over the top of the cabbage and spread evenly. Pour water over the top.
4. Push the sausage pieces down into the rice mixture, spreading them around evenly as possible.
5. Cook on Low for 4–6 hours.

Extra Good Mashed Potatoes

Zona Mae Bontrager, Kokomo, IN
Mary Jane Musser, Manheim, PA
Elsie Schlabach, Millersburg, OH
Carol Sommers, Millersburg, OH
Edwina Stoltzfus, Narvon, PA
Barbara Hershey, Lancaster, PA

Makes 12 servings

Prep. Time: 45 minutes
Cooking Time: 5–6 hours
Ideal slow-cooker size: 5- to 6-qt.

5 lbs. potatoes, peeled and cooked
2 cups milk, heated to scalding
2 Tbsp. butter, melted in hot milk
8-oz. fat-free cream cheese, softened
1½ cups fat-free sour cream
1 tsp. onion salt or garlic salt
1 tsp. salt
¼–½ tsp. pepper

1. Mash all ingredients together in a large mixing bowl until smooth.
2. Pour into slow cooker.
3. Cover. Cook on Low 4–6 hours, or until heated through.

Slow Cooker Crème Brûlée

Phyllis Good, Lancaster, PA

Makes 4–6 servings

Prep. Time: 20 minutes
Cooking Time: 2–4 hours
Chilling Time: 5 hours
Ideal slow-cooker size: 6-qt. oval

5 egg yolks
2 cups heavy cream
½ cup sugar
1 Tbsp. high-quality vanilla extract
pinch salt
¼ cup superfine sugar
fresh berries, for garnish

1. Get a baking dish that fits in your slow cooker. Put it in the slow cooker and pour water around it until the water comes halfway up the sides of the dish. Push the dish down if you need to (as it would be when it's full of the crème brûlée), to see the water level. Remove the dish and set aside.
2. In medium mixing bowl, beat egg yolks.
3. Slowly pour in cream and sugar while mixing. Add vanilla and salt.
4. Pour mixture into the baking dish.
5. Carefully place dish into water in slow cooker, being careful not to get water in the cream mixture.
6. Cover cooker and cook on High for 2–4 hours, until set but still a little jiggly in the middle.
7. Very carefully remove hot dish from hot slow cooker and let it cool on the counter. Refrigerate for 2 hours.
8. Sprinkle the superfine sugar evenly over the top. Broil for 3–10 minutes, until the sugar is bubbly and browning. Watch carefully! Or if you own a kitchen torch, use that instead to caramelize the sugar.
9. Return crème brûlée to refrigerator for at least 2 more hours. Serve cold with a few beautiful berries to garnish.

SPRING

Week 13

THIS WEEK'S
Menu

Sunday: Easy Ham Steaks
Monday: Greek Chicken Pita Filling
Tuesday: Hearty Brunch Casserole
Wednesday: Greek Chicken Pizza
Thursday: French Dip
Friday: Can't Beet Beef Stew!
Saturday: Cherry Tomato Spaghetti Sauce

Recommended Side Dish: Baked Corn
Special Dessert: Black and Blue Cobbler

Shopping List

PROTEIN

2½ lbs. ham steaks

5–6 lbs. boneless, skinless
   chicken thighs

3–4 lb. chuck roast

DAIRY and REFRIGERATED

½ cup plain yogurt

1½ cups shredded extra-
   sharp cheddar cheese

½ cup freshly grated
   Parmesan cheese

2 cups feta cheese

9 eggs

2¾ cups plus 2 Tbsp. milk

3 Tbsp. butter

8- or 12-oz. pkg. prepared
   pizza dough

butter, *optional*

shredded mozzarella
   cheese, *optional*

PRODUCE

3 medium onions

2 large onions

2 spring onions

¼ cup red onion, *optional*

2 large carrots

2 large parsnips

2 ribs celery

4 large beets, or 2 15½-oz.
   jars

10–12 tomato slices

½ cup sliced mushrooms

½ cup diced bell pepper or
   broccoli florets

4 qts. cherry tomatoes

¼ cup fresh finely chopped
   dill

1 qt. fresh corn, or 2 1-lb.
   bags frozen

2 cups fresh blueberries, or
   frozen

Download this shopping list to your
smartphone!
(x.co/ShopList)

2 cups fresh blackberries, or frozen

1 tsp. grated orange peel

CANNED/DRY GOODS

20-oz. can pineapple ring slices

6-oz. jar maraschino cherries

15½-oz. can petite diced tomatoes

1 can beef consommé

1 can Progresso French onion soup

8 slices firm white bread

1½ cups cornflakes

6 French rolls

½ cup kalamata olives, pitted

spaghetti

pita bread

DO YOU HAVE THESE ON HAND?

dried oregano

dry mustard

lemon pepper

seasoning salt

dried parsley

salt

pepper

garlic powder

onion powder

bay leaf

coarse salt

dried rosemary

dried thyme

dried basil

ground cinnamon

ground nutmeg

8 cloves garlic

4 cups beef broth

olive oil

vegetable oil

Worcestershire sauce

1½ cups plus 4 Tbsp. sugar

brown sugar

1 cup plus 3 Tbsp. flour

baking powder

SPIRITS

1 can or bottle of beer

Easy Ham Steaks

Hope Comerford,
Clinton Township, MI

Makes 8 servings

Prep. Time: 5 minutes
Cooking Time: 5 hours
Ideal slow-cooker size: 5-qt.

2½ lbs. ham steaks
20-oz. can pineapple ring
 slices
6-oz. jar maraschino cherries
3 Tbsp. brown sugar

1. Place ham steaks into the slow cooker.
2. Arrange the pineapple slices on top of the steaks.
3. Pour the jar of maraschino cherries over the top, juice included.
4. Sprinkle the brown sugar over the top.
5. Cover. Cook on Low for 5 hours.

Greek Chicken Pita Filling

Judi Manos, West Islip, NY
Jeanette Oberholtzer,
Manheim, PA

Makes 6–8 servings

Prep. Time: 10 minutes
Cooking Time: 6–8 hours
Ideal slow-cooker size: 2- to 3-qt.

1 medium onion, chopped
5–6 lbs. boneless, skinless
 chicken thighs
2 tsp. lemon pepper
½ tsp. dried oregano

½ cup plain yogurt
pita bread

1. Combine first 3 ingredients in slow cooker. Cover and cook on Low 6–8 hours, or until chicken is tender.
2. Just before serving, remove chicken and shred with two forks.
3. Add shredded chicken back into slow cooker and stir in oregano and yogurt.
4. Serve as a filling for pita bread.

Hearty Brunch Casserole

Phyllis Good, Lancaster, PA

Makes 12–15 servings

Prep. Time: 30 minutes
Cooking Time: 4 hours
Chilling Time: 8 hours
Ideal slow-cooker size: 4-qt.

8 slices firm white bread,
 crusts removed
1 cup cubed leftover ham,
 divided

2 spring onions, sliced, *divided*
½ cup sliced mushrooms, *divided*
½ cup diced bell pepper, or broccoli florets, *divided*
1½ cups shredded extra-sharp cheddar cheese, *divided*
½ cup freshly grated Parmesan cheese, *divided*
5 eggs
1¾ cups whole milk
¼ tsp. dry mustard
½ tsp. seasoning salt
1 Tbsp. dried parsley

Topping:
1½ cups cornflakes
3 Tbsp. butter, melted

1. Grease the slow cooker crock. You are going to make layers. Cover bottom of crock with 4 slices of bread, cutting to fit. Slight overlap is okay (but don't omit any bread or that will alter the final texture!).

2. Top with half the meat, half the veggies, and half the cheeses.

3. Repeat layers once more, ending with cheese.

4. Whisk together eggs, milk, dry mustard, seasoning salt, and parsley. Mix well and pour over layers.

5. Cover and refrigerate for 8 hours, or overnight.

6. Remove from refrigerator 30 minutes before baking.

7. Place crock in cooker. Cook on Low for 3½ hours.

8. Combine cornflakes and butter and sprinkle over casserole. Drape several paper towels over the crock and then put the lid back on. The paper towels will catch condensation and keep it off the cornflake topping. Cook an additional 30 minutes on Low.

Greek Chicken Pizza

Hope Comerford,
Clinton Township, MI

Makes 4 to 6 servings

Prep. Time: 20–25 minutes
Cooking Time: 2½–3 hours
Standing Time: 2 hours before you begin
Ideal slow-cooker size: 6-qt.

8- or 12-oz. pkg. prepared pizza dough, depending how thick you like your pizza crust
1 Tbsp. olive oil
3 cloves garlic, minced
¼ tsp. oregano
¼ tsp. salt
dash pepper
leftover chicken, chopped
½ cup kalamata olives, pitted, chopped
¼ cup red onion, diced or sliced, *optional*
10–12 slices of tomato
2 cups feta cheese

1. Take the prepared pizza dough out of the refrigerator and let it come up to room temperature.

2. Once the dough is at room temperature, grease the inside of your crock and then stretch the dough out around the bottom of your crock, making sure it goes up about an inch on the sides.

3. Bake the crust, uncovered, on High for 1 hour.

4. Prick the crust gently with a fork all around the bottom. Mix together the olive oil, garlic, oregano, salt, and pepper. If you have a pastry brush, brush it all over the bottom of the crust. If not, wash your hand, drizzle the mixture around, and spread it around the crust with your fingers.

5. Drop the leftover chopped chicken evenly over the crust.

6. Next, spread the kalamata olives, onion, and tomato slices evenly over the pizza crust.

7. Top it with the feta cheese.

8. Cover and cook on High for about 2 hours, or until the crust begins to brown around the edges.

9. Uncover, being careful not to let the condensation on the lid drip onto the pizza.

10. Let stand for 10 minutes. Cut into wedges and serve.

French Dip

Hope Comerford,
Clinton Township, MI

Makes 8–10 servings

Prep. Time: 10 minutes
Cooking Time: 7–9 hours
Ideal slow-cooker size: 6-qt.

1 can Progresso French onion
  soup
1 can beef consommé
1 bottle/can beer
8 dashes Worcestershire
  sauce
1 medium onion, chopped into
  rings
1½ tsp. garlic powder
1½ tsp. onion powder
3–4 lb. chuck roast
6 French rolls
butter and shredded
  mozzarella cheese for rolls,
  optional

1. Pour the French onion
soup, beef consommé, beer,
and Worcestershire sauce in
the crock.
2. Add the onion, garlic
powder, and onion powder.
Put the chuck roast on top.
3. Cook on Low 7–9 hours.
4. Serve on French rolls,
toasted with butter and
melted mozzarella cheese if
desired.

Can't Beet Beef Stew!

Bob Coffey, New Windsor, NY

Makes 6–8 servings

Prep. Time: 30 minutes
Cooking Time: 6 hours
Ideal slow-cooker size: 5- or 6-qt.

4 large beets, roasted in the
  oven at 425° until tender,
  then cooled, peeled, and
  diced—or if you don't
  have time for that much
  food prep, 2 15½-oz. jars
  prepared beets, drained
2 large onions, diced
3 cloves garlic, diced
2 large carrots, peeled and
  diced
2 large parsnips, peeled and
  diced
2 ribs celery, diced
15½-oz. can petite diced
  tomatoes, undrained
1 bay leaf
leftover beef, cut into pieces
4 cups beef broth
¼ cup finely chopped fresh dill
coarse salt and pepper, to
  taste

1. Grease interior of slow-
cooker crock.
2. If roasting beets yourself,
halve them. Place face down
in single layer in greased
baking pan. Cover and bake
at 425°F until tender, about
20 minutes. Uncover and
allow to cool until you can
handle them. Peel. Dice.
3. Place onion and garlic in
crock. Stir in beets.
4. Add rest of ingredients,
except dill, salt, and pepper to
crock.
5. Cover. Cook on Low 6
hours, or until vegetables are
tender.
6. Stir in dill. Season to
taste with salt and pepper.
7. Fish out the bay leaf
before serving.

Cherry Tomato Spaghetti Sauce

Beverly Hummel, Fleetwood, PA

Makes 8–10 servings

Prep. Time: 20 minutes
Cooking Time: 4–5 hours
Ideal slow-cooker size: 6-qt.

4 qts. cherry tomatoes
1 medium onion, chopped
2 cloves garlic, minced
3 tsp. sugar
1 tsp. dried rosemary
2 tsp. dried thyme
1 tsp. dried oregano
1 tsp. dried basil
1 tsp. salt
½ tsp. coarsely ground black
  pepper
cooked spaghetti

1. Grease interior of slow-
cooker crock.
2. Stem tomatoes and cut
them in half. Place in slow
cooker.
3. Add chopped onions and
garlic to cooker.
4. Stir in sugar, herbs, and
seasonings, mixing well.
5. Cover. Cook on Low 4–5
hours, or until the veggies are
as tender as you like them.
6. For a thicker sauce,
uncover the cooker for the
last 30–60 minutes of cooking
time.
7. Serve over just-cooked
spaghetti.

Baked Corn

Velma Stauffer, Akron, PA

Makes 8 servings

Prep. Time: 5–10 minutes
Cooking Time: 3 hours
Ideal slow-cooker size: 3- or 4-qt.

1 qt. fresh corn, or 2 1-lb. bags frozen
2 eggs, beaten
1 tsp. salt
1 cup milk
⅛ tsp. pepper
2 tsp. vegetable oil
3 Tbsp. sugar
3 Tbsp. flour

1. Grease interior of slow-cooker crock.
2. Combine all ingredients well in greased slow cooker.
3. Cover. Cook on Low 3 hours.

Black and Blue Cobbler

Renee Shirk, Mount Joy, PA

Makes 6 servings

Prep. Time: 20 minutes
Cooking Time: 2–2½ hours
Ideal slow-cooker size: 5-qt.

1 cup flour
1½ cups sugar, *divided*
1 tsp. baking powder
¼ tsp. salt
¼ tsp. ground cinnamon
¼ tsp. ground nutmeg
2 eggs, beaten
2 Tbsp. milk
2 Tbsp. vegetable oil

2 cups fresh or frozen blueberries
2 cups fresh or frozen blackberries
¾ cup water
1 tsp. grated orange peel

1. Grease interior of slow-cooker crock.
2. Combine flour, ¾ cup sugar, baking powder, salt, cinnamon, and nutmeg in a good-sized bowl.
3. Combine eggs, milk, and oil in another bowl. Stir into dry ingredients just until moistened.

4. Spread the batter evenly over bottom of greased slow cooker.
5. In saucepan, combine berries, water, orange peel, and ¾ cup sugar. Bring to boil. Remove from heat and pour over batter. Cover.
6. Cook on High 2–2½ hours, or until toothpick inserted into batter comes out clean. Turn off cooker.
7. Uncover and let stand 30 minutes before serving.

SUMMER

Week 1

THIS WEEK'S
Menu

Sunday: Stuffed Green Peppers
Monday: Marinated Asian Chicken Salad
Tuesday: Tamale Pie
Wednesday: Chicken Vegetable Soup
Thursday: Sausage and Apples
Friday: Asparagus Fettucine
Saturday: Sausage Comfort Casserole

Recommended Side Dish: Festive Apple Salad
Special Dessert: Cherry Delight

Shopping List

PROTEIN
1¾ lbs. lean ground beef

6 boneless skinless chicken
   breast halves

2 lbs. spicy precooked sausage

FROZEN
1 cup frozen corn

DAIRY and REFRIGERATED
½ cup reduced-fat shredded
   mozzarella cheese

1 cup grated fat-free
   cheddar cheese

¼ cup shredded Parmesan
   cheese

3 oz. shredded sharp
   cheddar cheese

4 Tbsp. crumbled blue
   cheese or shredded baby
   Swiss, *optional*

1 egg

1¾ cups fat-free milk

½ cup apple juice

1 stick plus 1 Tbsp. butter

2 oz. cream cheese

PRODUCE
6 large green bell peppers

1 large head lettuce

1 large head romaine
   lettuce

1 large onion

¼ cup chopped onions

2 carrots

2 ribs celery

½ lb. fresh asparagus

1½ lbs. potatoes

1 Tbsp. plus 1 tsp. grated
   fresh ginger

¼ cup fresh cilantro

2 large apples

Download this shopping list to your
smartphone!
(x.co/ShopList)

Salad:

1 large head lettuce, shredded

2 carrots, julienned

½ cup roasted peanuts, chopped

¼ cup fresh cilantro, chopped

½ pkg. maifun rice noodles, fried in hot oil

1. Mix marinade ingredients in a small bowl.

2. Place chicken in slow cooker and pour marinade over chicken, coating each piece well.

3. Cover. Cook on Low 6–8 hours or High 3–4 hours.

4. Remove chicken from slow cooker and cool. Reserve juices. Shred chicken into bite-sized pieces.

5. In a small bowl, combine dressing ingredients with ½ cup of the juice from the slow cooker.

6. In a large serving bowl toss together the shredded chicken, lettuce, carrots, peanuts, cilantro, and noodles.

7. Just before serving, drizzle with the salad dressing. Toss well and serve.

Tamale Pie

Jeannine Janzen, Elbing, KS

Makes 8 servings

Prep. Time: 20 minutes
Cooking Time: 4 hours
Ideal slow-cooker size: 4-qt.

¾ cup cornmeal

1½ cups fat-free milk

1 egg, beaten

1 lb. leftover browned ground beef

1¼-oz. envelope dry chili seasoning mix

16-oz. can diced tomatoes

16-oz. can corn, drained

1 cup grated fat-free cheddar cheese

1. Combine cornmeal, milk, and egg.

2. Stir in meat, chili seasoning mix, tomatoes, and corn until well blended. Pour into slow cooker.

3. Cover. Cook on High 1 hour, then on Low 3 hours.

4. Sprinkle with cheese. Cook another 5 minutes until cheese is melted.

Chicken Vegetable Soup

Barbara Walker, Sturgis, SD
Sheridy Steele, Ardmore, OK

Makes 6 servings

Prep. Time: 15 minutes
Cooking Time: 3–4 hours
Ideal slow-cooker size: 4-qt.

28-oz. can low-sodium diced tomatoes, undrained
2 cups low-sodium, reduced fat chicken broth
1 cup frozen corn
2 ribs celery, chopped
6-oz. can tomato paste
¼ cup dry lentils, rinsed
1 Tbsp. sugar
1 Tbsp. Worcestershire sauce
2 tsp. dried parsley flakes
1 tsp. dried marjoram
2 cups cooked leftover chicken

1. Combine all ingredients in slow cooker except chicken.
2. Cover. Cook on Low 3–4 hours. Stir in chicken one hour before end of cooking time.

Sausage and Apples

Linda Sluiter, Schererville, IN

Makes 4 servings

Prep. Time: 10 minutes
Cooking Time: 1–3 hours
Ideal slow-cooker size: 8-qt.

2 lb. spicy precooked sausage
2 large apples, cored and sliced
¼ cup brown sugar
½ cup apple juice

1. Cut sausage into 2-inch pieces.
2. Place all ingredients in slow cooker and mix together well.
3. Cover and cook on Low 1–3 hours, or until heated through and until apples are as tender as you like them.

Asparagus Fettuccine

Melva Baumer, Mifflintown, PA

Makes 2 servings

Prep. Time: 15 minutes
Cooking Time: 15–20 minutes

4 oz. uncooked fettuccine
½ lb. fresh asparagus, cut in 1-inch pieces
¼ cup chopped onions
1 garlic clove, minced
1 Tbsp. butter
2 oz. cream cheese, cubed
¼ cup fat-free milk
¼ cup shredded Parmesan cheese
1½ tsp. lemon juice
¼ tsp. salt
⅛ tsp. pepper

1. Cook fettuccine according to package directions. Drain.
2. In large skillet, sauté asparagus, onions, and garlic in butter until tender.
3. Add cream cheese, milk, Parmesan cheese, lemon juice, salt, and pepper.
4. Cook and stir over medium heat for 5 minutes or until cheese is melted and sauce is blended.
5. Toss fettuccine with asparagus mixture.

Sausage Comfort Casserole

Kay M. Zurcher, Minot, ND

Makes 4 servings

Prep. Time: 30 minutes
Cooking Time: 6 hours
Ideal slow-cooker size: 4- to 5-qt.

1 14-oz. can chicken broth, *divided*
1½ lbs. potatoes, sliced ¼-inch thick, *divided*
salt and pepper, *optional*
1 large onion, thinly sliced, *divided*
leftover sausage, cut into bite-sized pieces
3 oz. sharp cheddar cheese, shredded, *divided*

1. Spray slow cooker with nonstick cooking spray.
2. Pour ½ cup chicken broth into slow cooker. Spread one half of the potatoes on the bottom of the slow cooker. Sprinkle with salt and pepper if you wish.
3. Layer in half of the onions, half of the sausage, and half of the cheese.
4. Repeat the potato, salt and pepper if you wish, onion, sausage, and cheese 1 more time.

5. Pour the remaining chicken broth over top.

6. Cover and cook on Low 6 hours or until potatoes and onions are done to your liking.

Tip: Do not stir but check potatoes to make sure they are finished, but not overcooked.

Festive Apple Salad

Susan Kasting, Jenks, OK

Makes 8 servings

Prep. Time: 15 minutes

Dressing:
2 Tbsp. olive oil
2 Tbsp. vinegar, or lemon juice
2 Tbsp. Dijon mustard
1½–3 Tbsp. sugar
salt and pepper
4–6 Tbsp. chopped walnuts or cashews
1 Granny Smith apple, chopped
1 large head romaine lettuce, chopped
4 Tbsp. crumbled blue cheese, or shredded baby Swiss, *optional*

1. In the bottom of a large salad bowl, make dressing by mixing together the oil, vinegar, mustard, sugar, salt, and pepper.

2. Add the nuts and apple and stir to coat. Put lettuce and blue cheese on top without stirring.

3. Mix it all together when ready to serve.

Cherry Delight

Anna Musser, Manheim, PA
Marianne J. Troyer, Millersburg, OH

Makes 10–12 servings

Prep. Time: 5 minutes
Cooking Time: 2–4 hours
Ideal slow-cooker size: 2½-qt.

21-oz. can cherry pie filling
1 pkg. yellow cake mix
1 stick butter, melted

⅓ cup chopped walnuts, *optional*

1. Place pie filling in greased slow cooker.

2. Combine dry cake mix and butter (mixture will be crumbly). Sprinkle over filling. Sprinkle with walnuts.

3. Cover and cook on Low 4 hours, or on High 2 hours. Allow to cool, then serve in bowls with dips of ice cream.

Variation: For a less rich, less sweet dessert, use only half the cake mix and only ¼ cup butter, melted.

SUMMER

Week 2

THIS WEEK'S
Menu

Sunday: Zesty Italian Beef
Monday: Slow-Cooker Tex-Mex Chicken
Tuesday: Forgotten Minestrone
Wednesday: Chicken Tortilla Casserole
Thursday: Sloppy Beef Sandwiches
Friday: Quick 'n Easy Meat-Free Lasagna
Saturday: Beef Slow-Cooker Pizza

Recommended Side Dish: Macaroni Salad
Special Dessert: Easy Chocolate Clusters

Shopping List

PROTEIN

3–4 lb. rump roast

2 lbs. boneless, skinless
chicken breasts

2 lbs. 95% lean ground beef

FROZEN

1 cup frozen corn

DAIRY and REFRIGERATED

1 cup nonfat Mexican-style
shredded cheese

3 cups grated low-fat
cheddar cheese

2 cups shredded mozzarella
cheese

¼ cup grated Parmesan cheese

15 oz. ricotta cheese

12 hard-boiled eggs

6 eggs

1 Tbsp. butter

PRODUCE

1 green bell pepper

1 red bell pepper

4 medium onions

2 small onions

1 cup diced onions

1 medium zucchini

2 cups finely chopped
cabbage

½ cup chopped lettuce

1 cup diced celery

1 cup diced carrots

CANNED/DRY GOODS

28-oz. can diced tomatoes

16-oz. can garbanzo beans

10¾-oz. can 98% fat-free
cream of mushroom soup

2 4-oz. cans mild chopped
green chilies

28-oz. jar spaghetti sauce

Download this shopping list to your
smartphone!
(x.co/ShopList)

14-oz. can low-fat, low-sodium spaghetti sauce

14-oz. can fat-free pizza sauce

10¾-oz. can fat-free chicken broth

16-oz. jar low-sodium salsa

1½ cups chunky salsa

1 envelope dry onion soup mix

1 cup uncooked small elbow, shell or macaroni

6–7 uncooked lasagna noodles

12 oz. dry kluski noodles

1 lb. macaroni noodles

whole wheat sandwich rolls

10 6-inch flour tortillas

2 lbs. white chocolate coating

2 cups semisweet chocolate

4-oz. pkg. sweet German chocolate

24-oz. jar roasted peanuts

DO YOU HAVE THESE ON HAND?

garlic powder

dried basil

dried oregano

2 cups mayonnaise

paprika, *optional*

red pepper, *optional*

2 Tbsp. dry taco seasoning mix

minced dried parsley

salt

dried thyme

pepper

rubbed sage

1 beef bouillon cube

canola oil

flour

2 cups sugar

½ cup vinegar, or lemon juice

prepared mustard

Zesty Italian Beef

Carol Eveleth, Wellman, IA

Makes 8–10 servings

Prep. Time: 5 minutes
Cooking Time: 4–10 hours
Ideal slow-cooker size: 3½-qt.

1 envelope dry onion soup mix
½ tsp. garlic powder
1 tsp. dried basil
½ tsp. dried oregano
¼ tsp. paprika, *optional*
½ tsp. red pepper, *optional*
2 cups water
3–4 lb. rump roast

1. Combine soup mix and seasonings with 2 cups water in slow cooker. Add roast.
2. Cook on High 4–6 hours, or on Low 8–10 hours, or until meat is tender but not dry.
3. Allow meat to rest for 10 minutes before slicing. Top slices with cooking juices.

Slow Cooker Tex-Mex Chicken

Kim Stoltzfus, Parkesburg, PA

Makes 6 servings

Prep. Time: 15–20 minutes
Cooking Time: 2–6 hours
Ideal slow-cooker size: 3½-qt.

2 lbs. boneless, skinless chicken breasts, cut into ¾-inch-wide strips
2 Tbsp. dry taco seasoning mix
2 Tbsp. flour
1 green bell pepper, cut into strips
1 red bell pepper, cut into strips
1 cup frozen corn
1½ cups chunky salsa
1 cup shredded nonfat Mexican-style cheese

1. Toss chicken with seasoning and flour in slow cooker.
2. Gently stir in vegetables and salsa.
3. Cook on Low 4–6 hours, or on High 2–3 hours, until chicken and vegetables are cooked through but are not dry or mushy.
4. Stir before serving.
5. Serve topped with cheese.

Forgotten Minestrone

Phyllis Attig, Reynolds, IL

Makes 8 servings

Prep. Time: 15 minutes
Cooking Time: 7½–9½ hours
Ideal slow-cooker size: 7-qt.

leftover beef
6 cups water

28-oz. can diced tomatoes, undrained
1 beef bouillon cube
1 medium onion, chopped
2 Tbsp. minced dried parsley
1½ tsp. salt
1½ tsp. dried thyme
½ tsp. pepper
1 medium zucchini, thinly sliced
2 cups finely chopped cabbage
16-oz. can garbanzo beans, drained
1 cup uncooked small elbow, or shell, macaroni

1. Combine beef, water, tomatoes, bouillon, onion, parsley, salt, thyme, and pepper in slow cooker.
2. Cover. Cook on Low 7–9 hours, or until meat is tender.
3. Stir in zucchini, cabbage, beans, and macaroni. Cover and cook on High 30–45 minutes, or until vegetables are tender.

Chicken Tortilla Casserole

Jeanne Allen, Rye, CO

Makes 8–10 servings

Prep. Time: 30 minutes
Cooking Time: 3–6 hours
Ideal slow-cooker size: 5- or 6-qt.

Leftover chicken cut in 1-inch pieces
10 6-inch flour tortillas, cut in about ½x2-inch strips, *divided*
2 medium onions, chopped
1 tsp. canola oil

10¾-oz. can fat-free chicken broth
10¾-oz. can 98% fat-free cream of mushroom soup
2 4-oz. cans mild green chilies, chopped
1 egg
1 cup grated low-fat cheddar cheese

1. Spray the crock with cooking spray.
2. Scatter half the tortilla strips in bottom of slow cooker.
3. Mix remaining ingredients together, except the second half of the tortilla strips and the cheese.
4. Layer half the chicken mixture into the cooker, followed by the other half of the tortillas, followed by the rest of the chicken mix.
5. Cover. Cook on Low 4–6 hours or on High 3–5 hours.
6. Add cheese to top of dish during last 20–30 minutes of cooking.
7. Uncover and allow casserole to rest 15 minutes before serving.

Sloppy Beef Sandwiches

Colleen Konetzni,
Rio Rancho, NM

Makes 8 servings

Prep. Time: 30 minutes
Cooking Time: 2–3 hours
Ideal slow-cooker size: 3- or 4-qt.

2 lbs. 95% lean ground beef
1 medium onion, chopped
½ cup water
16-oz. jar low-sodium salsa
whole wheat sandwich rolls
2 cups grated fat-free cheddar
  cheese
½ cup chopped lettuce

1. Cook beef and onion in skillet with ½ cup water until meat is no longer pink. Stir with wooden spoon to break up clumps. Drain off drippings.
2. Place beef mixture into slow cooker. Add salsa. Mix well.
3. Cover. Cook on Low 2–3 hours.
4. Divide sandwich meat among buns and sprinkle with cheese and lettuce.

Quick 'n Easy Meat-Free Lasagna

Rhonda Freed, Lowville, NY

Makes 6 servings

Prep. Time: 10 minutes
Cooking Time: 3–4 hours
Ideal slow-cooker size: 4-qt.

28-oz. jar spaghetti sauce,
  your choice of flavor
6–7 uncooked lasagna noodles
2 cups shredded mozzarella
  cheese, *divided*
15 oz. ricotta cheese
¼ cup grated Parmesan
  cheese

1. Spread one-fourth of sauce in bottom of slow cooker.
2. Lay 2 noodles, broken into 1-inch pieces, over sauce.
3. In a bowl, mix together 1½ cups mozzarella cheese, the ricotta, and Parmesan cheeses.
4. Spoon half of cheese mixture onto noodles and spread out to edges.
5. Spoon in ⅓ of remaining sauce, and then 2 more broken noodles.
6. Spread remaining cheese mixture over top, then ½ the remaining sauce and all the remaining noodles.
7. Finish with remaining sauce.
8. Cover and cook on Low 3–4 hours, or until noodles are tender and cheeses are melted.
9. Add ½ cup mozzarella cheese and cook until cheese melts.

Beef Slow-Cooker Pizza

Wilma J. Haberkamp, Fairbank, IA

Makes 8 servings

Prep. Time: 20–30 minutes
Cooking Time: 1–2½ hours
Ideal slow-cooker size: 6-qt.

leftover "sloppy beef"
2 small onions, chopped
14-oz. can fat-free pizza
  sauce
14-oz. can low-fat, low-sodium
  spaghetti sauce
1 tsp. garlic powder
1¼ tsp. black pepper
1 tsp. dried oregano
¼ tsp. rubbed sage
12 oz. dry kluski noodles

1. In a large bowl, mix together leftover "sloppy beef," onions, pizza sauce, spaghetti sauce, seasonings, and herbs.
2. Boil noodles according to directions on package until tender. Drain.
3. Layer half of beef sauce in bottom of cooker. Spoon in noodles. Top with remaining beef sauce.
4. Cook on Low 1–1½ hours if ingredients are hot when placed in cooker. If the sauce and noodles are at room temperature or have just been refrigerated, cook on High 2–2½ hours.

Macaroni Salad

Frances and Cathy Kruba,
Dundalk, MD
Marcia S. Myer, Manheim, PA

Makes 8–10 servings

Prep. Time: 30 minutes
Cooking Time for pasta: 15 minutes

1 lb. macaroni, cooked and
  cooled
1 cup diced celery
1 cup diced onions
1 cup diced carrots
12 hard-boiled eggs, diced

2 cups sugar
½ cup vinegar, or lemon juice
2 cups mayonnaise

Dressing:
5 eggs
1 Tbsp. prepared mustard
1 Tbsp. butter
½–1 tsp. salt

1. Mix together macaroni, celery, onions, carrots, hard-boiled eggs, sugar, and vinegar or lemon juice. Add mayonnaise.

2. In a saucepan, mix eggs, mustard, butter, and salt. Cook on medium heat until thickened and steaming, stirring constantly. Do not boil.

3. Remove from heat and cool 5 minutes. Add to macaroni mixture.

Easy Chocolate Clusters

Marcella Stalter, Flanagan, IL

Makes 3½ dozen clusters

Prep. Time: 5 minutes
Cooking Time: 2 hours
Ideal slow-cooker size: 4-qt.

2 lbs. white coating chocolate, broken into small pieces
2 cups (12 oz.) semisweet chocolate chips
4-oz. pkg. sweet German chocolate
24-oz. jar roasted peanuts

1. Combine white coating chocolate, chocolate chips, and German chocolate. Cover and cook on High 1 hour. Reduce heat to Low and cook 1 hour longer, or until chocolate is melted, stirring every 15 minutes.

2. Stir in peanuts. Mix well.

3. Drop by teaspoonfuls onto wax paper. Let stand until set. Store at room temperature.

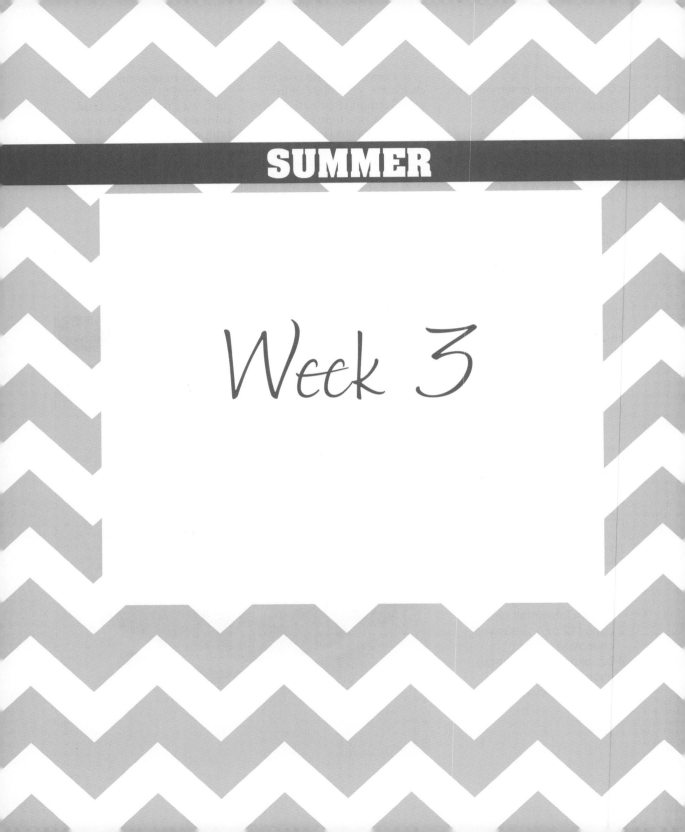

SUMMER

Week 3

THIS WEEK'S
Menu

Sunday: Beef Brisket Barbecue
Monday: Chicken with Tropical Barbecue Sauce
Tuesday: BBQ Beef Enchiladas
Wednesday: Barbecue Chicken for Buns
Thursday: Easy Crock Taco Filling
Friday: Sweet and Sour Meatballs
Saturday: Pizza Rice Casserole

Recommended Side Dish: Cornbread from Scratch
Special Dessert: Pineapple Upside-Down Cake

Shopping List

PROTEIN
3–4-lb. boneless beef brisket
3 whole chicken breasts
2 lbs. ground beef

DAIRY and REFRIGERATED
2 Tbsp. orange juice
5 cups shredded cheese of
   your choice
2 eggs
¾ cup cottage cheese,
   optional
1 cup milk
2 sticks butter

PRODUCE
2 small onions
1 large onion
½ cup chopped onion
1 cup chopped red onion
½ cup chopped celery
¾ cup chopped green bell
pepper

CANNED/DRY GOODS
15-oz. can enchilada sauce,
   green or red
15-oz. bottle sweet barbecue
   sauce
2 cups barbecue sauce
2 15-oz. cans chili beans
15-oz. can Santa Fe,
   Mexican, or Fiesta corn
20-oz. can pineapple
   chunks
1 8-oz. can pineapple slices
1 can black beans
8 sandwich rolls
12–14 small flour tortillas
1¼ cups bread crumbs
2 cups uncooked long-grain
   rice

Download this shopping list to your
smartphone!
(x.co/ShopList)

3 cups pizza sauce	cornstarch
6–8 maraschino cherries	1¼ cups flour
1 box dry yellow cake mix	¾ cup yellow cornmeal
steak rolls	1 cup plus 1½ teaspoons brown sugar
DO YOU HAVE THESE ON HAND?	¼ cup sugar
	baking powder
dry mustard	canola oil
pepper	vinegar of your choice
salt	apple cider vinegar
cayenne pepper, *optional*	¼ cup molasses
garlic powder, *optional*	Worcestershire sauce
garlic salt	prepared mustard
3 tsp. beef bouillon granules, or 2 beef bouillon cubes	hot pepper sauce
	1¾ cups ketchup

Beef Brisket Barbecue

Sharon Timpe, Jackson, WI

Makes 8 servings

Prep. Time: 15 minutes
Cooking Time: 6¼–7¼ hours
Ideal slow-cooker size: 4- to 5-qt.

2 cups barbecue sauce,
   divided
1 small onion, chopped
3 tsp. beef bouillon granules,
   or 2 beef bouillon cubes
3–4-lb. boneless beef brisket
8 sandwich rolls

1. In the bottom of your slow cooker combine 1 cup barbecue sauce, chopped onion, and bouillon.
2. Place beef brisket on top.
3. Cover and cook on Low 6–7 hours, or until brisket shreds easily.
4. Remove brisket from cooker. Using 2 forks, shred the meat.
5. Tilt cooker and spoon off fat from cooking broth. Discard fat.
6. Pour cooking broth into a bowl. Again, spoon off any remaining fat and discard.
7. Measure out 1 cup of cooking broth. Pour back into slow cooker, along with remaining cup of barbecue sauce. Blend broth and sauce well.
8. Return shredded meat to slow cooker. Stir into sauce thoroughly.
9. Cover and cook on High for 15 minutes, or until meat is hot.
10. Serve over sandwich rolls.

Tip: You can also serve the barbecue on small buns as a snack or appetizer. Serving from the slow cooker keeps the meat hot, and guests can help themselves whenever they want to.

Chicken with Tropical Barbecue Sauce

Lois Stoltzfus, Honey Brook, PA

Makes 6 servings

Prep. Time: 5 minutes
Cooking Time: 3–9 hours
Ideal slow-cooker size: 4-qt.

¼ cup molasses
2 Tbsp. cider vinegar
2 Tbsp. Worcestershire sauce
2 tsp. prepared mustard
⅛–¼ tsp. hot pepper sauce
2 Tbsp. orange juice
3 whole chicken breasts,
   halved

1. Combine molasses, vinegar, Worcestershire sauce, mustard, hot pepper sauce, and orange juice.
2. Place chicken in slow cooker. Brush sauce over the chicken.
3. Cover. Cook on Low 7–9 hours, or on High 3–4 hours.

BBQ Beef Enchiladas

Hope Comerford,
Clinton Township, MI

Makes 8 servings

Prep. Time: 10 minutes
Cooking Time: 4–6 hours
Ideal slow-cooker size: 5 qt.

15-oz. can enchilada sauce, green or red
15-oz. bottle sweet barbecue sauce
12–14 small flour tortillas
leftover shredded beef
1 can black beans, drained, rinsed
1 cup chopped red onion
3 cups shredded cheese of your choice

1. Spray the slow cooker crock with nonstick spray.
2. Mix together the enchilada sauce and barbecue sauce.
3. Line the bottom of the slow cooker with the flour tortillas. You may need to cut some in half.
4. Next, spread ⅓ of the beef, ⅓ of the black beans, ⅓ of the onion, ⅓ barbecue/enchilada sauce mixture, and ¼ of the shredded cheese over the bottom layer of tortillas. Repeat this process two more times, finishing with a little enchilada sauce for the top layer and spreading the remaining cheese on top.
5. Cook on Low for 4–6 hours.

Barbecue Chicken for Buns

Linda Sluiter, Schererville, IN

Makes 5 servings

Prep. Time: 25 minutes
Cooking Time: 3–4 hours
Ideal slow-cooker size: 4-qt.

leftover chicken, diced
½ cup chopped celery
¼ cup chopped onions
¼ cup chopped green bell peppers
1½ tsp. canola oil
¾ cup ketchup
¾ cups water
1½ tsp. brown sugar
1 Tbsp. vinegar
¾ tsp. dry mustard
¼ tsp. pepper
⅛ tsp. salt
steak rolls

1. Combine all ingredients in slow cooker.
2. Cover. Cook on Low 3–4 hours.
3. Pile into steak rolls and serve.

Easy Crock Taco Filling

Joanne Good, Wheaton, IL

Makes 6–8 servings

Prep. Time: 20 minutes
Cooking Time: 6–8 hours
Ideal slow-cooker size: 4-qt.

1 large onion, chopped
1¾ lbs. ground beef
2 15-oz. cans chili beans
15-oz. can Santa Fe corn, or Mexican, or Fiesta, corn
¾ cup water

Optional Ingredients:
¼ tsp. cayenne pepper
½ tsp. garlic powder

1. Brown ground beef and chopped onion in a nonstick skillet. Drain.
2. Mix all ingredients together in the slow cooker, blending well.
3. Cover and cook on Low for 6–8 hours.

Tips: 1. You may want to add more or less than ¾ cup water to this recipe, depending upon how hot and fast your slow cooker cooks and how tight-fitting its lid is.
2. Serve in warmed, soft corn tortillas or hard taco shells. Or serve as a taco dip with plain corn tortilla chips.
3. Good garnishes for this taco filling include sour cream, guacamole, shredded cheese, diced tomatoes, shredded lettuce, and salsa.

Sweet and Sour Meatballs

Elaine Unruh, Minneapolis, MN

Makes 8 main-dish servings, or 20 appetizer servings

Prep. Time: 45 minutes
Cooking Time: 6 hours
Ideal slow-cooker size: 4-qt.

Meatballs:
2 lbs. ground beef
1¼ cups bread crumbs
¼ tsp. salt
1 tsp. pepper
2–3 Tbsp. Worcestershire sauce
1 egg
½ tsp. garlic salt
¼ cup finely chopped onions

Sauce:
20-oz. can pineapple chunks, juice reserved
3 Tbsp. cornstarch
¼ cup cold water
1 cup ketchup
2 Tbsp. Worcestershire sauce
¼ tsp. salt
¼ tsp. pepper
¼ tsp. garlic salt
½ cup chopped green bell pepper

1. Combine all meatball ingredients. Shape into 60 meatballs. Brown in skillet, rolling so all sides are browned. Place meatballs in slow cooker.
2. Pour juice from pineapples into skillet. Stir into drippings.
3. Combine cornstarch and cold water. Add to skillet and stir until thickened.
4. Stir in ketchup and Worcestershire sauce. Season with salt, pepper, and garlic salt. Add green peppers and pineapples. Pour over meatballs.
5. Cover. Cook on Low 6 hours.

Pizza Rice Casserole

Jennie Martin, Richfield, PA

Makes 4–6 servings

Prep. Time: 20 minutes
Cooking Time: 6 hours
Ideal slow-cooker size: 5-qt.

leftover taco beef
1 small onion, chopped
2 cups uncooked long-grain rice
3 cups pizza sauce
2 cups shredded cheese, your choice of flavor
¾ cup cottage cheese, *optional*
3 cups water

1. Mix all ingredients in slow cooker.
2. Cover and cook on High for 6 hours, or until the rice is tender.

Cornbread from Scratch

Dorothy M. Van Deest, Memphis, TN

Makes 6 servings

Prep. Time: 15 minutes
Cooking Time: 2–3 hours
Ideal slow-cooker size: 6-qt.

1¼ cups flour
¾ cup yellow cornmeal
¼ cup sugar
4½ tsp. baking powder
1 tsp. salt
1 egg, slightly beaten
1 cup milk
5⅓ Tbsp. (⅓ cup) butter,
    melted, or oil

1. In mixing bowl sift together flour, cornmeal, sugar, baking powder, and salt. Make a well in the center.

2. Pour egg, milk, and butter into well. Mix into the dry mixture until just moistened.

3. Pour mixture into a greased 2-quart mold. Cover with a plate. Place on a trivet or rack in the bottom of slow cooker.

4. Cover. Cook on High 2–3 hours.

Pineapple Upside-Down Cake

Vera M. Kuhns,
Harrisonburg, VA

Makes 10 servings

Prep. Time: 20 minutes
Cooking Time: 4–5 hours
Ideal slow-cooker size: 4-qt.

1 stick butter, or margarine,
    melted
1 cup brown sugar
1 8-oz. can pineapple slices,
    drained, reserving juice
6–8 maraschino cherries
1 box dry yellow cake mix

1. Combine butter and brown sugar. Spread over bottom of well-greased cooker.

2. Add pineapple slices and place cherries in the center of each one.

3. Prepare cake batter according to package directions, using pineapple juice for part of liquid. Spoon cake batter into cooker over top fruit.

4. Cover cooker with two tea towels and then with its own lid. Cook on High 1 hour, and then on Low 3–4 hours.

SUMMER

Week 4

THIS WEEK'S
Menu

Sunday: Tracy's Barbecued Chicken Wings
Monday: Terrific Turkey Breast
Tuesday: Beef Pitas
Wednesday: Barbecued Turkey for Sandwiches
Thursday: Ham 'n Cola
Friday: Beef Marinara Casserole
Saturday: Barbecued Ham Sandwiches

Recommended Side Dish: Best Baked Beans
Special Dessert: Brownies with Nuts

Shopping List

PROTEIN
3 lbs. chicken wings
2½-lb. turkey breast
2 lbs. ground beef
3–4 lb. precooked ham
8 strips bacon

DAIRY and REFRIGERATED
1 cup nonfat sour cream
3 cups shredded mozzarella
  or parmesan
½ stick butter

PRODUCE
2 large onions
1 medium onion
3 small onions
2 cups chopped onion
2½ cups chopped tomatoes
2 Tbsp. diced green bell
  pepper

CANNED/DRY GOODS
2 6-oz. cans tomato paste
5 15-oz. cans baked beans
1 qt. marinara sauce
¼ cup cola-flavored soda
large pita breads
3 cups uncooked long-grain
  rice
bread and buns
23-oz. pkg. brownie mix

DO YOU HAVE THESE ON HAND?
salt
dry mustard
black pepper
dried rosemary
dried sage
dried oregano
ground cloves
4 cloves garlic

Download this shopping list to your smartphone!
(x.co/ShopList)

2 cups fat-free, low-sodium
  chicken broth

vegetable oil

canola oil

cider vinegar

red wine vinegar

vinegar of your choice

½ cup molasses

prepared mustard

prepared horseradish

1½ cups ketchup

¼ cup flour

1⅓ cups plus 3 Tbsp. brown
  sugar

sugar

Worcestershire sauce

½ cup sweet pickle relish

1 cup chopped nuts

SPIRITS

½ cup red or white wine

½ cup white wine, *optional*

Tracy's Barbecued Chicken Wings

Tracy Supcoe, Barclay, MD

Makes 4–6 servings

Prep. Time: 35 minutes
Cooking Time: 5–6 hours
Ideal slow-cooker size: 4-qt.

3 lbs. chicken wings, skin removed
2 large onions, chopped
2 6-oz. cans tomato paste
2 large cloves garlic, minced
¼ cup Worcestershire sauce
¼ cup cider vinegar
¼ cup brown sugar
2 Tbsp. sugar
½ cup sweet pickle relish
½ cup red or white wine
¼ tsp. salt
2 tsp. dry mustard

1. Cut off wing tips. Cut wings at joint. Place in slow cooker.
2. Combine remaining ingredients. Add to slow cooker. Stir.
3. Cover. Cook on Low 5–6 hours.

Terrific Turkey Breast

Dawn Day, Westminster, CA

Makes 10 servings

Prep. Time: 30 minutes
Cooking Time: 6¼–8¼ hours
Ideal slow-cooker size: 5-qt.

2½-lb. turkey breast
2 Tbsp. canola oil
2 cups chopped onions
2 cloves garlic, chopped
1 tsp. black pepper
1 tsp. salt
1 tsp. dried rosemary
½ tsp. dried sage
2 cups fat-free, low-sodium chicken broth
¼ cup flour
½ cup white wine, *optional*

1. Brown turkey breast in oil in skillet. Remove from skillet and place in slow cooker.
2. Sauté onions and garlic in reserved drippings. Stir in seasonings, broth, and wine and mix well.
3. Pour seasoned broth over turkey in slow cooker.
4. Cover. Cook on Low 6–8 hours or just until turkey is tender.
5. Remove turkey from cooker and allow to rest for 10 minutes on warm platter.
6. Remove 1 cup broth from cooker and place in bowl. Mix ¼ cup flour into broth in bowl until smooth. Stir back into broth in cooker until smooth. Cover and cook on High for 10 minutes, or until broth is thickened.
7. Meanwhile, slice turkey. Serve with gravy or au jus.

Beef Pitas

Dede Peterson, Rapid City, SD

Makes 8 servings

Prep. Time: 15 minutes
Cooking Time: 2–3 hours
Ideal slow-cooker size: 2-qt.

2 lbs. ground beef
1 tsp. dried oregano
¼ tsp. black pepper
2½ cups chopped fresh
  tomatoes
2 Tbsp. diced fresh green bell
  pepper
1 cup nonfat sour cream
1 Tbsp. red wine vinegar
1 Tbsp. vegetable oil
large pita breads, heated and
  cut in half

1. Place meat in slow cooker. Sprinkle with oregano and black pepper.
2. Cook on Low 2–3 hours. Remove half of the beef and refrigerate for later this week.
3. In a separate bowl, combine tomatoes, green pepper, sour cream, vinegar, and oil.
4. Fill pitas with meat. Top with vegetable and sour cream mixture.

Barbecued Turkey for Sandwiches

Joanna Bear, Salisbury, MD

Makes 4–5 servings

Prep. Time: 10 minutes
Cooking Time: 1 hour
Ideal slow-cooker size: 1½- to 2-qt.

½ cup ketchup
¼ cup brown sugar
1 Tbsp. prepared mustard
1 Tbsp. Worcestershire sauce
2 cups leftover turkey, cut into
  bite-sized chunks
1 small onion, finely chopped,
  optional
buns

1. Mix ketchup, sugar, mustard, and Worcestershire sauce together in the slow cooker. Add turkey, and onion, if you wish. Toss to coat well.
2. Cover and cook on High 1 hour, or until heated through.
3. Serve on buns.

Ham 'n Cola

Carol Peachey, Lancaster, PA

Makes 8–10 servings

Prep. Time: 5 minutes
Cooking Time: 2–10 hours
Ideal slow-cooker size: 4- to 5-qt.

½ cup brown sugar
1 tsp. dry mustard
1 tsp. prepared horseradish
¼ cup cola-flavored soda
3–4-lb. precooked ham

1. Combine brown sugar, mustard, and horseradish. Moisten with just enough cola to make a smooth paste. Reserve remaining cola.
2. Rub entire ham with mixture. Place ham in slow cooker and add remaining cola.
3. Cover. Cook on Low 6–10 hours, or on High 2–3 hours.

Beef Marinara Casserole

Hope Comerford,
Clinton Township, MI

Makes 6–8 servings

Prep. Time: 20 minutes
Cooking Time: 6 hours
Ideal slow-cooker size: 5-qt.

1 medium onion, chopped
leftover ground beef
3 cups uncooked long-grain rice
1 qt. marinara sauce

3 cups shredded mozzarella or parmesan
4 cups water

1. Place chopped onion in a nonstick skillet and brown.
2. Mix all ingredients in slow cooker.
3. Cover and cook on High for 6 hours, or until the rice is tender.

Barbecued Ham Sandwiches

Jane Steiner, Orrville, OH

Makes 4–6 full-sized servings

Prep. Time: 5–7 minutes
Cooking Time: 5 hours
Ideal slow-cooker size: 3-qt.

leftover ham slices
1 small onion, finely diced
½ cup ketchup
1 Tbsp. vinegar
3 Tbsp. brown sugar
bread or buns

1. Place half of meat in greased slow cooker.
2. Combine other ingredients except the bread. Pour half of mixture over meat. Repeat layers.
3. Cover. Cook on Low 5 hours.
4. Serve on bread of your choice.

Best Baked Beans

Nadine Martinitz, Salina, KS

Makes 8–10 servings

Prep. Time: 15 minutes
Cooking Time: 2–6 hours
Ideal slow-cooker size: 6-qt.

8 strips bacon, diced
1 small onion, chopped
5 15-oz. cans pork and beans
2 Tbsp. Worcestershire sauce
⅓ cup brown sugar
½ cup molasses
½ cup ketchup
dash of ground cloves

1. Sauté bacon in skillet until crisp. Remove bacon but retain drippings in skillet.
2. Brown chopped onion in drippings until translucent.
3. Combine all ingredients in slow cooker. Stir well.
4. Cover. Cook on Low 5–6 hours, or on High 2–3 hours.

Brownies with Nuts

Dorothy M. Van Deest,
Memphis, TN

Makes 24 brownies

Prep. Time: 10–15 minutes
Cooking Time: 3 hours
Ideal slow-cooker size: 5-qt.

½ stick butter, melted
1 cup chopped nuts, *divided*
23-oz. pkg. brownie mix

1. Pour melted butter into a baking insert designed to fit into your slow cooker. Swirl butter around to grease sides of insert.

2. Sprinkle butter with half the nuts.

3. In a bowl, mix brownies according to package directions. Spoon half the batter into the baking insert, trying to cover the nuts evenly.

4. Add remaining half of nuts. Spoon in remaining batter.

5. Place insert in slow cooker. Cover insert with 8 paper towels.

6. Cover cooker. Cook on High 3 hours. Do not check or remove cover until last hour of cooking. Then insert toothpick into center of brownies. If it comes out clean, the brownies are finished. If it doesn't, continue cooking another 15 minutes. Check again. Repeat until pick comes out clean.

7. When finished cooking, uncover cooker and baking insert. Let brownies stand 5 minutes.

8. Invert insert onto serving plate. Cut brownies with a plastic knife (so the crumbs don't drag). Serve warm.

Week 5

THIS WEEK'S
Menu

Sunday: Shredded Beef for Tacos
Monday: Lemon Honey Chicken
Tuesday: Hearty Italian Sandwiches
Wednesday: Shredded Chicken Salad
Thursday: Pasta Sauce with Shredded Beef
Friday: Slow-Cooked Steak Fajitas
Saturday: Slow-Cooker Fajita Stew

Recommended Side Dish: Marinated Asparagus
Special Dessert: Sour Cherry Cobbler

Shopping List

PROTEIN

6-lb. round roast

5–6-lb. whole roasting
   chicken

½-lb. bulk Italian sausage

1½-lb. beef flank steak

DAIRY and REFRIGERATED

¾ cup orange juice

¾ cup fat-free sour cream

1 egg

½ cup shredded cheese of
   your choice

½–1 cup shredded
   Monterey Jack cheese,
   optional

¼ cup milk

2 Tbsp. butter

PRODUCE

1 small onion

2 medium onions

1 large onion

1½ cups chopped onion

½ cup chopped onion,
   optional

3 green bell peppers

4 red bell peppers

6–8 cups chopped lettuce

1 cup chopped lettuce,
   optional

1 cup diced tomatoes

1 cup diced tomtaoes,
   optional

1 cup sugar snap peas

½ cup bean sprouts

2 lbs. asparagus

1 Tbsp. minced fresh
   parsley

1 jalapeño pepper

3 serrano chilies

1 lemon

Download this shopping list to your
smartphone!

(x.co/ShopList)

4 cups fresh sour pitted
  cherries, or frozen

CANNED/DRY GOODS
15-oz. can tomato sauce
14½-oz. can stewed
  tomatoes
15-oz. can crushed tomatoes
15-oz. can low-sodium diced
  tomatoes with garlic and
  onion
14-oz. can diced tomatoes
¾ cup low-sodium salsa
1 lb. pasta
12 6-inch flour tortillas
1-oz. envelope dry fajita
  seasoning mix
taco shells
sandwich rolls

**DO YOU HAVE THESE ON
HAND?**
salt
pepper
garlic powder

dried minced onion
onion powder
dried oregano
dried basil
ground coriander
ground cumin
chili powder
ground cinnamon
8 cloves garlic
oil of your choice
vegetable oil
olive oil
5 tsp. lemon juice
soy sauce
cider vinegar
honey
sugar
brown sugar
½ cup whole wheat flour
1 cup all-purpose flour
cornstarch
baking powder
almond extract
¼ cup sliced almonds,
  optional

Shredded Beef for Tacos

Dawn Day, Westminster, CA

Makes 10–12 servings

Prep. Time: 15 minutes
Cooking Time: 6–8 hours
Ideal slow-cooker size: 4-qt.

6-lb. round roast, cut into
  large chunks
1½ cups onion, chopped
6 Tbsp. oil pf your choice
3 serrano chilies, chopped
6 cloves garlic, minced
2 tsp. salt
3 cup water
taco shells

optional toppings: diced
tomatoes, chopped onions,
chopped lettuce, shredded
cheese of your choice

1. Brown meat and onion
in oil. Transfer to slow cooker.
2. Add chilies, garlic, salt,
and water.
3. Cover. Cook on High 6–8
hours.
4. Pull meat apart with two
forks until shredded.
5. Serve in taco shells with
toppings of your choice.

Lemon Honey Chicken

Carolyn W. Carmichael,
Berkeley Heights, NJ

Makes 4–6 servings

Prep. Time: 5 minutes
Cooking Time: 8 hours
Ideal slow-cooker size: 4-qt.

1 lemon
5–6-lb. whole roasting
  chicken, rinsed
½ cup orange juice
½ cup honey

1. Pierce lemon with fork.
Place in chicken cavity. Place
chicken in slow cooker.
2. Combine orange juice
and honey. Pour over
chicken.
3. Cover. Cook on Low 8
hours. Remove lemon and
squeeze over chicken.
4. Carve chicken and serve.

Hearty Italian Sandwiches

Rhonda Lee Schmidt,
Scranton, PA
Robin Schrock, Millersburg, OH

Makes 4 servings

Prep. Time: 15 minutes
Cooking Time: 6 hours
Ideal slow-cooker size: 4-qt.

2–3 cups leftover shredded
  beef
½ lb. bulk Italian sausage
1 large onion, chopped

1 large green bell pepper,
  chopped
1 large red bell pepper,
  chopped
½ tsp. salt
½ tsp. pepper

1. In skillet, brown sausage.
Drain. Mix in the leftover beef.

2. Place ⅓ onions and
peppers in slow cooker. Top
with half of meat mixture.
Repeat layers. Sprinkle with
salt and pepper.

3. Cover. Cook on Low 6
hours, or until vegetables are
tender.

Serving Suggestion: With
a slotted spoon, serve about
1 cup mixture on each
sandwich roll. Top with
optional shredded Monterey
Jack cheese.

Shredded Chicken Salad

Hope Comerford,
Clinton Township, MI

Makes 4–6 servings

Prep. Time: 10 minutes

6–8 cups chopped lettuce
leftover chicken

Toppings:
1 cup diced tomatoes
1 cup sugar snap peas
½ cup bean sprouts

Dressing:
½ cup olive oil
¼ cup orange juice
1 Tbsp. honey
1 tsp. lemon juice
½ tsp. salt
¼ tsp. pepper

1. To assemble salad, start
with dividing the lettuce
between plates or bowls and
topping each with a portion
of chicken.

2. Add the toppings to each
plate/bowl.

3. Mix together the
dressing ingredients. Drizzle
the dressing over each salad.

Lemon Honey Chicken, (page 154)

Pasta Sauce with Shredded Beef

Hope Comerford,
Clinton Township, MI

Servings: 4–5 servings

Prep. Time: 5 minutes
Cooking Time: 5 hours
Ideal slow-cooker size: 4-qt.

1½ cups leftover shredded beef
15-oz. can tomato sauce
14½-oz. can stewed tomatoes
15-oz. can crushed tomatoes
2½ cups water
2 Tbsp. garlic powder
1 Tbsp. dried minced onion
1 Tbsp. onion powder
¼ tsp. pepper
1 tsp. salt
½ tsp. dried oregano
½ tsp. dried basil
1 lb. pasta of your choice

1. Place all ingredients except the pasta into the crock and stir.
2. Cook on Low for 5 hours.
3. Serve over your favorite type of pasta.

Slow-Cooked Steak Fajitas

Virginia Graybill, Hershey, PA

Makes 12 servings

Prep. Time: 25–30 minutes
Cooking Time: 4½–6½ hours
Ideal slow-cooker size: 4-qt.

1½-lb. beef flank steak
15-oz. can low-sodium diced tomatoes with garlic and onion, undrained
1 jalapeño pepper, seeded and chopped
2 cloves garlic, minced
1 tsp. ground coriander
1 tsp. ground cumin
1 tsp. chili powder
½ tsp. salt
2 medium onions, sliced
2 medium green bell peppers, julienned
2 medium sweet red bell peppers, julienned
1 Tbsp. minced fresh parsley
2 tsp. cornstarch
1 Tbsp. water
12 6-inch flour tortillas, warmed
¾ cup fat-free sour cream
¾ cup low-sodium salsa

1. Slice steak thinly into strips across grain. Place in slow cooker.
2. Add tomatoes, jalapeño, garlic, coriander, cumin, chili powder, and salt.
3. Cover. Cook on Low 3–4 hours.
4. Add onions, peppers, and parsley.
5. Cover. Cook on Low 1–2 hours longer, or until meat is tender.
6. Combine cornstarch and water until smooth. Gradually stir into slow cooker.
7. Cover. Cook on High 30 minutes, or until slightly thickened.
8. Using a slotted spoon, spoon about ½ cup of meat mixture down the center of each tortilla.
9. Add 1 Tbsp. sour cream and 1 Tbsp. salsa to each.
10. Fold bottom of tortilla over filling and roll up.

Slow-Cooker Fajita Stew

Sara Puskar, Abingdon, MD
Nancy Wagner Graves, Manhattan, KS

Makes 4 servings

Prep. Time: 20 minutes
Cooking Time: 2½ hours
Ideal slow-cooker size: 3- or 4-qt.

1 small onion, chopped
1 red bell pepper, cut into 1-inch pieces
1-oz. envelope dry fajita seasoning mix (about 2 Tbsp.)
14-oz. can diced tomatoes, undrained
leftover steak
¼ cup flour
¼ cup water

1. Place the onion and bell pepper into the slow cooker.
2. Mix together fajita seasoning and undrained tomatoes. Pour over the onions and peppers.
3. Cover. Cook on Low 2 hours.
4. Add in the leftover steak.
5. Combine flour and water in a small bowl. Stir well to mix.
6. Gradually add to slow cooker.
7. Cover. Cook on High 30 minutes until thickened, stirring occasionally and until steak is heated through.

Tip: This is delicious served over hot rice.

Marinated Asparagus

Rebecca Meyerkorth,
Wamego, KS

Makes 8–10 servings

Prep. Time: 20 minutes
Cooking Time: 5–10 minutes
Chilling Time: 2–12 hours

Marinade:

½ cup brown sugar
½ cup cider vinegar
½ cup soy sauce
½ cup vegetable oil
4 tsp. lemon juice
1 tsp. garlic powder

2 lbs. asparagus
¼ cup sliced almonds,
   optional

1. In saucepan, stir together brown sugar, vinegar, soy sauce, oil, juice, and garlic powder.
2. Bring to a boil and simmer 5 minutes. Cool.
3. Meanwhile, microwave or cook asparagus until just crisp tender. Plunge it in cold water to stop the cooking. Drain well.
4. In a large resealable plastic bag, put asparagus and marinade. Zip bag and turn to coat asparagus.
5. Refrigerate at least 2 hours or overnight, turning occasionally.
6. Drain and discard marinade.
7. Place asparagus on plate to serve. Sprinkle with sliced almonds, if desired.

Sour Cherry Cobbler

Margaret W. High, Lancaster, PA

Makes 6–8 servings

Prep. Time: 20 minutes
Cooking Time: 2 hours
Ideal slow-cooker size: 6-qt.

½ cup whole wheat flour
¾ cup all-purpose flour,
   divided
1 Tbsp. sugar, plus ⅔ cup
   sugar, *divided*
1 tsp. baking powder
¼ tsp. salt
¼ tsp. ground cinnamon
¼ tsp. almond extract
1 egg
¼ cup milk
2 Tbsp. butter, melted
4 cups fresh pitted sour
   cherries, or thawed and
   drained if frozen

1. In mixing bowl, combine whole wheat flour and ½ cup all-purpose flour. Mix in 1 Tbsp. sugar, baking powder, salt, and cinnamon.
2. Separately, combine almond extract, egg, milk, and butter. Stir into dry ingredients just until moistened.
3. Spread batter in bottom of greased slow cooker.
4. Separately, mix remaining ¼ cup flour with ⅔ cup sugar. Add cherries. Sprinkle cherry mixture evenly over batter in slow cooker.
5. Cover and cook on High 2 hours or until lightly browned at edges and juice is bubbling from cherries.

SUMMER

Week 6

THIS WEEK'S
Menu

Sunday: Lemony Turkey Breast
Monday: Turkey Enchiladas
Tuesday: 4-Bean Turkey Chili
Wednesday: Slow-Cooker Fresh Veggie Lasagna
Thursday: Super Easy Chicken
Friday: Wild Rice Soup
Saturday: Company Casserole
Recommended Side Dish: Whole Wheat Oatmeal Bread
Special Dessert: Slow-Cooker Peach Crisp

Shopping List

PROTEIN

6-lb. bone-in turkey breast

10 boneless, skinless
   chicken breast halves

12-oz. pkg. shelled frozen
   shrimp

DAIRY and REFRIGERATED

3 cups shredded cheese,
   your choice of flavor

1½ cups shredded
   mozzarella cheese

⅓ cup shredded Parmesan
   cheese

½ cup ricotta cheese

2 eggs

4 Tbsp. butter

1 cup skim milk or
   buttermilk

PRODUCE

1 large onion

1 cup chopped red onions

½ cup minced fresh onions

8 green onions

1 medium zucchini

½ lb. winter squash

1 cup mushrooms

½ cup minced celery

4 cups baby spinach

1 medium lemon

1 Tbsp. chopped fresh
   parsley, *optional*

CANNED/DRY GOODS

10-oz. can low-sodium
   tomato sauce

4-oz. can chopped green
   chilies

Download this shopping list to your
smartphone!
(x.co/ShopList)

6-oz. can low-sodium tomato paste

12-oz. can chili beans

12-oz. can kidney beans

12-oz. can black beans

12-oz. can pinto beans

12-oz. can low-sodium tomatoes

2 4-oz. cans sliced mushrooms

4 cups canned peaches

10–12 corn tortillas

1 cup marinara sauce

4 no-boil lasagna noodles

2 pkgs. dry Italian dressing mix

½ cup dry wild rice

1¼ cups uncooked rice

¼ cup biscuit baking mix

DO YOU HAVE THESE ON HAND?

lemon pepper

garlic salt

chili powder

garlic powder

dried oregano

salt

ground cinnamon

cornstarch

3½ cups fat-free, reduced-sodium chicken broth

1½ cups chicken stock, *optional*

6 cups fat-free, low-sodium chicken stock

Worcestershire sauce

⅓ cup light soy sauce

2 Tbsp. peanut oil, or butter

honey

⅔ cup plus ½ cup rolled, or quick, dry oats

1 pkg. active dry yeast

⅔ cup plus ½ cup slivered almonds

¼ cup wheat germ

2¾ cups whole wheat flour from hard wheat (also called bread flour)

3 Tbsp. wheat gluten

¾ cup brown sugar

Lemony Turkey Breast

Joyce Shackelford, Green Bay, WI
Carolyn Baer, Conrath, WI

Makes 12 servings

Prep. Time: 15 minutes
Cooking Time: 7–8 hours
Ideal slow-cooker size: 6-qt.

6-lb. bone-in turkey breast,
  cut in half and skin removed
1 medium lemon, halved
1 tsp. lemon pepper
1 tsp. garlic salt
4 tsp. cornstarch
½ cup fat-free, reduced-
  sodium chicken broth

1. Place turkey, meaty side up, in slow cooker sprayed with nonfat cooking spray.
2. Squeeze half of lemon over turkey. Sprinkle with lemon pepper and garlic salt.
3. Place lemon halves under turkey.
4. Cover. Cook on Low 7–8 hours or just until turkey is tender.
5. Remove turkey. Discard lemons.
6. Allow turkey to rest 15 minutes before slicing.

Turkey Enchiladas

Hope Comerford,
Clinton Township, MI

Makes 4–6 servings

Prep. Time: 20 minutes
Cooking Time: 3–4 hours
Ideal slow-cooker size: 3-qt.

10–12 corn tortillas
10-oz. can low-sodium tomato
  sauce
4-oz. can chopped green
  chilies
1 cup chopped red onions
2 Tbsp. Worcestershire sauce
1–2 Tbsp. chili powder
¼ tsp. garlic powder
1 cup leftover turkey, diced

3 cups shredded cheese, your
  choice of flavor

1. Spray the bottom of your crock with nonstick spray.
2. Cover the bottom of your crock with 3–4 of the corn tortillas. You may need to cut some in half to make them fit well.

3. Combine tomato sauce, chilies, onions, Worcestershire sauce, chili powder, and garlic powder. Stir in the turkey.

4. Pour half of this mixture onto the layer of tortillas. Sprinkle with ⅓ of the shredded cheese. Repeat this process again, finishing with a layer of tortillas and cheese on top.

5. Cover. Cook on Low for 3–4 hours.

6. Turn the slow cooker off and let stand for about 10–15 minutes before serving.

4-Bean Turkey Chili

Dawn Day, Westminster, CA

Makes 10 servings

Prep. Time: 30 minutes
Cooking Time: 4–5 hours
Ideal slow-cooker size: 4-qt.

remaining leftover turkey, chopped
1 large onion, chopped
6-oz. can low-sodium tomato paste
2 Tbsp. chili powder
12-oz. can chili beans, undrained
12-oz. can kidney beans, undrained
12-oz. can black beans, undrained
12-oz. can pinto beans, undrained
12-oz. can low-sodium tomatoes with juice
1 Tbsp. chopped fresh parsley, *optional*

1. Combine leftover turkey, onion, and tomato paste in slow cooker.

2. Add chili powder, beans, and tomatoes. Mix well.

3. Cover. Cook on Low 4–5 hours.

4. Serve with grated low-fat cheddar cheese.

5. Sprinkle individual servings with fresh parsley, if you wish.

Slow-Cooker Fresh Veggie Lasagna

Deanne Gingrich, Lancaster, PA

Makes 4–6 servings

Prep. Time: 30 minutes
Cooking Time: 4–5 hours
Ideal slow-cooker size: 4-qt.

1½ cups shredded mozzarella cheese
½ cup ricotta cheese
⅓ cup shredded Parmesan cheese
1 egg, lightly beaten
1 tsp. dried oregano
¼ tsp. garlic powder
1 cup marinara sauce, *divided*, plus more for serving
1 medium zucchini, diced, *divided*
4 no-boil lasagna noodles
4 cups baby spinach, *divided*
1 cup mushrooms, sliced, *divided*

1. Combine mozzarella, ricotta, Parmesan, egg, oregano and garlic powder in a bowl. Set aside.

2. Spread 2 Tbsp. marinara sauce in the slow cooker.

3. Sprinkle with ½ of the diced zucchini and ⅓ of the cheese mixture.

4. Break 2 noodles into large pieces to cover cheese layer.

5. Spread 2 Tbsp. sauce, ½ of the spinach, and ½ of the mushrooms atop cheese.

6. Repeat layers, ending with the cheese mixture and sauce. Press layers down firmly.

7. Cover and cook on Low 4–5 hours. Allow to rest 20 minutes before cutting and serving. Serve with extra sauce.

Super Easy Chicken

Mary Seielstad, Sparks, NV

Makes 10 servings

Prep. Time: 5 minutes
Cooking Time: 5–6 hours
Ideal slow-cooker size: 4-qt.

10 boneless, skinless chicken breast halves
2 pkgs. dry Italian dressing mix
1½ cups warm water or chicken stock

1. Place chicken in slow cooker. Sprinkle with dressing mix. Pour water or stock around chicken.

2. Cover. Cook on Low 5–6 hours, or until juices run clear.

Wild Rice Soup

Joyce Shackelford, Green Bay, WI

Makes 8 servings

Prep. Time: 25 minutes
Cooking Time: 3–4 hours
Ideal slow-cooker size: 4-qt.

2 Tbsp. butter
½ cup dry wild rice
6 cups fat-free, low-sodium chicken stock
½ cup minced fresh onions
½ cup minced celery
½ lb. winter squash, peeled, seeded, cut into ½-inch cubes
2 cups leftover chicken, chopped
½ cup browned, slivered almonds

1. Melt butter in small skillet. Add rice and sauté 10 minutes over low heat. Transfer to slow cooker.

2. Add all remaining ingredients except chicken and almonds.

3. Cover. Cook on Low 3–4 hours, or until vegetables are cooked to your liking. One hour before serving, stir in chicken.

4. Top with browned slivered almonds just before serving.

Company Casserole

Vera Schmucker, Goshen, IN

Makes 6 servings

Prep. Time: 15–25 minutes
Cooking Time: 2–6 hours
Ideal slow-cooker size: 4- or 5-qt.

1¼ cups uncooked rice
2 Tbsp. butter, melted
3 cups fat-free, low-sodium chicken broth
1 cup water
remaining leftover chicken, chopped
2 4-oz. cans sliced mushrooms, drained
⅓ cup light soy sauce
12-oz. pkg. shelled frozen shrimp, thawed
8 green onions, chopped, 2 Tbsp. reserved
⅔ cup slivered almonds

1. Combine rice and butter in slow cooker. Stir to coat rice well.

2. Add remaining ingredients except shrimp, almonds, and 2 Tbsp. green onions.

3. Cover. Cook on Low 5–6 hours or on High 2–3 hours, until rice is tender.

4. Fifteen minutes before the end of cooking time, stir in shrimp.

5. Sprinkle almonds and green onions over top before serving.

Whole Wheat Oatmeal Bread

Phyllis Good, Lancaster, PA

Makes 1 loaf

Prep. Time: 30 minutes
Cooking Time: 2½–3 hours
Ideal slow-cooker size: 6-qt.

1 Tbsp. (1 pkg.) active dry yeast

¼ cup warm water, heated to 110–120°F
1 cup skim milk, or 1 cup buttermilk, heated to 110–120°F
½ cup rolled, or quick, dry oats
2 Tbsp. peanut oil, or 2 Tbsp. butter, melted
2 Tbsp. honey
1 egg
¼ cup wheat germ
1 tsp. salt
2¾ cups whole wheat flour from hard wheat (also called bread flour), *divided*
3 Tbsp. wheat gluten

1. Grease a loaf pan that fits into your slow cooker, or a 1-lb. can that will stand upright in your cooker with the cooker lid on.

2. Put yeast, water, milk, oats, oil or butter, honey, egg, and wheat germ in good-sized mixing bowl. Mix together. Let stand until bubbly, about 10 minutes.

3. Stir in salt, about 2 cups flour, and gluten. When the mixture becomes too stiff to stir with a wooden spoon, use your hands to scrape and turn the dough until it forms a ball. If it remains too sticky, add a bit of the remaining flour.

4. When a ball forms, turn it onto a lightly floured countertop. Knead until smooth and elastic, about 5–8 minutes. Work in more of the remaining flour if you need it.

5. Turn dough immediately into the loaf pan or coffee can. Cover with greased aluminum foil. Let stand 5 minutes.

6. Place covered pan or can into the slow cooker on top of a trivet or metal jar rings. Cover the cooker. Bake on High 2½–3 hours. You'll know the bread is done when its sides brown and look crispy and its top is lightly brown and soft.

7. Remove pan from cooker. Let stand uncovered for 5 minutes. Then turn the pan or can upside down and take the bread out. Let it cool before slicing it.

Slow-Cooker Peach Crisp

Amanda Gross, Souderton, PA

Makes 6 servings

Prep. Time: 15 minutes
Cooking Time: 4–5 hours
Ideal slow-cooker size: 6-qt.

¼ cup biscuit baking mix
⅔ cup quick or rolled oats
1½ tsp. ground cinnamon
¾ cup brown sugar
4 cups canned peaches, cut in quarters or slices, juice reserved
½ cup peach juice from can

1. Mix together biscuit mix, oats, cinnamon, and brown sugar in a bowl.

2. Place peaches and juice in greased slow cooker.

3. Add oat mix. Stir gently once or twice so as not to break the peaches.

4. Cook on Low 4–5 hours. Remove lid for the last 30 minutes of cooking.

SUMMER

Week 7

THIS WEEK'S
Menu

Sunday: Tex-Mex Luau
Monday: Chicken, Sweet Chicken
Tuesday: Asian Chicken Salad
Wednesday: Slow-Cooked Pork Chops with Green Beans
Thursday: Chicken Broccoli Alfredo
Friday: Pork-Veggie Stew
Saturday: BBQ Pork Sandwiches

Recommended Side Dish: Carrot Raisin Salad
Special Dessert: Peanut Butter Fudge Cake

Shopping List

PROTEIN

1½ lbs. frozen firm-textured
  fish filets

10 boneless skinless
  chicken thighs

10–12 boneless pork chops

2 slices bacon

FROZEN

2 cups frozen green beans,
  or fresh

DAIRY and REFRIGERATED

4 Tbsp. butter

½ cup grated mild cheddar
  cheese

⅔ cup plain yogurt

½ cup milk

PRODUCE

2 medium onions

2 medium sweet potatoes

4 medium potatoes

1 head lettuce

1 cup shredded Brussels
  sprouts

½ cup shredded carrots

1½ cups broccoli, or frozen

8 large carrots

2 lemons

CANNED/DRY GOODS

8-oz. jar orange marmalade

10¾-oz. can cream of
  mushroom soup

1 cup chow mein noodles

8-oz. pkg. noodles or
  spaghetti

hamburger buns

canned sliced jalapeños,
  optional

1 cup raisins

*Download this shopping list to your
smartphone!*
(x.co/ShopList)

DO YOU HAVE THESE ON HAND?

salt

pepper

bay leaf

ginger

garam masala

garlic powder

onion powder

dry mustard

4 whole peppercorns

grapeseed oil

rice wine vinegar

apple cider vinegar

low-sodium soy sauce

unsweetened cocoa powder

baking powder

½ cup flour

brown sugar

½ cup sugar

vanilla extract

honey

Worcestershire sauce

hot sauce

¼ cup peanut butter, smooth or chunky

1¼ cups ketchup

½ cup slivered almonds

1 Tbsp. lemon juice

4 Tbsp. mayonnaise

Tex-Mex Luau

Dorothy M. Van Deest,
Memphis, TN

Makes 6 servings

Prep. Time: 20 minutes
Cooking Time: 2–3 hours
Ideal slow-cooker size: 3- or 4-qt.

1½ lbs. frozen firm-textured
  fish fillets, thawed
2 medium onions, thinly sliced
2 lemons, *divided*
2 Tbsp. butter, melted
2 tsp. salt
1 bay leaf
4 whole peppercorns
1 cup water

1. Cut fillets into serving portions.
2. Combine onion slices and 1 sliced lemon in butter, along with salt, bay leaf, and peppercorns. Pour into slow cooker.
3. Place fillets on top of onion and lemon slices. Add water.
4. Cover. Cook on High 2–3 hours or until fish is flaky.
5. Before serving, carefully remove fish fillets with a slotted spoon. Place on heatproof plate.
6. Sprinkle with juice of half of the second lemon. Garnish with remaining lemon slices.
7. Serve hot or chill and serve cold.

Chicken, Sweet Chicken

Anne Townsend,
Albuquerque, NM

Makes 8–10 servings

Prep. Time: 15 minutes
Cooking Time: 5–6 hours
Ideal slow-cooker size: 3-qt.

2 medium sweet potatoes,
  peeled and cut into ¼-inch
  thick slices
10 boneless, skinless chicken
  thighs
8-oz. jar orange marmalade
¼ cup water
¼–½ tsp. salt
½ tsp. pepper

1. Place sweet potato slices in slow cooker.

2. Rinse and dry chicken pieces. Arrange on top of the potatoes.

3. Spoon marmalade over the chicken and potatoes.

4. Pour water over all. Season with salt and pepper.

5. Cover and cook on High 1 hour, and then turn to Low and cook 4–5 hours, or until potatoes and chicken are both tender.

Asian Chicken Salad

Hope Comerford,
Clinton Township, MI

Makes 4 servings

Prep. Time: 20 minutes

1 head lettuce, shredded
1 cup shredded Brussels sprouts
½ cup shredded carrots
2 cups leftover chicken, chopped or sliced into thin strips

Dressing:
½ cup grapeseed oil
½ cup rice wine vinegar
1 tsp low-sodium soy sauce
2 tsp. honey
1 tsp. ginger
½ tsp. garam masala

Toppings:
½ cup slivered almonds
1 cup chow mein noodles

1. Mix together the lettuce, Brussels sprouts, and carrots and divide between plates or bowls. Top each with a portion of the leftover chicken.

2. Mix together the dressing ingredients. Drizzle over each salad.

3. Top each salad with slivered almonds and chow mein noodles.

Slow-Cooked Pork Chops with Green Beans

Vonnie Oyer, Hubbard, OR

Makes 10–12 servings

Prep. Time: 10 minutes
Cooking Time: 4–8 hours
Ideal slow-cooker size: 3-qt.

10–12 boneless pork chops
salt and pepper, to taste
2 cups green beans, frozen or fresh
2 slices bacon, cut up
½ cup water
1 Tbsp. lemon juice

1. Place pork chops in bottom of slow cooker. Add salt and pepper to taste.

2. Top with remaining ingredients in the order listed.

3. Cover and cook on Low 4–8 hours, or until meat and green beans are tender but not dry or overcooked.

Chicken Broccoli Alfredo

Mahlon Miller, Hutchinson, KS

Makes 4 servings

Prep. Time: 30 minutes
Cooking Time: 1–2 hours
Ideal slow-cooker size: 3-qt.

8-oz. pkg. noodles, or spaghetti (half a 16-oz. pkg.)
1½ cups fresh or frozen broccoli
2 cups leftover chicken, cubed
10¾-oz. can cream of mushroom soup
½ cup grated mild cheddar cheese

1. Cook noodles according to package directions, adding broccoli during the last 4 minutes of the cooking time. Drain.

2. Combine all ingredients in slow cooker.

3. Cover and cook on Low 1–2 hours, or until heated through and until cheese is melted.

Pork-Veggie Stew

Ruth E. Martin, Loysville, PA

Makes 4 servings

Prep. Time: 15 minutes
Cooking Time: 6 hours
Ideal slow-cooker size: 4-qt.

3–4 leftover pork chops, diced
4 medium potatoes, peeled
  and cut into 2-inch pieces
3 large carrots, peeled and
  cut into 2-inch pieces
½ cup ketchup
1¼ cups water, *divided*

1. Lightly spray slow cooker with nonstick cooking spray.
2. Place all ingredients except ketchup and ¼ cup water in slow cooker.
3. Cover and cook on High 5 hours. One hour before serving, combine ketchup with ¼ cup water. Pour over stew. Cook one more hour.

BBQ Pork Sandwiches

Hope Comerford,
Clinton Township, MI

Makes 4–6 servings

Prep. Time: 5 minutes
Cooking Time: 3 hours
Ideal slow-cooker size: 2-qt.

remaining leftover pork,
  chopped
¾ cup ketchup
2 Tbsp. brown sugar
1 Tbsp. Worcestershire sauce
1 Tbsp. apple cider vinegar

1 tsp. garlic powder
1 tsp. onion powder
½ tsp. salt
½ tsp. ginger
¼ tsp. dry mustard
⅛ tsp. pepper
4 dashes of hot sauce
hamburger buns
sliced jalapeños, *optional*

1. Place all ingredients except sliced jalapeños in your slow cooker and stir.
2. Cook on Low for 3 hours.
3. Serve on buns with jalapeño slices on top.

Carrot Raisin Salad (page 173)

Carrot Raisin Salad

Shelia Heil, Lancaster, PA

Makes 6 servings

Prep. Time: 10 minutes
Chilling Time: 4–12 hours

5 large carrots, shredded
1 cup raisins
⅔ cup plain yogurt
4 Tbsp. mayonnaise
2 tsp. honey

1. Combine ingredients in a medium non-metallic bowl.
2. Chill for several hours or overnight. Serve cold.

Peanut Butter Fudge Cake

Beverly Hummel, Fleetwood, PA

Makes 6 servings

Prep. Time: 20 minutes
Cooking Time: 2–3 hours
Ideal slow-cooker size: 3-qt.

¼ cup brown sugar
½ cup flour
2 Tbsp. unsweetened cocoa powder
½ tsp. salt
1 tsp. baking powder
½ cup milk
2 Tbsp. butter, melted
½ tsp. vanilla extract
¼ cup peanut butter, your choice of chunky or smooth

Topping:
2 Tbsp. unsweetened cocoa powder
½ cup sugar
1 cup boiling water

1. To make cake, combine brown sugar, flour, cocoa powder, salt, and baking powder in a good-sized bowl.
2. Add milk, melted butter, vanilla, and peanut butter and stir until smooth.
3. Pour into greased slow cooker.
4. To make topping, mix cocoa powder, sugar, and boiling water together.
5. Pour over mixture in slow cooker. Do not stir.
6. Cover. Cook on High 1½–2 hours, or until toothpick inserted in center of cake comes out clean.
7. Serve warm. If you've refrigerated any leftovers, warm them in the microwave before eating.

SUMMER

Week 8

THIS WEEK'S
Menu

Sunday: Cheeseburger Pie
Monday: Lazy Cabbage Rolls
Tuesday: Chicken with Feta
Wednesday: Open-Face Italian Beef Sandwiches
Thursday: Lemon Rice Soup
Friday: Italian Beef Hoagies
Saturday: Barbecued Lentils

Recommended Side Dish: Greek Pasta Salad
Special Dessert: Gooey Cookie Dessert

Shopping List

PROTEIN

2 lbs. ground turkey

8 boneless, skinless chicken thighs

3-lb. boneless beef chuck roast

1 pkg. vegetarian hot dogs

FROZEN

3½ cups full-fat vanilla ice cream

DAIRY and REFRIGERATED

12 oz. shredded cheddar cheese

7–8 oz. crumbled feta cheese

10 slices provolone cheese

4 deli slices mozzarella cheese

¼ cup plain Greek yogurt

½ cup cream

2 eggs plus 3 egg yolks

16½-oz. roll refrigerator ready-to-bake chocolate chip cookie dough

PRODUCE

2 medium onions

1 large onion

1½ cups sliced onions

¼ cup chopped onion

onion, sliced into rings, *optional*

1-lb. head of cabbage

1 red or green bell pepper

2 Tbsp. chopped fresh parsley

¼ cup diced carrots

¼ cup diced celery

12 basil leaves

1 cup baby arugula

Download this shopping list to your smartphone!

(x.co/ShopList)

1 beefsteak tomato

4 medium plum tomatoes

lettuce, *optional*

tomatoes, sliced, *optional*

CANNED/DRY GOODS

14-oz. can diced tomatoes

16-oz. can tomato sauce

19-oz. can tomato-basil soup

15-oz. can garbanzo beans

6-oz. can pitted black olives

1 cup dry pasta

1 lb. dry lentils

2 cups barbecue sauce

¾ cup long-grain brown rice

⅔ cup uncooked brown rice

10 ½–inch-thick slices Italian
  bread

4 hoagie rolls

pickles, *optional*

DO YOU HAVE THESE ON HAND?

garlic powder

onion powder

salt

pepper

dried oregano

dried basil

cayenne pepper

2 cloves garlic

6 cups chicken broth

cornstarch

brown sugar

Worcestershire sauce

honey

olive oil

½ cup balsamic vinegar

¼ cup mayonnaise

½ cup plus 2 Tbsp. lemon
  juice

Cheeseburger Pie

Hope Comerford,
Clinton Township, MI

Makes 4–6 servings

Prep. Time: 20 minutes
Cooking Time: 4 hours
Ideal slow-cooker size: 3–4 qt.

2 lbs. ground turkey
1 medium onion, chopped
2 tsp. garlic powder
2 tsp. onion powder
12 oz. shredded cheddar
   cheese
¼ cup mayonnaise
¼ cup plain Greek yogurt
½ cup cream
2 eggs

Toppings:
lettuce
pickles
onion, sliced into rings
sliced tomatoes

1. Brown the turkey and onion together in a skillet. Set aside half of the turkey and refrigerate for later this week.
2. Grease interior of slow-cooker crock.
3. Pour the turkey into the bottom of the slow cooker. Top with 6 oz. of the shredded cheese.
4. Mix together the mayonnaise, Greek yogurt, cream, and eggs. Pour this on top of the turkey and cheese.
5. Top with the rest of the cheese.
6. Cover. Cook on Low for 4 hours.

7. Serve on top of a piece of lettuce and top with pickles, onions, and tomato slices, if desired.

Lazy Cabbage Rolls

Janie Steele, Moore, OK

Makes 6 servings

Prep. Time: 36 minutes
Cooking Time: 2–5½ hours
Ideal slow-cooker size: 5- or 6-qt.

leftover browned turkey
salt and pepper, to taste
1 large onion, chopped
1 clove garlic, minced
1-lb. cabbage head, chopped
   into 1-inch squares
⅔ cup uncooked brown rice
2 14½-oz. cans diced
   tomatoes, undrained
16-oz. can tomato sauce

1. Grease interior of slow-cooker crock.
2. Crumble turkey over bottom of cooker. Season with salt and pepper. (Season each layer with salt and pepper, except tomatoes and tomato sauce.)
3. Add a layer of onion. Follow that with garlic, and then cabbage.
4. Spread uncooked rice over cabbage.
5. Pour tomatoes and sauce on top. Cook on High 2–3 hours or on Low 4–5½ hours, or until cabbage and rice are tender.

6. Let stand 15 minutes before serving to let the dish firm up.

Chicken with Feta

Susan Tjon, Austin, TX

Makes 8 servings

Prep. Time: 15 minutes
Cooking Time: 4 hours
Ideal slow-cooker size: 4- or 5-qt.

8 boneless, skinless chicken thighs
2 Tbsp. lemon juice, *divided*
3–4 oz. feta cheese, crumbled
1 red or green bell pepper, chopped

1. Grease interior of slow-cooker crock.
2. Place thighs on bottom of crock. If you need to create a second layer, stagger the thighs so they don't completely overlap each other.
3. Sprinkle with 1 Tbsp. lemon juice.
4. Crumble feta cheese evenly over thighs. (If you've made 2 layers, lift up the top layer and sprinkle cheese over those underneath.)
5. Top with remaining lemon juice.
6. Cover. Cook on Low for 4 hours, or until instant-read meat thermometer registers 160°-165°F when inserted in thighs.
7. Sprinkle chicken with chopped bell pepper just before serving.

Open-Face Italian Beef Sandwiches

Edith Romano,
Westminster, MD

Makes 10 servings

Prep. Time: 20–30 minutes
Cooking Time: 6–8 hours
Ideal slow-cooker size: 5- or 6-qt.

3-lb. boneless beef chuck roast, partially frozen
1½ cups sliced onions
19-oz. can tomato-basil soup
2 Tbsp. cornstarch
2 Tbsp. brown sugar
¼ tsp. dried oregano
¼ tsp. dried basil
⅛ tsp. cayenne pepper
2 Tbsp. Worcestershire sauce
10½-inch-thick slices Italian bread
10 slices provolone cheese
2 Tbsp. chopped fresh parsley

1. Grease interior of slow-cooker crock.
2. Cut beef diagonally across grain into thin slices. Place beef in crock, along with onions.
3. In medium bowl, combine soup, cornstarch, brown sugar, oregano, basil, cayenne pepper, and Worcestershire sauce. Mix until smooth.
4. Pour sauce over beef and onions. Stir well so all pieces of meat are covered with sauce.
5. Cover. Cook on Low 6–8 hours, or until beef is tender.

6. For each serving, place 1 slice of bread on plate. Top with 1 slice of cheese. Spoon about ¾ cup beef mixture over cheese. Sprinkle with parsley and serve immediately.

Lemon Rice Soup

Hope Comerford,
Clinton Township, MI

Makes 4 servings

Prep. Time: 5 minutes
Cooking Time: 3 hours, 10 minutes
Ideal slow-cooker size: 3-qt.

6 cups chicken broth
¾ cup long-grain brown rice
¼ cup diced carrots
¼ cup diced celery
¼ cup chopped onion
1 cup leftover chicken, chopped
1 tsp. salt
½ tsp. pepper
3 egg yolks, beaten
¼ cup lemon juice

1. Place the broth, rice, carrots, celery, onion, leftover chicken, salt, and pepper into your slow cooker. Cook on Low for 3 hours.
2. Remove 1 cup of the broth. Slowly whisk in the egg yolks and lemon juice. Return this slowly to the crock, whisking the whole time.
3. Continue to cook on Low for 10 more minutes.

Italian Beef Hoagies

Hope Comerford,
Clinton Township, MI

Makes 4 hoagies

Prep. Time: 10 minutes
Cooking Time: 15 minutes

4 hoagie rolls
leftover beef, warmed
4 deli slices mozzarella
   cheese
12 basil leaves
1 cup baby arugula
1 beefsteak tomato, sliced
½ cup balsamic vinegar
2 tsp. honey

1. Preheat the oven to 400°F.
2. On a foil-lined baking sheet, place each hoagie roll, open-faced.
3. On one side, place beef and on the other side, a slice of mozzarella cheese.
4. Cook for about 10 minutes or until cheese is melted.
5. Meanwhile bring the balsamic vinegar and honey to a boil on the stove. Reduce to a simmer and continue to let it simmer until it becomes thick and reduces to about a ¼ cup.
6. When you take your hoagies out of the oven, top each with 3 basil leaves, a bit of arugula, a few slices of tomato, and drizzle the balsamic reduction over the top.

Barbecued Lentils

Sue Hamilton, Minooka, IL

Makes 8 servings

Prep. Time: 5 minutes
Cooking Time: 6–8 hours
Ideal slow-cooker size: 4-qt.

2 cups barbecue sauce
3½ cups water
1 lb. dry lentils
1 pkg. vegetarian hot dogs,
   sliced

1. Combine all ingredients in slow cooker.
2. Cover. Cook on Low 6–8 hours.

Greek Pasta Salad

Edie Moran, West Babylon, NY
Judi Manos, West Islip, NY

Makes 8 servings

Prep. Time: 15 minutes
Cooking Time for pasta: 15 minutes

2 cups cooked pasta, rinsed
    and cooled (1 cup dry)
4 medium plum tomatoes,
    chopped
15-oz. can garbanzo beans,
    rinsed and drained
1 medium onion, chopped
6-oz. can pitted black olives,
    drained
4-oz. pkg. feta cheese,
    crumbled
1 garlic clove, minced
½ cup olive oil
¼ cup lemon juice
1 tsp. salt
½ tsp. pepper

1. In a large bowl, combine
pasta, tomatoes, garbanzo
beans, onion, olives, feta
cheese, and garlic.
2. In a small bowl, whisk
together oil, lemon juice, salt,
and pepper. Pour over salad
and toss to coat.
3. Cover and chill in
refrigerator. Stir before
serving.

Tips: 1. I like to serve this
salad in a clear glass salad
bowl. 2. Add some baby
spinach leaves. Combine
vegetables with hot pasta
right after draining it.

Gooey Cookie Dessert

Sue Hamilton, Benson, AZ

Makes 8 servings

Prep. Time: 10 minutes
Cooking Time: 2 hours
Ideal slow-cooker size: 5-qt.

3½ cups full-fat vanilla ice
    cream (half of 1¾-qt.
    container)
16½-oz. roll refrigerator
    ready-to-bake chocolate
    chip cookie dough

1. Turn empty slow cooker
to High to preheat.
2. Place ice cream in warmed
crock, spreading and pushing
it to make it a layer. Lumps are
fine—they will melt.
3. Slice cookie dough into
12 slices.
4. Press the slices into the
ice cream.
5. Cover and cook on High
for 2 hours, until edges are
browning and the center is
cooked.

SUMMER

Week 9

THIS WEEK'S
Menu

Sunday: Tasty Drumsticks
Monday: Chickenetti
Tuesday: Just Peachy Ribs
Wednesday: Texas Cottage Pie
Thursday: Macaroni and Cheese
Friday: Beer Brats
Saturday: Sausage Beef Spaghetti Sauce

Recommended Side Dish: Sour Cream Potatoes
Special Dessert: Peaches and Cream Dessert

Shopping List

PROTEIN

5–6 lbs. chicken drumsticks

6 lbs. boneless pork spareribs

4 hot dogs, *optional*

10 fresh bratwurst

FROZEN

1 cup frozen corn

DAIRY and REFRIGERATED

¼ lb. white, or yellow, American cheese

1 cup shredded pepper jack cheese

3 cups shredded cheese: cheddar, or American, or Velveeta, or a combination

2 8-oz. pkg. cream cheese

2¾ cups milk

7–9 Tbsp. butter

8 oz. sour cream

1 egg

PRODUCE

⅛ cup chopped green bell pepper

¼ cup diced celery

1 small onion

2 Tbsp. finely chopped onion

10 medium red potatoes

CANNED/DRY GOODS

8-oz. can tomato sauce

10¾-oz. can cream of mushroom soup, or cream of celery soup

15-oz. can spiced cling peaches

15-oz. can black beans

14½-oz. can diced tomatoes with green chilies

Download this shopping list to your smartphone!

(x.co/ShopList)

Just Peachy Ribs

Amymarlene Jensen, Fountain, CO

Makes 6–8 servings

Prep. Time: 10 minutes
Cooking Time: 8–10 hours
Ideal slow-cooker size: 4-qt.

6 lbs. boneless pork spareribs
½ cup brown sugar
¼ cup ketchup
¼ cup white vinegar
1 garlic clove, minced
1 tsp. salt
1 tsp. pepper
2 Tbsp. soy sauce
15-oz. can spiced cling
  peaches, cubed, with juice

1. Cut ribs in serving-size pieces and brown in broiler or in saucepan in oil. Drain. Place in slow cooker.
2. Combine remaining ingredients. Pour over ribs.
3. Cover. Cook on Low 8–10 hours.

Texas Cottage Pie

Kathy Hertzler, Lancaster, PA

Makes 6 servings

Prep. Time: 25–30 minutes
Baking Time: 30–35 minutes

1 Tbsp. oil
leftover pork, chopped
½ tsp. salt
½ tsp. cumin
½ tsp. paprika
1 tsp. chili powder
¼ tsp black pepper
¼ tsp. cinnamon
1 tsp. chopped garlic
15-oz. can black beans,
  drained and rinsed
1 cup frozen corn
14½-oz. can diced tomatoes
  with green chilies
3 cups mashed potatoes
½ cup milk
1 cup shredded pepper jack
  cheese, *divided*

1. In a skillet, add the leftover pork, salt, seasonings, and garlic until warmed.
2. Cook 2 minutes more on medium heat.
3. Add black beans, corn, and tomatoes with chilies. Stir well.
4. Cover. Cook on low heat 15 minutes.
6. Meanwhile, warm mashed potatoes mixed with ½ cup milk in microwaveable bowl in microwave (2 minutes, covered, on Power 8), or in saucepan on stove top (covered and over very low heat for 5–10 minutes, stirring frequently to prevent sticking).
7. Stir ½ cup cheese into warmed mashed potatoes.
8. Transfer meat mixture to greased 7×10-inch baking dish.
9. Top with mashed potatoes, spreading in an even layer to edges of baking dish.
10. Sprinkle with the remaining ½ cup cheese.
11. Bake at 350°F for 30–35 minutes.

Macaroni and Cheese

Martha Hershey, Ronks, PA
Marcia S. Myer, Manheim, PA
LeAnne Nolt, Leola, PA
Ellen Ranck, Gap, PA
Mary Sommerfeld, Lancaster, PA
Kathryn Yoder, Minot, ND
Janie Steele, Moore, OK

Makes 6 servings

Prep. Time: 30 minutes
Cooking Time: 3–4 hours
Ideal slow-cooker size: 4-qt.

8-oz. pkg. dry macaroni, cooked
2 Tbsp. oil of your choice
13-oz. can evaporated milk
  (fat-free will work)
1½ cups milk
1 tsp. salt
3 cups (about ½ lb.) shredded
  cheese: cheddar, or
  American, or Velveeta, or a
  combination
2–4 Tbsp. butter, melted
2 Tbsp. finely chopped onion
4 hot dogs, sliced, *optional*

1. In slow cooker, toss cooked macaroni in oil. Stir in remaining ingredients except hot dogs.
2. Cover. Cook on Low 2–3 hours.
3. Add hot dogs if you wish. Cover. Cook 1 hour longer on Low (whether you've added hot dogs or not).

Serving Suggestion: If you wish, mix ½ cup bread crumbs and 2 Tbsp. melted butter together. Sprinkle over dish just before serving. Or top instead with crushed potato chips.

Beer Brats

Mary Ann Wasick, West Allis, WI

Makes 8–10 servings

Prep. Time: 10 minutes
Cooking Time: 6–7 hours
Ideal slow-cooker size: 4-qt.

10 fresh bratwurst
2 cloves garlic, minced
2 Tbsp. olive oil
12-oz. can beer

1. Brown sausages and garlic in olive oil in skillet. Pierce sausage casings and cook 5 more minutes. Transfer to slow cooker.
2. Pour beer into cooker to cover sausages.
3. Cover. Cook on Low 6–7 hours.

Sausage Beef Spaghetti Sauce

Jeannine Janzen, Elbing, KS

Makes 8–10 servings

Prep. Time: 15 minutes
Cooking Time: 6 hours
Ideal slow-cooker size: 5-qt.

leftover brats, chopped
28-oz. can crushed tomatoes
14 oz. water
1 tsp. garlic powder
½ tsp. pepper
1 Tbsp. or more parsley flakes
1 Tbsp. dried oregano
12-oz. can tomato paste
12-oz. can tomato puree
spaghetti

1. Place all ingredients but the spaghetti in the slow cooker.
2. Cover. Cook on Low for 6 hours.
3. Serve over cooked spaghetti.

Sour Cream Potatoes

Renee Baum, Chambersburg, PA

Makes 6–8 servings

Prep. Time: 30 minutes
Cooking/Baking Time: 60 minutes

10 medium red potatoes
8-oz. pkg. cream cheese
8 oz. sour cream
¼ cup milk
2 Tbsp. butter, *divided*
1 Tbsp. dried parsley flakes, or 2 Tbsp. chopped fresh parsley
1¼ tsp. garlic salt
¼ tsp. paprika

1. Peel and quarter potatoes. Place in a large saucepan and cover with water. Bring to a boil.
2. Reduce heat and cover and cook 15–20 minutes or until tender. Drain.
3. Mash the potatoes.
4. Add cream cheese, sour cream, milk, 1 Tbsp. butter,

parsley, and garlic salt; beat until smooth.

5. Spoon into a greased 2-qt. baking dish.

6. Dot with remaining butter. Sprinkle with paprika.

7. Bake, uncovered, at 350°F for 30–40 minutes or until heated through.

Peaches and Cream Dessert

Phyllis Good, Lancaster, PA

Makes 6 servings

Prep. Time: 10–15 minutes
Cooking Time: 2–3 hours
Standing Time: 30 minutes
Ideal slow-cooker size: 4- or 5-qt.

¾ cup all-purpose flour
1 egg
½ tsp. baking powder
½ tsp. salt
3-oz. box instant vanilla pudding
½ cup milk
3 Tbsp. butter, softened
1 qt. sliced peaches, drained, 3 Tbsp. juice reserved
8-oz. pkg. cream cheese, softened
2 Tbsp. sugar
½ tsp. cinnamon

1. Put flour, egg, baking powder, salt, dry pudding, milk, and butter in a mixing bowl. Beat well with electric mixer.

2. Pour batter into greased slow cooker.

3. Lay peach halves or slices on top.

4. Mix together cream cheese and 3 Tbsp. peach juice. Pour over peaches.

5. Mix sugar and cinnamon together. Sprinkle over cream cheese mixture.

6. Cover and cook on High for 2–3 hours, or until toothpick inserted in center comes out clean.

7. Allow to stand for 30 minutes with the lid off before serving.

Beer Brats (page 188)

Week 10

THIS WEEK'S Menu

Sunday: Big Juicy Burgers
Monday: Hope's Simple Italian Meat Loaf
Tuesday: Mile-High Shredded Beef Sandwiches
Wednesday: Twenty-Clove Chicken
Thursday: Green Chile Shredded Beef Stew
Friday: Hot Chicken Salad
Saturday: Chicken Tortilla Casserole

Recommended Side Dish: Mozzarella/Tomato/Basil Salad
Special Dessert: Gooey Chocolate Pudding Cake

Shopping List

PROTEIN

4 lbs. ground beef

3-lb. chuck roast, or round
steak

10 boneless, skinless
chicken breast halves

DAIRY and REFRIGERATED

3 eggs

1 cup sour cream

2 cups shredded cheese,
your choice of flavor

½ cup grated low-fat
cheddar cheese

1 pint buffalo mozzarella
cheese balls, or ¼–½ lb.
buffalo mozzarella cheese,
sliced

½ cup milk

PRODUCE

2 medium onions

1 small onion

2½ cups chopped onions

4 ribs celery

¼ cup chopped celery

½ cup sliced celery

2 carrots

1 jalapeño pepper

2 large tomatoes

½ cup basil leaves

2 lemons

fresh herbs, *optional*

CANNED/DRY GOODS

8-oz. can mild green chilies

4-oz. can chopped mild
green chilies

10¾-oz. can cream of
chicken soup

Download this shopping list to your
smartphone!
(x.co/ShopList)

10¾-oz. can cream of
  mushroom soup
10¾-oz. can 98% fat-free
  cream of mushroom soup
1 can water chestnuts
½ cup black olives
2 cups tomato juice
1 cup Italian bread crumbs
1 cup fettuccine
potato chips
5 6-inch flour tortillas
8 sandwich rolls
hamburger buns

DO YOU HAVE THESE ON HAND?
salt
pepper
Italian seasoning
dry mustard
chili powder
bay leaves
paprika
garlic powder
dried parsley
dried basil

dried oregano
crushed red pepper flakes
21 cloves garlic
minced garlic
2 cups reduced-sodium,
  98% fat-free beef broth
5 cups beef stock
6 oz. chicken broth
canola oil
olive oil
red wine vinegar
vinegar of your choice
Worcestershire sauce
ketchup
Tabasco sauce
3 Tbsp. brown sugar
1 cup sugar
1 cup dry all-purpose baking
  mix
unsweetened cocoa powder
vanilla extract
1 cup mayonnaise

SPIRITS
½ cup dry white wine
1 cup red wine

Big Juicy Burgers

Phyllis Good, Lancaster, PA

Makes 8 servings

Prep. Time: 15 minutes
Cooking Time: 7–9 hours
Ideal slow-cooker size: 4- or 5-qt.

1 cup chopped onions
¼ cup chopped celery
4 lbs. ground beef
1½ tsp. salt, *divided*
1 tsp. pepper
2 cups tomato juice
2 tsp. minced garlic
1 Tbsp. ketchup
1 tsp. Italian seasoning
hamburger buns

1. Place the chopped onions and celery in your slow cooker.
2. Place the beef, 1 tsp. salt, and pepper into a large mixing bowl. Use your hands to mix the salt and pepper into the beef. Divide the mixture in half. Wrap up half tightly and place in the refrigerator to use later this week. Divide the remaining dough into eight balls, each the same size.
3. Flatten the eight balls of beef so they look like hamburger patties. Place the patties in the slow cooker on top of the onions and celery. Try not to stack them. If you have to, stagger them so they don't lie exactly on top of each other. Wash your hands well.
4. In a medium-sized mixing bowl stir together the tomato juice, minced garlic, ketchup, Italian seasoning and ½ tsp. salt. Pour this sauce over the patties in your slow cooker.
5. Cover your slow cooker. Cook the burgers on Low for 7–9 hours.
6. Serve each Big Juicy Burger on a hamburger bun.

Hope's Simple Italian Meat Loaf

Hope Comerford,
Clinton Township, MI

Makes 6–8 servings

Prep. Time: 5 minutes
Cooking Time: 7–9 hours
Ideal slow-cooker size: 4-qt.

½ cup chopped onion
2 eggs, beaten

1 cup Italian bread crumbs
leftover ground beef mixture
3 Tbsp. ketchup
1 Tbsp. brown sugar

1. Grease your slow cooker and make a foil basket out of foil strips.

2. Add the onion, eggs, and bread crumbs to the turkey mixture. Form the turkey mixture into a loaf and place into the slow cooker.

3. Cook on Low for 7–9 hours.

4. Mix together the ketchup and brown sugar. Spread it on top of the loaf the last 30 minutes of cooking.

Mile-High Shredded Beef Sandwiches

Miriam Christophel,
Battle Creek, MI
Mary Seielstad, Sparks, NV

Makes 8 servings

Prep. Time: 35 minutes
Cooking Time: 7–9 hours
Ideal slow-cooker size: 4-qt.

3-lb. chuck roast, or round steak, trimmed of fat
2 Tbsp. oil of your choice
1 cup chopped onions
½ cup sliced celery
2 cups reduced-sodium, 98% fat-free beef broth
1 garlic clove
¾ cup ketchup

2 Tbsp. brown sugar
2 Tbsp. vinegar
1 tsp. dry mustard
½ tsp. chili powder
3 drops Tabasco sauce
1 bay leaf
¼ tsp. paprika
¼ tsp. garlic powder
1 tsp. Worcestershire sauce
8 sandwich rolls

1. In a skillet brown both sides of meat in oil. Add onions and celery and sauté briefly. Transfer to slow cooker. Add broth.

2. Cover. Cook on Low 6–8 hours, or until tender. Remove meat from cooker and cool. Shred beef.

3. Remove vegetables from cooker and drain, reserving 1½ cups broth. Combine vegetables and meat.

4. Return shredded meat and vegetables to cooker. Add broth and remaining ingredients and combine well.

5. Cover. Cook on High 1 hour. Remove bay leaf.

6. Pile into sandwich rolls and serve.

Twenty-Clove Chicken

Nancy Savage, Factoryville, PA

Makes 8–10 servings

Prep. Time: 20 minutes
Cooking Time: 5–6 hours
Ideal slow-cooker size: 5- to 6-qt.

½ cup dry white wine
4 Tbsp. dried parsley

4 tsp. dried basil
2 tsp. dried oregano
pinch of crushed red pepper flakes
20 cloves of garlic (about 2 bulbs)
4 ribs celery, chopped
10 boneless, skinless chicken breast halves
2 lemons, juice and zest
fresh herbs, *optional*

1. Combine wine, dried parsley, dried basil, dried oregano, and dried red pepper flakes in large bowl.

2. Add garlic cloves and celery. Mix well.

3. Transfer garlic and celery to slow cooker with slotted spoon.

4. Add chicken to herb mixture one piece at a time. Coat well. Place chicken on top of vegetables in slow cooker.

5. Sprinkle lemon juice and zest over chicken. Add any remaining herb mixture.

6. Cover. Cook on Low 5–6 hours or until chicken is no longer pink in center.

7. Garnish with fresh herbs if desired.

Green Chile Shredded Beef Stew

Hope Comerford, Clinton Township, MI

Makes 4–6 servings

Prep. Time: 10 minutes
Cooking Time: 6–7 hours
Ideal slow-cooker size: 4- to 5-qt.

5 cups beef stock
1 cup red wine
1 bay leaf
1 medium onion, chopped
2 carrots, chopped
1 rib celery, chopped
8-oz. can mild green chilies
1 jalapeño, seeded and diced
leftover beef

1. Add all ingredients to the slow cooker.
2. Cook on Low for 6–7 hours.

Hot Chicken Salad

Janie Steele, Moore, OK

Makes 6–8 servings

Prep. Time: 15–30 minutes
Cooking Time: 1½ hours
Ideal slow-cooker size: 4-qt.

10¾-oz. can cream of chicken soup
10¾-oz. can cream of mushroom soup
1 cup mayonnaise
1 small onion, chopped
½ tsp. salt
¼–½ tsp. pepper
4 cups leftover chicken, cubed
1 can water chestnuts, drained and chopped
1 cup sour cream
1 cup cooked and drained fettuccine pasta
2 cups shredded cheese, your choice of flavor
potato chips, crushed

1. Combine soups, mayonnaise, chopped onion, salt, and pepper in slow cooker. Mix until smooth.
2. Stir in leftover cubed chicken and water chestnuts.
3. Fold in sour cream and fettuccine.
4. Cover. Cook on High until bubbly, about 1½ hours.
5. Ten minutes before end of cooking time and before serving, sprinkle with shredded cheese and crushed potato chips. Continue cooking, uncovered.

Chicken Tortilla Casserole

Jeanne Allen, Rye, CO

Makes 4–5 servings

Prep. Time: 30 minutes
Cooking Time: 3–6 hours
Ideal slow-cooker size: 5- or 6-qt.

6 oz. chicken broth
5 6-inch flour tortillas, cut in strips about ½x2 inches, *divided*
remaining leftover chicken
1 medium onion, chopped
½ tsp. canola oil

10¾-oz. can 98% fat-free cream of mushroom soup

4-oz. can mild green chilies, chopped

1 egg

½ cup grated low-fat cheddar cheese

1. Pour reserved chicken broth in slow cooker sprayed with nonfat cooking spray.

2. Scatter half the tortilla strips in bottom of slow cooker.

3. Mix remaining ingredients together, except the second half of the tortilla strips and the cheese.

4. Layer half the chicken mixture into the cooker, followed by the other half of the tortillas, followed by the rest of the chicken mix.

5. Cover. Cook on Low 4–6 hours or on High 3–5 hours.

6. Add cheese to top of dish during last 20–30 minutes of cooking.

7. Uncover and allow casserole to rest 15 minutes before serving.

Mozzarella/ Tomato/Basil Salad

Phyllis Good, Lancaster, PA

Makes 6 servings

Prep. Time: 8 minutes

1 pint buffalo mozzarella cheese balls, or ¼–½ lb. buffalo mozzarella cheese, sliced

2 large tomatoes, sliced and quartered

½ cup black olives, sliced

½ cup basil leaves, torn

1 Tbsp. olive oil

1 Tbsp. red wine vinegar

¼ tsp. salt

⅛ tsp. pepper

1. If the mozzarella balls are in liquid, rinse and drain them. Place in a mixing bowl.

2. Add tomatoes, black olives, and basil leaves. Mix together gently.

3. Mix olive oil, vinegar, salt, and pepper together. Pour over salad ingredients and mix gently.

Gooey Chocolate Pudding Cake

Phyllis Good, Lancaster, PA

Makes 8 servings

Prep. Time: 15 minutes
Cooking Time: 2–3 hours
Ideal slow-cooker size: 3½-qt.

1 cup dry all-purpose baking mix

1 cup sugar, *divided*

3 Tbsp. unsweetened cocoa powder, plus ⅓ cup, *divided*

½ cup milk

1 tsp. vanilla extract

1⅔ cups hot water

1. Spray the inside of your slow cooker with cooking spray.

2. In a medium-sized mixing bowl, mix together the baking mix, ½ cup sugar, 3 Tbsp. cocoa powder, milk, and vanilla. Spoon the batter into your slow cooker and spread it out evenly.

3. In a small mixing bowl, mix the remaining ½ cup sugar, ⅓ cup cocoa powder, and the hot water together. Carefully pour this mixture over the batter. Do not stir.

4. Cover your slow cooker. Cook the cake on High for 2–3 hours.

5. After 2 hours, use a potholder to remove the lid. Carefully stick a toothpick into the center of the cake and pull it out. If the toothpick looks wet, the cake needs to keep cooking. If it has some dry crumbs on it, it's time to eat.

6. If the cake needs to cook longer, continue to test it with a toothpick every 15 minutes until it's done.

SUMMER

Week 11

THIS WEEK'S
Menu

Sunday: Chicken in Piquant Sauce
Monday: Three-Cheese Chicken Bake
Tuesday: Sharon's Chicken and Rice Casserole
Wednesday: Tomato Spaghetti Sauce
Thursday: Easy Sausage Sandwiches
Friday: Triple-Decker Tortilla
Saturday: Slow-Cooker Pizza

Recommended Side Dish: Picnic Pea Salad
Special Dessert: Tapioca Treat

Shopping List

PROTEIN
6 boneless, skinless chicken
  breast halves
4 sub-roll length sausages
1½ lbs. ground beef
8 oz. thinly sliced pepperoni
¼–½ cup fried and
  crumbled, bacon

FROZEN
10-oz. bag frozen peas
1 cup frozen whipped topping,
  or fresh whipped cream

DAIRY and REFRIGERATED
12 oz. creamed cottage
  cheese
2 cups shredded cheddar
  cheese
½ cup grated Parmesan
  cheese

3–4 cups shredded
  mozzarella cheese
½ cup shredded Monterey
  Jack or cheddar cheese
3 Tbsp. butter
8⅓ cups milk
½ cup sour cream
4 eggs
1 cup whipped cream, or
  frozen whipped topping

PRODUCE
2½ cups chopped onion
¼ cup chopped onion or
  green onions
½ cup chopped green bell
  pepper
¼ lb. fresh mushrooms, or
  4 oz. canned
4 lbs. fresh tomatoes, or
  28 oz. canned

Download this shopping list to your
smartphone!
(x.co/ShopList)

1 cup cherry tomatoes for garnish, *optional*	2 cups cooked pinto beans
½ cup chopped celery	1 cup salsa
avocado, *optional*	4 small flour tortillas
cilantro, *optional*	12-oz. bag kluski, or other sturdy noodles
1 cup grapes	1 cup Spanish peanuts
	1 cup small pearl tapioca

CANNED/DRY GOODS

16-oz. jar Russian or creamy French salad dressing	**DO YOU HAVE THESE ON HAND?**
12-oz. jar apricot preserves	dried basil
1 cup canned crushed pineapple	dried oregano
10¾-oz. can cream of chicken soup	salt
	pepper
10¾-oz. can cream of celery soup	dried dill weed
	2 bay leaves
8-oz. can sliced mushrooms	4 cloves garlic
2-oz. can sliced mushrooms	4 tsp. instant beef bouillon granules
12-oz. can tomato paste	1 Tbsp. dry onion soup mix
½ cup canned corn, or frozen	¼ cup chopped pimentos
	cornstarch
1 envelope dry onion soup mix	1½ cups sugar plus 2 Tbsp. sugar
½ lb. lasagna noodles	vanilla extract
½ cup raw long-grain rice	2 Tbsp. mayonnaise
4 sub rolls	

Chicken in Piquant Sauce

Beth Shank, Wellman, IA
Karen Waggoner, Joplin, MO
Carol Armstrong, Winston, OR
Lois Niebauer, Pedricktown, NJ
Jean Butzer, Batavia, NY
Veronica Sabo, Shelton, CT
Charlotte Shaffer, East Earl, PA

Makes 4–6 servings

Prep. Time: 10–15 minutes
Cooking Time: 3–4 hours
Ideal slow-cooker size: 3- to 4-qt.

16-oz. jar Russian or creamy
   French, salad dressing
12-oz. jar apricot preserves
1 envelope dry onion soup mix
6 boneless, skinless chicken
   breast halves

1. In a bowl, mix together
the dressing, preserves, and
dry onion soup mix.
2. Place the chicken breasts
in your slow cooker.
3. Pour the sauce over top
of the chicken.
4. Cover and cook on High
3 hours, or on Low 4 hours,
or until chicken is tender but
not dry.

Three-Cheese Chicken Bake

Dorothy M. Van Deest,
Memphis, TN

Makes 8–10 servings

Prep. Time: 25 minutes
Baking Time: 45 minutes

½ lb. lasagna noodles, *divided*
Mushroom Sauce:
½ cup chopped onion
½ cup chopped green bell
   pepper
3 Tbsp. butter
10¾-oz. can cream of chicken
   soup
⅓ cup milk
¼ lb. fresh mushrooms,
   sliced, or 4-oz. can
   mushroom pieces, drained
¼ cup chopped pimentos
½ tsp. dried basil
12 oz. (1½ cups) creamed
   cottage cheese, *divided*
3 cups leftover diced chicken,
   divided
2 cups shredded cheddar
   cheese, *divided*
½ cup grated Parmesan
   cheese, *divided*

1. Cook noodles until just
tender in large amount of
boiling water. Drain and rinse
in cold water.
2. Prepare mushroom sauce
by cooking onion and green
pepper in butter in medium-
sized saucepan.
3. Stir soup, milk,
mushrooms, pimentos, and
basil into sautéed vegetables.
4. Grease 9×13-inch baking
dish.
5. Place half of noodles
over bottom of baking dish.
6. Cover with half the
mushroom sauce.
7. Top with half the cottage
cheese.
8. Top with half the chicken.
9. Top with half the
cheddar and Parmesan
cheeses.
10. Repeat layers, using all
remaining ingredients.
11. Bake at 350°F for 45
minutes.

3. Meanwhile, grease interior of slow cooker.

4. Pour in ¼ of spaghetti sauce. Follow with half the noodles, and then half the browned ground beef. Top with ⅓ of the shredded cheese. Follow with half the pepperoni.

5. Repeat the layers, beginning with ⅓ of the sauce, followed by the rest of the noodles, the remaining ground beef, half the cheese, and the rest of the pepperoni.

6. Top with the remaining spaghetti sauce. Finish with the rest of the cheese.

7. Cover and cook on Low for 2–3 hours, or until heated through and until the cheese has melted.

Picnic Pea Salad

Mary Kathryn Yoder,
Harrisonville, MO

Makes 4–6 servings

Prep. Time: 30 minutes
Chilling Time: 1 hour

10-oz. pkg. frozen peas, thawed
¼ cup chopped onion or green onions
½ cup chopped celery
½ cup sour cream
2 Tbsp. mayonnaise
1 tsp. salt
1 tsp. dill weed
¼ tsp. pepper
1 cup Spanish peanuts
¼–½ cup fried and crumbled bacon
1 cup cherry tomatoes for garnish, *optional*

1. Mix peas, onion, celery, sour cream, mayonnaise, salt, dill weed, and pepper. Chill.

2. Just before serving, stir in peanuts. Garnish with bacon and tomatoes.

Tapioca Treat

Phyllis Good, Lancaster, PA

Makes 10–12 servings

Prep. Time: 15 minutes
Cooking Time: 3 hours and 20 minutes
Chilling Time: 3 hours or so
Ideal slow-cooker size: 4- or 5-qt.

8 cups (2 qts.) milk
1 cup small pearl tapioca
1–1½ cups sugar
4 eggs
1 tsp. vanilla extract
1 cup grapes
1 cup canned crushed pineapple
1 cup frozen whipped topping, thawed, or whipped cream from a can

1. Mix the milk, tapioca, and sugar in your slow cooker with a whisk.

2. Cover your slow cooker. Cook the tapioca on High for 3 hours.

3. Crack the eggs into a mixing bowl. Beat them well with a whisk. Add the vanilla to the eggs.

4. Scoop out a little of the hot milk from the slow cooker. Carefully add the hot milk to the egg mixture. Stir the hot milk into the eggs.

5. Add the egg mixture to the slow cooker. Use a rubber spatula to scrape the bowl.

6. Cover your slow cooker. Cook the tapioca on High for 20 more minutes.

7. Chill the tapioca completely. This may take 3 hours or so.

8. While it's chilling, use a kitchen shears to cut the grapes in half.

9. Use a can opener to open the crushed pineapple. Drain off the juice.

10. After the tapioca has chilled completely, stir in the grapes, pineapple, and whipped topping or cream. Serve cold.

SUMMER

Week 12

THIS WEEK'S
Menu

Sunday: Sloppy Joes
Monday: Carne Asada
Tuesday: Sloppy Joe and Macaroni Casserole
Wednesday: Carne Asada Soup
Thursday: BBQ Balls
Friday: Slow-Cooker Ratatouille
Saturday: Hash Brown Dinner

Recommended Side Dish: Fresh Corn and Tomato Salad
Special Dessert: Perfectly Peachy Cake

Shopping List

PROTEIN

2 lbs. ground beef

4–5 lb. flank steak

2 lbs. 99% fat-free ground
   turkey

FROZEN

½ cup frozen corn

3 cups frozen hash brown
   potatoes

1-lb. pkg. frozen California
   blend vegetables

vanilla ice cream, or
   whipped cream

DAIRY and REFRIGERATED

crumbled queso fresco

2 cups shredded cheddar
   cheese

¾ lb. cubed cheese of your
   choice

½ lb. fresh mozzarella

6 eggs

1 cup milk

2 Tbsp. butter

PRODUCE

2 large onions

3 medium onions

½ cup chopped onion

4–6 green onions (scallions)

½ cup chopped green bell
   pepper

1 green bell pepper

1 red bell pepper

2 avocados

chopped fresh cilantro

1¾ cups fresh basil

¼ cup fresh parsley

1 medium eggplant

2 cups mushrooms

4 tomatoes

Download this shopping list to your
smartphone!
(x.co/ShopList)

Perfectly Peachy Cake

Ruthie Schiefer, Vassar, MI

Makes 4–6 servings

Prep. Time: 20 minutes
Cooking Time: 6–8 hours
Ideal slow-cooker size: 3-qt.

¾ cup biscuit baking mix
¼ cup brown sugar, packed
⅓ cup sugar
2 eggs, beaten
2 tsp. vanilla extract
¼ cup evaporated milk
2 Tbsp. butter, melted
3 peaches, peeled, pitted, and mashed
¾ tsp. ground cinnamon
vanilla ice cream or whipped cream, for serving

1. In large bowl, combine baking mix and sugars.
2. Stir in eggs and vanilla until blended. Mix in milk and butter.
3. Fold in peaches and cinnamon until well mixed.
4. Spoon mixture into lightly greased slow cooker. Lay a double layer of paper towels across the top of the cooker (to absorb condensation).
5. Cover and cook on Low 6–8 hours.
6. Serve warm with a scoop of ice cream or a dollop of whipped cream.

Fresh Corn and Tomato Salad (page 212)

Week 13

THIS WEEK'S

Menu

Sunday: Teriyaki Salmon
Monday: Salmon Cheese Casserole
Tuesday: Herby Chicken
Wednesday: Perfect Pork Chops
Thursday: Green Enchiladas
Friday: Chops and Beans
Saturday: Chicken Tortilla Soup

Recommended Side Dish: Summer Salad
Special Dessert: Slow Cooker Berry Cobbler

Shopping List

PROTEIN
4 salmon filets

6-lb. whole roaster chicken

3½ lbs. boneless, center loin
   pork chops

2 slices bacon, browned and
   crumbled

DAIRY and REFRIGERATED
3 eggs

1 cup grated cheese of your
   choice

1½ cups mozzarella cheese

½ cup fat-free cheddar
   cheese

2 Tbsp. shredded Parmesan
   cheese

¼ cup skim milk

PRODUCE
1 large onion

1 cup chopped onions

½ cup chopped celery

½ cup chopped cucumber

2 medium tomatoes

2–4 sprigs thyme, or dried

fresh sprigs parsley, *optional*

2 lemons

lemon slices, *optional*

2 cups raspberries, or frozen

2 cups blueberries, or frozen

½ cup chopped grapes

CANNED/DRY GOODS
4-oz. can mushrooms

2 10-oz. cans green
   enchilada sauce

2 1-lb. cans pork and beans

15-oz. can no-salt-added
   black beans

15-oz. can Mexican stewed
   tomatoes

Download this shopping list to your
smartphone!
(x.co/ShopList)

4-oz. can chopped green chilies

6-oz. can no-salt-added tomato sauce

2¼-oz. can sliced black olives

1½ cups cooked garbanzo beans

½ cup salsa

1½ cups bread crumbs

8 large tortillas

1 oz. (12 chips) tortilla chips

¾ cups dry couscous

DO YOU HAVE THESE ON HAND?

ground ginger

pepper

dried minced onion

bay leaf

dried thyme

salt

minced garlic

dried oregano

dried basil

coriander

onion powder

dried parsley

cinnamon

1½ tsp. reduced-sodium bouillon granules of your choice

olive oil

canola oil

½ or lemon juice, or vinegar

¼ cup plus 2 Tbsp. no-salt-added ketchup

prepared mustard

prepared mustard with white wine

Dijon mustard

Worcestershire sauce

4 Tbsp. teriyaki sauce

4 Tbsp. hoisin sauce

low-sodium soy sauce

1 Tbsp. lemon juice

brown sugar

sugar

baking powder

1¼ cups all-purpose flour

Teriyaki Salmon

Hope Comerford,
Clinton Township, MI

Makes 4 servings

Prep. Time: 10 minutes
Cooking Time: 1–2 hours
Ideal slow-cooker size: 3- to 4-qt.

4 salmon filets
4 Tbsp. teriyaki sauce
4 Tbsp. hoisin sauce
1 Tbsp. low-sodium soy sauce
1 Tbsp. brown sugar
2 tsp. ground ginger
⅛ tsp. pepper

1. Lay out six pieces of foil, big enough to wrap the salmon filets in. Lay the salmon filets on top of each of them.

2. Mix together all remaining ingredients. Divide this mixture evenly over each salmon filet and spread to coat evenly.

3. Close the packets up tightly and place them in the crock.

4. Cover and cook on Low for 1–2 hours. The fish should flake easily when done.

Salmon Cheese Casserole

Wanda S. Curtin, Bradenton, FL

Makes 6 servings

Prep. Time: 5 minutes
Cooking Time: 3–4 hours
Ideal slow-cooker size: 2-qt.

leftover salmon, flaked
4-oz. can mushrooms,
  drained

1½ cups bread crumbs
2 eggs, beaten
1 cup grated cheese of your
  choice
1 Tbsp. lemon juice
1 Tbsp. dried minced onion

1. Flake fish in bowl, removing bones. Stir in remaining ingredients. Pour into lightly greased slow cooker.

2. Cover. Cook on Low 3–4 hours.

Herby Chicken

Joyce Bowman, Lady Lake, FL

Makes 8–10 servings

Prep. Time: 10 minutes
Cooking Time: 5–7 hours
Ideal slow-cooker size: 7-qt.

6-lb. whole roaster chicken
1 lemon, cut into wedges
1 bay leaf
2–4 sprigs fresh thyme, or ¾
  tsp. dried thyme
salt and pepper, to taste

1. Remove giblets from chicken.

2. Put lemon wedges and bay leaf in cavity.

3. Place whole chicken in slow cooker.

4. Scatter sprigs of thyme over the chicken. Sprinkle with salt and pepper.

5. Cover and cook on Low 5–7 hours, or until chicken is tender.

Serving Suggestion: Serve hot with pasta or rice, or debone and freeze for your favorite casseroles or salads.

Perfect Pork Chops

Brenda Pope, Dundee, OH

Makes 2 servings

Prep. Time: 20 minutes
Cooking Time: 3–4 hours
Ideal slow-cooker size: 4-qt.

1 large onion
3½ lb. boneless, center loin pork chops, frozen
fresh ground pepper, to taste
1½ tsp. reduced-sodium bouillon granules of your choice
½ cup hot water
4 Tbsp. prepared mustard with white wine
fresh parsley sprigs, or lemon slices, *optional*

1. Cut off ends of onion and peel. Cut onion in half

crosswise to make 4 thick wheels. Place in bottom of slow cooker.

2. Sear both sides of frozen chops in heavy skillet. Place in cooker on top of onions. Sprinkle with pepper.

3. Dissolve bouillon cube in hot water. Stir in mustard. Pour into slow cooker.

4. Cover. Cook on High 3–4 hours.

5. Serve topped with fresh parsley sprigs or lemon slices, if desired.

Green Enchiladas

Jennifer Yoder Sommers, Harrisonburg, VA

Makes 8 servings

Prep. Time: 5–7 minutes
Cooking Time: 2–4 hours
Ideal slow-cooker size: 3-qt.

2 10-oz. cans green enchilada sauce, *divided*
8 large tortillas, *divided*
2 cups leftover chopped chicken, *divided*
1½ cups mozzarella cheese

1. Pour a little enchilada sauce on the bottom of your slow cooker.

2. Layer 1 tortilla, ¼ cup of chicken, and ¼ cup of sauce into slow cooker.

3. Repeat layers until all these ingredients are used completely.

4. Sprinkle mozzarella cheese over top.

5. Cover and cook on Low 2–4 hours.

Tip: Green enchilada sauce can be found in the Mexican foods section in most grocery stores.

Chops and Beans

Mary L. Casey, Scranton, PA

Makes 6 servings

Prep. Time: 20 minutes
Cooking Time: 4–5 hours
Ideal slow-cooker size: 4-qt.

leftover pork, chopped
2 1-lb. cans pork and beans
¼ cup plus 2 Tbsp no-salt-added ketchup
2 slices bacon, browned and crumbled
½ cup chopped onions, sautéed
1 Tbsp. Worcestershire sauce
2 Tbsp. brown sugar
2 tsp. prepared mustard
one lemon, sliced

1. Place all ingredients in the slow cooker. Stir well.

2. Cover. Cook on Low 4–5 hours.

Chicken Tortilla Soup

Becky Harder, Monument, CO

Makes 4 servings

Prep. Time: 15 minutes
Cooking Time: 5–6 hours
Ideal slow-cooker size: 3-qt.

15-oz. can no-salt-added
   black beans, undrained
15-oz. can Mexican stewed
   tomatoes
½ cup salsa of your choice
4-oz. can chopped green
   chilies
6-oz. can no-salt-added
   tomato sauce
remaining leftover chicken
1 oz. (about 12 chips) tortilla
   chips
½ cup fat-free cheddar
   cheese

   1. Combine all ingredients
except chicken, chips, and
cheese in large slow cooker.
   2. Cover. Cook on Low 5–6
hours. Add leftover chicken
the last hour of cooking.
   3. To serve, put a handful
of chips in each individual
soup bowl. Ladle soup over
chips. Top with cheese.

Serving Suggestion: garnish
with avocado and lime
wedge.

Summer Salad

June S. Groff, Denver, PA

Makes 8 servings

Prep. Time: 20 minutes
Cooking Time for couscous: 10 minutes

1½ cups cooked garbanzo
   beans, drained
½ cup chopped onion
½ cup chopped celery
½ cup chopped cucumber
½ cup chopped red grapes
2 medium tomatoes, chopped
2¼-oz. can sliced black
   olives, drained
¾ cup dry couscous, cooked
   and cooled

Dressing:
½ cup olive oil
½ cup lemon juice, or vinegar
⅛ tsp. minced garlic
1 Tbsp. Dijon mustard
¼ tsp. dried oregano
¼ tsp. dried basil
1 Tbsp. sugar

⅛ tsp. coriander
⅛ tsp. onion powder
1 tsp. dried parsley
2 Tbsp. shredded Parmesan cheese

1. Toss salad ingredients together.
2. Mix dressing ingredients together. Pour dressing over salad mixture and toss.
3. Top with Parmesan cheese.

Slow-Cooker Berry Cobbler

Wilma J. Haberkamp, Fairbank, IA
Virginia Graybill, Hershey, PA

Makes 8 servings

Prep. Time: 15–20 minutes
Cooking Time: 2–2½ hours
Ideal slow-cooker size: 5-qt.

1¼ cups all-purpose flour, *divided*

2 Tbsp. sugar, plus 1 cup sugar, *divided*
1 tsp. baking powder
¼ tsp. ground cinnamon
1 egg, lightly beaten
¼ cup skim milk
2 Tbsp. canola oil
⅛ tsp. salt
2 cups unsweetened raspberries, fresh, or thawed if frozen, and drained
2 cups unsweetened blueberries, fresh, or thawed if frozen, and drained

1. In mixing bowl, combine 1 cup flour, 2 Tbsp. sugar, baking powder, and cinnamon.
2. In a separate bowl, combine egg, milk, and oil. Stir into dry ingredients until moistened. Batter will be thick.
3. Spray slow cooker with cooking spray. Spread batter evenly on bottom of slow cooker.
4. In another bowl combine salt, remaining flour, remaining sugar, and berries. Toss to coat berries.
5. Spread berries over batter.
6. Cook on High 2–2½ hours, or until toothpick inserted into cobbler comes out clean.

FALL

Week 1

THIS WEEK'S
Menu

Sunday: Barbara Jean's Junior Beef
Monday: Teriyaki Chicken
Tuesday: Your-Choice-of-Vegetables Soup
Wednesday: Teriyaki Chicken Tacos
Thursday: Apple Raisin Ham
Friday: Sweet Potatoes, Ham, and Oranges
Saturday: Lemon Dijon Fish

Recommended Side Dish: Winter Squash with Herbs and Butter
Special Dessert: Triple-Chocolate Lava Cake

Shopping List

PROTEIN

5-lb. beef roast (chuck or English)
8 skinless chicken thighs
2½-lb. boneless ham
1½ lbs. orange roughy fillets
3 Tbsp. orange juice concentrate

DAIRY and REFRIGERATED

2 cups grated cheddar or Swiss cheese
7 Tbsp. butter
3 eggs
2 cups 2% milk
⅓ cup orange juice

PRODUCE

1 medium onion
½ lb. mushrooms
fresh ginger

3 cups your choice of fresh vegetables (corn, peas, carrots, broccoli, green beans, cauliflower, mushrooms), or frozen coleslaw or broccoli slaw
2–3 sweet potatoes
3 seedless oranges
1 small butternut squash
1 small acorn squash
1 small golden nugget squash
4–8 sprigs of fresh rosemary, basil, tarragon, or thyme

CANNED/DRY GOODS

small jar dill pickles
1 qt. dill pickle juice (from 1-qt. jar of dill pickles)
lemon juice

Download this shopping list to your smartphone!
(x.co/ShopList)

15-oz. can diced tomatoes	seasoned salt
4–6 hamburger rolls	garlic powder
16 corn tortillas	allspice
long grain rice, small pearl	cinnamon
barley, orzo, or small pasta	bay leaves
shells	brown sugar
15-oz. pkg. devil's food cake	honey
mix	cornstarch
3-oz. pkg. instant chocolate	olive oil
pudding	canola oil
21-oz. can apple pie filling	sesame oil
2 cups semisweet chocolate	rice vinegar
chips	Worcestershire sauce
golden raisins	soy sauce
	low-sodium soy sauce
DO YOU HAVE THESE ON	Dijon mustard
HAND?	2 cloves garlic
salt	3 cups vegetable, beef, or
cayenne pepper	chicken stock
black pepper	

Barbara Jean's Junior Beef

Barbara Jean Fabel, Wausau, WI

Makes 4–6 servings

Prep. Time: 10 minutes
Cooking Time: 5–6 hours
Ideal slow-cooker size: 4-qt.

5-lb. beef roast (chuck or English)

½ tsp. salt

½ tsp. cayenne pepper

½ tsp. black pepper

1 tsp. seasoned salt

1 medium onion, chopped

juice from 1-qt. jar of dill pickles

4 dill pickles, chopped

4–6 hamburger rolls

½ lb. fresh mushrooms, sliced and sautéed

2 cups grated cheddar or Swiss cheese

1. Combine all ingredients except rolls, mushrooms, and cheese in slow cooker.

2. Cover. Cook on High 4–5 hours.

3. Shred meat using two forks. Reduce heat to Low and cook 1 hour, or until meat is very tender.

4. Serve on hamburger buns with sautéed mushrooms and grated cheddar or Swiss cheese.

Teriyaki Chicken

Colleen Konetzni, Rio Rancho, NM

Makes 4 servings

Prep. Time: 10 minutes
Cooking Time: 6–7 hours
Ideal slow-cooker size: 4-qt.

8 skinless chicken thighs

½ cup soy sauce

2 Tbsp. brown sugar

2 Tbsp. grated fresh ginger

2 cloves garlic, minced

1. Wash and dry chicken. Arrange in slow cooker.

2. Combine remaining ingredients in bowl. Pour over chicken.

3. Cover. Cook on High 1 hour. Reduce heat to Low and cook 5–6 hours, or until chicken is fork-tender.

Serving Suggestion: Serve over rice with a fresh salad.

Your-Choice-of-Vegetables Soup

Dawn Day, Westminster, CA

Makes 4–6 servings

Prep. Time: 10 minutes
Cooking Time: 6 hours
Ideal slow-cooker size: 4- to 5-qt.

3 cups vegetable, beef, or chicken stock
3 cups vegetables (use any or all of corn, peas, carrots, broccoli, green beans, cauliflower, mushrooms), either fresh or frozen
leftover beef
15-oz. can diced tomatoes
1 bay leaf
⅛ cup uncooked long-grain rice or small pearl barley, or ¼ cup cooked orzo or small shells

1. Combine all ingredients in slow cooker except rice, barley, or pasta.

2. Cover. Cook on Low 6 hours.

3. One hour before end of cooking time, stir in rice or barley. Or 30 minutes before end of cooking time, stir in cooked pasta.

Teriyaki Chicken Tacos

Hope Comerford, Clinton Township, MI

Makes 4 servings

Prep. Time: 10 minutes
Cooking Time: 5 minutes

leftover teriyaki chicken

16 corn tortillas
2 cups coleslaw or broccoli slaw

Dressing:
⅛ cup olive oil
⅛ cup rice vinegar
1 tsp. low-sodium soy sauce
1 tsp. brown sugar
½ tsp. sesame oil
½ tsp. garlic powder
¼ tsp. salt

1. Warm the leftover chicken and corn tortillas.

2. Meanwhile, mix together the ingredients for the dressing. Pour it over the coleslaw or broccoli slaw and mix well.

3. Fill each taco with some teriyaki chicken and top with slaw.

Apple Raisin Ham

Betty B. Dennison, Grove City, PA

Makes 6 servings

Prep. Time: 10–15 minutes
Cooking Time: 4–5 hours
Ideal slow-cooker size: 4-qt.

2½-lb. fully cooked boneless ham
21-oz. can apple pie filling
⅓ cup golden raisins
⅓ cup orange juice
¼ tsp. ground cinnamon
2 Tbsp. water

1. Cut ham into six equal slices.
2. In a mixing bowl, combine pie filling, raisins, orange juice, cinnamon, and water.
3. Place 1 slice of ham in your slow cooker. Spread 1/6 of the apple mixture over top.
4. Repeat layers until you have used all the ham and apple mixture.
5. Cover and cook on Low 4–5 hours.

Sweet Potatoes, Ham, and Oranges

Phyllis Good, Lancaster, PA

Makes 4 servings

Prep. Time: 15 minutes
Cooking Time: 4–5 hours
Ideal slow-cooker size: 3- to 4-qt.

2–3 sweet potatoes, peeled and sliced
¼-inch-thick ham slice, cut into 4 pieces from leftover ham
3 seedless oranges, peeled and sliced
3 Tbsp. orange juice concentrate
3 Tbsp. honey
¼ tsp. ground allspice
⅛ tsp. pepper
½ cup brown sugar
1 Tbsp. cornstarch

1. Place sweet potatoes in slow cooker.
2. Arrange ham and orange slices on top.
3. Combine remaining ingredients. Drizzle over ham and oranges.
4. Cover. Cook on Low 4–5 hours, or just until the sweet potatoes are as tender as you like them.

Lemon Dijon Fish

June S. Groff, Denver, PA

Makes 4 servings

Prep. Time: 10 minutes
Cooking Time: 3 hours
Ideal slow-cooker size: 2-qt.

1½ lbs. orange roughy fillets
2 Tbsp. Dijon mustard
3 Tbsp. butter, melted
1 tsp. Worcestershire sauce
1 Tbsp. lemon juice

1. Cut fillets to fit in slow cooker.
2. In a bowl, mix remaining ingredients together. Pour sauce over fish. (If you have to stack the fish, spoon a portion of the sauce over the first layer of fish before adding the second layer.)
3. Cover and cook on Low 3 hours, or until fish flakes easily but is not dry or overcooked.

Winter Squash with Herbs and Butter

Sharon Timpe, Jackson, WI

Makes 6–8 servings

Prep. Time: 30 minutes
Cooking Time: 3–8 hours
Ideal slow-cooker size: 3- to 4-qt.

3 lbs. whole winter squash, mixed kinds, ideally 1 small butternut, 1 small golden nugget, 1 small acorn squash
4 Tbsp. butter
4–5 Tbsp. honey
4–8 sprigs fresh herbs, such as tarragon, basil, thyme, and/or rosemary
salt, to taste

1. Peel and halve squash, removing seeds and strings. Cut squash in ¼-inch slices.
2. In lightly greased slow cooker, make layers of squash half-moons, butter, drizzles of honey, and herb sprigs.
3. Cover and cook on High for 3–4 hours or Low for 6–8 hours, until squash is tender.
4. Sprinkle lightly with salt to taste before serving.

Triple-Chocolate Lava Cake

Carol Sherwood, Batavia, NY

Makes 12 servings

Prep. Time: 15 minutes
Cooking Time: 3–4 hours
Ideal slow-cooker size: 4-qt.

15-oz. pkg. devil's food cake mix
1⅔ cups water
3 eggs
½ cup canola oil
2 cups cold 2% milk
3-oz. pkg. instant chocolate pudding
2 cups semisweet chocolate chips

1. In a large bowl, combine cake mix, water, eggs, and oil. Beat on low speed for 30 seconds. Beat on medium speed for 2 minutes.
2. Transfer to greased slow cooker.
3. In another bowl, whisk milk and pudding mix for 2 minutes. Let stand for 2 minutes or until soft set.
4. Spoon pudding over cake batter in cooker. Sprinkle with chocolate chips.
5. Cover and cook on High for 3–4 hours or until a toothpick inserted in cake portion comes out with moist crumbs. Serve warm.

Week 2

THIS WEEK'S
Menu

Sunday: Baked Ziti
Monday: Mexican Haystacks
Tuesday: Simple Chicken Thighs
Wednesday: Mexican Haystack Nachos
Thursday: Chicken Rice Soup
Friday: Autumn Brisket
Saturday: Baked Rice Dinner

Recommended Side Dish: Beets with Capers
Special Dessert: Pumpkin Bread Pudding

Shopping List

PROTEIN

2 lbs. ground beef

4 lbs. skinless chicken
  thighs

3-lb. boneless beef brisket

DAIRY and REFRIGERATED

1 lb. cottage cheese

2 Tbsp. Parmesan cheese

½ lb. mozzarella cheese

8 oz. shredded cheese of
  your choice

8 Tbsp. butter

2 cups heavy cream

5 eggs

sour cream, *optional*

plain Greek yogurt, *optional*

shredded Monterey Jack,
  optional

guacamole, *optional*

PRODUCE

1 large onion

1 medium onion

1 small onion

½ cup chopped onion,
  optional

2 ribs celery

1 lb. head of cabbage

1 large sweet potato

4–6 baking potatoes, *optional*

1 medium Granny Smith
  apple

8 cups fresh diced beets

fresh parsley

diced apples, *optional*

pineapple chunks, *optional*

shredded lettuce, *optional*

chopped tomatoes, *optional*

green onions, *optional*

Download this shopping list to your
smartphone!
(x.co/ShopList)

CANNED/DRY GOODS

59 oz. spaghetti sauce

1 lb. ziti

2 8-oz. cans tomato sauce

2 15-oz. cans chili beans
  with chili gravy or red
  beans

2 10-oz. cans mild enchilada
  sauce or mild salsa

2 10¾-oz. cans cream of
  celery soup

1 10¾-oz. can French onion
  soup

1 10¾-oz. can beef
  consommé

capers

French baguette

Craisins

tortilla chips

corn chips, *optional*

wild rice

long-grain rice

raisins, *optional*

shredded coconut, *optional*

pepper

salt

dried minced garlic

chili powder

garlic salt

red pepper flakes

dried thyme

dried rosemary

cinnamon

nutmeg

sugar

olive oil

vegetable oil

red wine vinegar

honey

soy sauce

5 cloves garlic

3¼ cups chicken broth

vanilla extract

caraway seeds, *optional*

cornstarch, *optional*

SPIRITS

pumpkin spice liqueur

DO YOU HAVE THESE ON HAND?

parsley flakes

Baked Ziti

Phyllis Good, Lancaster, PA

Makes 8–10 servings

Prep. Time: 15–20 minutes
Cooking Time: 4 hours
Standing Time: 15 minutes
Ideal slow-cooker size: 5-qt.

1 lb. cottage cheese
2 Tbsp. Parmesan cheese
1 egg
1 tsp. parsley flakes
⅛ tsp. pepper
⅛ tsp. salt
1 tsp. dried minced garlic
45-oz. jar of your favorite
  spaghetti sauce, *divided*
14-oz. jar of your favorite
  spaghetti sauce, *divided*
1 lb. ziti, uncooked
½ lb. mozzarella cheese,
  grated

1. Blend cottage cheese, Parmesan cheese, egg, parsley, pepper, salt, and garlic together.

2. Pour 2 cups spaghetti sauce into your greased slow cooker.

3. Drop ⅓ of the uncooked ziti over the spaghetti sauce.

4. Spoon ⅓ of the cottage cheese mixture over the ziti.

5. Repeat the layers 2 more times. You should have 1 cup spaghetti sauce left.

6. Pour the remaining tomato sauce over top.

7. Cover. Cook on Low 4 hours.

8. Thirty minutes before the end of the cooking time, sprinkle the top of the ziti mixture with mozzarella cheese. Do not cover.

Continue cooking 30 more minutes.

9. Let stand 15 minutes before serving to let everything firm up.

Tip: Use leftovers of this as a side dish this week.

Mexican Haystacks

Phyllis Good, Lancaster, PA

Makes 10–12 servings

Prep. Time: 20 minutes
Cooking Time: 1–3 hours
Ideal slow-cooker size: 5-qt.

2 lbs. ground beef
1 small onion, chopped
2 8-oz. cans tomato sauce
2 15-oz. cans chili beans with
  chili gravy, or red beans
2 10-oz. cans mild enchilada
  sauce, or mild salsa
½ tsp. chili powder
1 tsp. garlic salt
pepper, to taste
cooked rice, or baked
  potatoes (made in a second
  slow cooker!)

**Condiments (choose some
or all):**
raisins
diced apples
fresh pineapple chunks
shredded lettuce
chopped tomatoes
shredded coconut
shredded Monterey Jack
  cheese
corn chips

1. Brown beef in a skillet.
Using a slotted spoon, lift
it out of the drippings and
into the slow cooker. Discard
drippings.
2. Stir onion, tomato sauce,
chili beans, enchilada sauce,
chili powder, garlic salt, and
pepper into the beef in the
slow cooker.
3. Cover. Cook on Low 2–3
hours, or on High 1 hour.
4. Serve over baked
potatoes or rice. Then add as
many condiments on top as
you want.

Simple Chicken Thighs

Phyllis Good, Lancaster, PA

Makes 4–6 servings

Prep. Time: 10 minutes
Cooking Time: 4–6 hours
Chilling Time: 3–12 hours
Ideal slow-cooker size: 4-qt.

4 lbs. bone-in chicken thighs,
  skin removed
3 Tbsp. olive oil
4 Tbsp. red wine vinegar
¼ cup honey
¼ cup soy sauce
1 garlic clove, minced
½ tsp. freshly ground pepper
¼ cup chopped fresh parsley
cornstarch, *optional*

1. Place chicken in a
shallow glass pan in a single
layer.
2. In a small bowl, combine
oil, vinegar, honey, soy sauce,
garlic, pepper, and parsley.
3. Pour over chicken.
Marinate in the fridge for at
least 3 hours and up to 12.
4. Place chicken with
marinade in slow cooker.
Cover and cook on Low for
4–6 hours.
5. Either lift the chicken
thighs out of the resulting
sauce and serve, or thicken
the sauce with a mixture of 1
Tbsp. cornstarch and 3 Tbsp.
water whisked together, and
then whisked through the hot
sauce. Serve thickened sauce
as a gravy on the side.

Mexican Haystack Nachos

Hope Comerford,
Clinton Township, MI

Makes 6 servings

Prep. Time: 8 minutes
Cooking Time: 10–15 minutes

leftover Mexican Haystacks
  chili
tortilla chips
8 oz. shredded cheese, (your
  choice of flavor
½ cup chopped onions,
  optional

Additional Toppings:
sour cream or Greek yogurt
green onions, chopped
guacamole

1. Warm the leftover
Mexican Haystacks chili.
2. Preheat your oven to
400°F.
3. Spray your baking sheet
with nonstick spray then
arrange as many chips as you
wish across the baking sheet.
4. Top with warmed chili,
then add the onions if you
wish and cover with shredded
cheese.
5. Bake for 10–15 minutes,
or until cheese is melted.
6. Top with any additional
toppings you wish.

Chicken Rice Soup

Karen Ceneviva, Seymour, CT

Makes 4–6 servings

Prep. Time: 15 minutes
Cooking Time: 4–8 hours
Ideal slow-cooker size: 3½-qt.

¼ cup wild rice, uncooked
¼ cup long-grain rice, uncooked
1 tsp. vegetable oil
3¼ cups chicken broth
¾ cup celery (about 2 ribs), chopped in ½-inch-thick pieces
½ medium onion, chopped
1 tsp. dried thyme leaves
⅛ tsp. red pepper flakes
leftover chicken

1. Mix wild and white rice with oil in slow cooker.
2. Cover. Cook on High 15 minutes.
3. Add broth, vegetables, and seasonings.
4. Cover. Cook 4–5 hours on High or 7–8 hours on Low. 1 hour before serving, add the chicken.

Autumn Brisket

Karen Ceneviva, Seymour, CT

Makes 8 servings

Prep. Time: 20–30 minutes
Cooking Time: 4–9 hours
Ideal slow-cooker size: 6-qt.

3-lb. boneless beef brisket
salt, to taste
pepper, to taste
1-lb. head cabbage, cut into wedges
1 large (¾ lb.) sweet potato, peeled and cut into 1-inch pieces
1 large onion, cut in wedges
salt, to taste
pepper, to taste
1 medium Granny Smith apple, cored and cut into 8 wedges
2 10¾-oz. cans cream of celery soup
1 cup water
2 tsp. caraway seeds, *optional*

1. Place brisket in slow cooker.
2. Shake salt and pepper over meat to taste.
3. Top with cabbage, sweet potato, and onion.
4. Season to taste with salt and pepper.
5. Place apple wedges over vegetables.
6. In a medium bowl combine soup, water, and caraway seeds if you wish.
7. Spoon mixture over brisket and vegetables.

Baked Rice Dinner

Kay Magruder, Seminole, OK

Makes 4 servings

Prep. Time: 15 minutes
Baking Time: 1–1½ hours

¾ stick (6 Tbsp.) butter
10¾-oz. can French onion soup
10¾-oz. can beef consommé
1 cup long-grain rice, uncooked
2–3 cups bite-sized pieces of leftover brisket

1. Butter 1–1½-qt. baking dish. Cut remaining butter into chunks. Place in baking dish.
2. Add soup, consommé, rice, and meat.
3. Cover. Bake at 350°F for 1–1½ hours, or until liquid is absorbed.

Beets with Capers

Mary Clair Wenger, Kimmswick, MO

Makes 6 servings

Prep. Time: 20 minutes
Cooking Time: 3–4 hours
Ideal slow-cooker size: 3-qt.

8 cups diced fresh beets, peeled or not
3 Tbsp. olive oil
4 cloves garlic, chopped
¼ tsp. fresh ground pepper
1/2 tsp. salt
1 tsp. dried rosemary
1–2 Tbsp. capers with brine

1. In slow cooker, mix together beets, olive oil, garlic, pepper, salt, and rosemary.
2. Cover and cook on High until beets are tender, 3–4 hours.
3. Stir in capers and brine. Taste for salt. Serve hot or room temperature.

Pumpkin Bread Pudding

Hope Comerford, Clinton Township, MI

Makes 6–8 servings

Prep. Time: 8 minutes
Cooking Time: 4–6 hours
Ideal slow-cooker size: 3-qt.

1 French baguette, cut into ½-inch cubes and left out overnight to dry out.
½ cup Craisins
¼ cup pumpkin spice liqueur
4 eggs
1 tsp. vanilla extract
½ tsp. cinnamon
¼ tsp. salt
⅛ tsp. nutmeg
½ cup sugar
2 Tbsp. butter, melted
2 cups heavy cream

1. Spray your crock with nonstick spray.
2. In a small bowl, soak your Craisins in the pumpkin liqueur.
3. In a bigger bowl, mix together the eggs, vanilla extract, cinnamon, salt, nutmeg, sugar, melted butter, and heavy cream.
4. Stir in the pumpkin liqueur and soaked Craisins last.
5. Add in the bread and stir.
6. Pour everything into the crock.
7. Place a towel under the lid and cook on Low for 4–6 hours.

FALL

Week 3

THIS WEEK'S
Menu

Sunday: Zucchini Hot Dish
Monday: Easy Chicken
Tuesday: Stuffed Ground Beef
Wednesday: Basic Meat Curry Sauce
Thursday: Stuffed Acorn Squash
Friday: Italian Sausage Dinner
Saturday: Edie's Paella

Recommended Side Dish: Saucy Mushrooms
Special Dessert: Extra-Crisp Apple Crisp

Shopping List

PROTEIN

2½ lbs. ground beef

4 lbs. frozen chicken breasts

8–10 Italian sausage links

DAIRY and REFRIGERATED

1–2 cups shredded cheddar
  cheese

½ lb. sharp cheddar cheese,
  cubed

2 sticks butter

PRODUCE

5 large onions

1 small onion

1 large red onion

4–5 6-inch-long zucchini

2 cups shredded cabbage

2 acorn squash

5 large apples

5–6 large tart apples

1 pint grape tomatoes

4–5 tomatoes

1 lb. fingerling potatoes

1 lb. whole small mushrooms

fresh rosemary, or dried

CANNED/DRY GOODS

10¾-oz. can cream of
  mushroom soup

15½-oz. can black beans

15½-oz. can pinto beans

15½-oz. can great northern
  beans

2 pkgs. dry Italian dressing
  mix

2 cups dry bread cubes

2 cups tomato juice

apricot preserves

1½ cups instant rice

long-grain rice

1 cup rolled or quick oats

Download this shopping list to your
smartphone!
(x.co/ShopList)

DO YOU HAVE THESE ON HAND?

salt

pepper

curry powder

ground ginger

cardamom

ground nutmeg

ground cinnamon

Italian seasoning

garlic powder

dried thyme

cornstarch

1½ cups chicken broth or white wine, *optional*

flour

1 cup brown sugar

5–6 cloves garlic

lemon juice

olive oil

8 cups chicken stock or broth

SPIRITS

¾ cup red wine

Zucchini Hot Dish

Sharon Wantland,
Menomonee Falls, WI

Makes 4 servings

Prep. Time: 15–20 minutes
Cooking Time: 2–3 hours
Ideal slow-cooker size: 1½-qt.

2½ lbs. ground beef, *divided*
1 large onion, chopped
salt and pepper, to taste
4–5 6-inch-long zucchini,
   sliced
10¾-oz. can cream of
   mushroom soup
1–2 cups shredded cheddar
   cheese

1. Brown ground beef with onions, along with salt and pepper, in a nonstick skillet until crumbly. Drain. Put ½ lb. away for the Stuffed Ground Beef later this week and 1 lb. away for the Stuffed Acorn Squash later this week.
2. Layer zucchini and beef mixture alternately in slow cooker.
3. Top with soup. Sprinkle with cheese.
4. Cover and cook on Low 2–3 hours, or until the zucchini is done to your liking.

Easy Chicken

Hope Comerford,
Clinton Township, MI

Makes 8 servings

Prep. Time: 5 minutes
Cooking Time: 8 hours
Ideal slow-cooker size: 3-qt.

4 lbs. frozen chicken breasts
2 pkgs. dry Italian dressing
   mix
½ cup chopped onion
1½ cups warm water, chicken
   broth, or white wine

1. Place frozen chicken in the slow cooker and sprinkle with dry Italian dressing and onion.
2. Warm liquid and pour over the chicken.
3. Cook on Low for 8 hours.

Stuffed Ground Beef

Mary B. Sensenig,
New Holland, PA

Makes 4 servings

Prep. Time: 10 minutes
Cooking Time: 4–6 hours
Ideal slow-cooker size: 4-qt.

½ lb. leftover ground beef
2 cups cabbage, shredded
salt and pepper, to taste

2 cups dry bread cubes
2 cups tomato juice

1. Take the ½ lb. ground beef out of the refrigerator you browned earlier this week.
2. Spray the inside of the cooker with nonstick cooking spray. Layer ingredients in slow cooker in this order: ground beef, cabbage, salt and pepper, bread filling.
3. Pour tomato juice over top.
4. Cook on Low 4–6 hours, or until cabbage is just tender.

Basic Meat Curry Sauce

Carol Eveleth, Hillsdale, WY

Makes 8 servings

Prep. Time: 20 minutes
Cooking Time: 2–3 hours
Ideal slow-cooker size: 3-qt.

2 large onions, chopped
1–2 cloves garlic, minced

2 Tbsp. lemon juice
2–4 tsp. curry powder
1–2 cups leftover chicken, chopped into bite-sized pieces
rice

1. Grease interior of slow-cooker crock.

2. Mix onions, garlic, lemon juice, and curry powder in crock.

3. Stir in the chicken until all pieces are well coated.

4. Cover. Cook on Low 2–3 hours, or until onions are as tender as you like them.

5. If you'd like a thickened sauce, mix 2 Tbsp. flour into meat and sauce at end of cooking time. Cook on High 10 minutes, or until sauce bubbles and thickens.

6. Serve over steamed rice.

Stuffed Acorn Squash

Phyllis Good, Lancaster, PA

Makes 6–8 servings

Prep. Time: 45 minutes
Cooking Time: 5–8 hours
Ideal slow-cooker size: 6-qt.

2 acorn squash
1 lb. leftover ground beef
1 small onion, chopped
5 cups chopped, unpeeled apples, *divided*
4 tsp. curry powder
½ tsp. cardamom
½ tsp. ginger
scant ½ tsp. black pepper
½ lb. sharp cheddar cheese, cubed

6 Tbsp. apricot preserves
1–1¼ tsp. salt
2 Tbsp. butter
scant ½ tsp. ground cinnamon
scant ½ tsp. ground nutmeg

1. Wash the squash, and then cut in half from top to bottom. Scrape out the seeds and stringy stuff. (A grapefruit spoon works well because of its teeth. But a regular spoon with some pressure behind it works, too.) Cut each half in half again.

2. Put four quarters into the bottom of the slow cooker side by side, cut side up. Set the other four quarters on top, but staggered so they're not sitting inside the four pieces on the bottom. Add about 2 Tbsp. water to the cooker. Cover. Turn the cooker to Low and let it go for 3–6 hours, or until you can stick a fork into the skin of the squash halves with very little resistance.

3. Sometime during those 3–6 hours, warm the leftover 1 lb. ground beef and stir 2 cups chopped apples into beef and onions.

4. Mix in curry powder, cardamom, ginger, and black pepper.

5. Then add the cubed cheese, apricot preserves, and salt. Stir together gently. Set aside until squash is done softening up.

6. When squash is tender, divide the meat mixture among the 8 quarters evenly.

7. Put the filled quarters back into the cooker in staggered layers.

8. Cover. Cook on High for 45–60 minutes, or until the stuffing is heated through and the cheese is melted.

9. Sauté the remaining 3 cups apple slices in butter just until they're tender. Season lightly with cinnamon and nutmeg.

10. Remove the filled squash from cooker. Place a quarter on each serving plate. Top each with sautéed apples.

Italian Sausage Dinner

Hope Comerford,
Clinton Township, MI

Makes 8–10 servings

Prep. Time: 5 minutes
Cooking Time: 6 hours
Ideal slow-cooker size: 4-qt.

1 pint grape tomatoes
1 lb. fingerling potatoes
1 large red onion, quartered
8–10 Italian sausage links
1 Tbsp. olive oil
1½ tsp. Italian seasoning
1 tsp. garlic powder
salt and pepper, to taste
½ cup chicken stock or broth

1. If desired, brown sausages in a skillet. In the bottom of the crock, place the grape tomatoes, potatoes, and onion pieces, and then place the sausage links on top.

2. Drizzle the olive oil over the contents of the crock and sprinkle with the Italian seasoning, garlic powder, salt and pepper. Pour the chicken stock/broth in last.

3. Cook on Low for 6 hours.

Edie's Paella

Joy Sutter, Perkasie, PA

Makes 6–8 servings

Prep. Time: 20 minutes
Cooking Time: 4 hours
Ideal slow-cooker size: 6-qt.

1 large onion, chopped

2 Tbsp. olive oil
4–5 tomatoes, chopped
7½ cups chicken broth or stock
15½-oz. can black beans, drained and rinsed
15½-oz. can pinto beans, drained and rinsed
15½-oz. can great northern beans, drained and rinsed
¾ tsp. salt
½ tsp. black pepper
1½ tsp. fresh rosemary leaves or ½ tsp. dried
1½ cups instant rice
leftover Italian sausage, cut into chunks
leftover chicken (however much is leftover)

1. Grease interior of slow-cooker crock.

2. Add onion, tomatoes, chicken broth, black beans, pinto beans, great northern beans, salt, and pepper. Stir together until well mixed.

3. Cover. Cook on Low 4 hours. An hour before cooking time is up, add in the leftover chicken, leftover sausage, and stir in rosemary and rice.

Saucy Mushrooms

Donna Lantgen, Arvada, CO

Makes 4 servings

Prep. Time: 15 minutes
Cooking Time: 4½–6½ hours
Ideal slow-cooker size: 3-qt.

1 lb. small whole fresh mushrooms, cleaned
4 cloves garlic, minced
¼ cup chopped onion

THIS WEEK'S
Menu

Sunday: Butterfly Steaks
Monday: Snowmobile Soup
Tuesday: King Turkey
Wednesday: Our Favorite Tetrazzini
Thursday: Apricot Salsa Salmon
Friday: Country-Style Ribs
Saturday: Rib and Rice Bowls

Recommended Side Dish: Cheesy Creamed Corn
Special Dessert: Chocolate Blueberry Dessert

Shopping List

PROTEIN

4-lb. butt beef, or venison,
  or tenderloin

5–6-lb. turkey breast, bone
  in and skin on

12 oz. frozen salmon fillets

5–6 lbs. pork shoulder ribs

FROZEN

3 16-oz. pkgs. frozen corn

DAIRY and REFRIGERATED

2 cups milk

2 lbs. plus 1 cup shredded
  cheddar cheese

½ cup shredded sharp
  cheddar cheese

2 sticks butter

1 cup plain fat-free yogurt

8 oz. cream cheese

Parmesan cheese, grated,
  optional

PRODUCE

1 small onion

2 medium onions

2–3 green onions

5 large potatoes

1 rib celery

1 medium green bell pepper

CANNED/DRY GOODS

10¾-oz. can cream of
  mushroom soup

10¾-oz. can cream of
  chicken soup

8-oz. can sliced ripe olives

8-oz. can mushroom stems/
  pieces

4-oz. jar chopped pimento

Download this shopping list to your
smartphone!
(x.co/ShopList)

5 oz. spaghetti	cayenne pepper
¼ cup apricot jam	sesame seeds
¼ cup roasted salsa verde	sugar
12–14 servings rice	apple cider vinegar
21-oz. can blueberry pie filling	rice vinegar
	low-sodium soy sauce
15-oz. pkg. chocolate cake mix	½ cup soy sauce
	olive oil
	sesame oil

DO YOU HAVE THESE ON HAND?

	canola oil
ground cinnamon	1 cup chicken broth
garlic powder	ketchup
celery seeds	Worcestershire sauce
black pepper	1 dried chili pepper
salt	red chili paste
ground ginger	4 cloves garlic
dry mustard	
	SPIRITS
lemon pepper	1 cup white wine

Butterfly Steaks

Mary Louise Martin, Boyd, WI

Makes 8–10 servings

Prep. Time: 30 minutes
Cooking Time: 2–4 hours
Standing Time: 2 hours
Ideal slow-cooker size: 7-qt. oval

4-lb. butt beef, or venison,
   tenderloin
4½ tsp. garlic powder, *divided*
2 tsp. celery seeds
1 tsp. black pepper
1 Tbsp. salt
½ cup apple cider vinegar
¾ cup canola oil
½ cup soy sauce
⅓ cup olive oil
1 tsp. ground ginger
1 tsp. dry mustard
rice

1. Cut tenderloin into ¾–1-inch-thick slices. Cut each slice through the center but not the whole way through. Flatten into a butterfly-shaped steak and lay in large glass baking dish.

2. In a bowl, mix 4 tsp. garlic powder, celery seeds, pepper, salt, vinegar, and canola oil for marinade. Pour over steaks in a glass pan.

3. Cover, and marinate in fridge for 2 hours, stirring occasionally.

4. Meanwhile, grease interior of slow-cooker crock.

5. Place marinated steaks on broiler pan and broil at 400°F just until lightly browned. Place steaks in slow cooker. Stagger the pieces so they don't directly overlap each other.

6. Mix soy sauce, olive oil, ginger, dry mustard, and remaining ½ tsp. garlic powder. Pour over meat, making sure to spoon sauce on any steaks on the bottom layer.

7. Cook on Low 2–4 hours.

8. Serve with rice.

Snowmobile Soup

Jane Geigley, Honey Brook, PA

Makes 4–6 servings

Prep. Time: 20 minutes
Cooking Time: 5–6 hours
Ideal slow-cooker size: 4- to 6-qt.

1 small onion, chopped
5 large potatoes, julienned
   like french fries (you can
   leave the skins on)
10¾-oz. can cream of
   mushroom soup
1 soup can milk
2 lbs. shredded cheddar
   cheese
1 tsp. salt
¼ tsp. pepper
leftover steak

1. Stir onion, potatoes, soup, milk, cheese, salt, and pepper into your slow cooker.
2. Cover. Cook on Low 5–6 hours, or until potatoes are as soft as you like them. The last hour of cooking, add in the leftover steak.

King Turkey

Phyllis Good, Lancaster, PA

Makes 10–12 servings

Prep. Time: 20 minutes
Cooking Time: 5–7 hours
Ideal slow-cooker size: 4- to 5-qt.

5–6-lb. turkey breast, bone in
   and skin on
1 medium onion, chopped
1 rib celery, chopped
4 Tbsp. (½ stick) butter,
   melted
a good shower of salt, to taste
a sprinkling of lemon pepper,
   to taste
1 cup chicken broth
1 cup white wine

1. Wash turkey breast. Pat dry. Put onion and celery in cavity. Place in greased slow cooker.
2. Pour melted butter over turkey. Season with salt and lemon pepper.
3. Pour broth and wine around turkey.
4. Cover. Cook on Low 5–7 hours, or just until meat thermometer registers 165°F. (Make sure thermometer does not touch the bone.)
5. Let stand 15 minutes before carving.

Our Favorite Tetrazzini

Carolyn Spohn, Shawnee, KS

Makes 6–8 servings

Prep. Time: 30 minutes
Baking Time: 40 minutes

5 oz. spaghetti, broken
1 medium onion, chopped
1 medium green bell pepper,
   chopped
10¾-oz. can cream of chicken
   soup
⅓ cup milk
1 cup plain fat-free yogurt
3–4 cups diced leftover turkey
8-oz. can sliced ripe olives,
   drained
8-oz. can mushroom stems/
   pieces, drained
4-oz. jar chopped pimento,
   drained
Parmesan cheese, grated,
   optional
1 cup grated cheddar cheese

1. Cook spaghetti according to package directions. Drain well.
2. Sauté onion and green pepper in nonstick skillet until soft.
3. Mix soup, milk, and yogurt together in large mixing bowl until smooth.
4. Stir into soup mixture the onion and green pepper, spaghetti, meat, olives, mushrooms, and pimento. Fold together until well mixed.
5. Pour into greased 9×13-inch baking dish.
6. Bake at 350°F for 30 minutes, or until bubbly.
7. If you wish, sprinkle with Parmesan cheese. Then sprinkle with shredded cheddar cheese. Bake 10 more minutes.

Apricot Salsa Salmon

Sue Hamilton, Benson, AZ

Makes 2 servings

Prep. Time: 5 minutes
Cooking Time: 1–1½ hours
Ideal slow-cooker size: 4-qt.

12 oz. frozen salmon fillets
   (do NOT thaw)
¼ cup apricot jam
¼ cup roasted salsa verde

1. Grease interior of slow-cooker crock.

2. Remember not to thaw the salmon! Place frozen salmon skin side down in bottom of cooker.

3. Mix together jam and salsa. Spread mixture over salmon.

4. Cover. Cook on Low for 1–1½ hours or until an instant-read meat thermometer registers 135°F when stuck into center of fillet.

Country-Style Ribs

Patricia Howard,
Green Valley, AZ

Makes 6–8 servings

Prep. Time: 10–15 minutes
Cooking Time: 4–7 hours
Ideal slow-cooker size: 6-qt.

5–6 lbs. pork shoulder ribs
¾ cup ketchup
¾ cup water
1 tsp. salt
1 tsp. coarsely ground black
   pepper
dash cayenne pepper
1 Tbsp. chopped dried chili
   pepper
2 Tbsp. apple cider vinegar
2 Tbsp. Worcestershire sauce

1. Grease interior of slow-cooker crock.

2. Place ribs in crock. If you need to make a second layer, stagger pieces so they don't directly overlap each other.

3. Mix together all other ingredients in a bowl.

4. Spoon mixture over ribs, making sure that those on the bottom get covered with some sauce, too.

5. Cover. Cook on Low 5–7 hours, or on High 3–4 hours, or until instant-read meat thermometer registers 145°–150°F when stuck in center of ribs (but not against bone).

Rib and Rice Bowls

Hope Comerford,
Clinton Township, MI

Makes 4 servings

Prep. Time: 10 minutes
Cooking Time: 10 minutes

Leftover rib meat, cut up
4 servings of rice, cooked
  according to package
  directions

Sauce:
4 Tbsp. red chili paste (sub
  sriracha if you can't find)
4 cloves garlic, minced
2 Tbsp. rice vinegar
2 Tbsp. low-sodium soy sauce
2 tsp. sesame oil
2 tsp. sesame seeds
2 tsp. sugar
2–3 scallions, chopped

1. Warm up rib meat and cook rice according to the package directions.
2. Mix together all the ingredients except the scallions for the sauce. If it's too spicy for you, add in some ketchup to cut it down.
3. In 4 bowls, divide up the rice. Place a portion of rib meat on top of each. Drizzle the sauce over the top of each bowl. Top with some scallions.

Serving Suggestion: Add some peas or other mixed veggies to each bowl to get your veggies in.

Cheesy Creamed Corn

A. Catherine Boshart,
Lebanon, PA

Makes 12 servings

Prep. Time: 5 minutes
Cooking Time: 4 hours
Ideal slow-cooker size: 2- to 4-qt.

3 16-oz. pkgs. frozen corn
8 oz. cream cheese, room
  temperature, cubed
4 Tbsp. (½ stick) butter
¼ cup water
¼ cup milk
2 Tbsp. sugar
½ cup shredded sharp
  cheddar cheese

1. Combine all ingredients in lightly greased slow cooker.
2. Cover and cook on Low for 4 hours, stirring twice in the first hour.

Chocolate Blueberry Dessert

Sharon Timpe, Jackson, WI

Makes 6–8 servings

Prep. Time: 5 minutes
Cooking Time: 3 hours
Ideal slow-cooker size: 3-qt.

21-oz. can blueberry pie filling
15-oz. pkg. chocolate cake mix
4 Tbsp. (1 stick) butter, melted
1 tsp. ground cinnamon

1. Pour pie filling in lightly greased slow cooker.
2. Combine dry cake mix and cinnamon. Mix in melted butter.
3. Sprinkle over pie filling.
4. Cover and cook on Low for 3 hours. Allow to cool a bit before serving with ice cream or whipped cream.

FALL

Week 5

THIS WEEK'S
Menu

Sunday: Italian Chicken Fajita Wraps
Monday: Apple and Onion Beef Pot Roast
Tuesday: Italian Chicken Quesadillas
Wednesday: Creamy Vegetable Beef Stew
Thursday: Sweet and Saucy Pork Tenderloin
Friday: Chili Rellenos Casserole
Saturday: Pork Fried Rice

Recommended Side Dish: Boston Brown Bread
Special Dessert: Pumpkin Pie Pudding

Shopping List

PROTEIN

3 lbs. boneless, skinless
  chicken breasts

3-lb. boneless beef roast

4–5-lb. pork tenderloin

FROZEN

vanilla ice cream, *optional*

DAIRY and REFRIGERATED

14 oz. shredded cheddar cheese

¾ cup shredded Monterey
  Jack cheese

4 Tbsp. butter

1⅓ cups milk

10 eggs

1½ cups low-fat cottage
  cheese

1 cup buttermilk

freshly grated Parmesan
  cheese, *optional*

fresh mozzarella cheese
  slices, *optional*

sour cream, *optional*

guacamole, *optional*

vanilla whipped cream,
  optional

PRODUCE

2 green bell peppers

2 red bell peppers

2 large onions

½ cup chopped onion

chopped onion, *optional*

1 large tart apple

2 green onions

1 cup diced potatoes

1 cup diced carrots

lemon wedges, *optional*

shredded lettuce, *optional*

chopped tomatoes, *optional*

chopped fresh basil, *optional*

Download this shopping list to your
smartphone!
(x.co/ShopList)

diced tomatoes, *optional*

diced cucumbers, *optional*

CANNED/DRY GOODS

2 16-oz. bottles Italian
 dressing

21-oz. can apple pie filling

15-oz. can solid-pack
 pumpkin

12-oz. can evaporated milk

4-oz. can chopped green
 chilies

2 cups salsa

4 cups tomato juice

½ cup sweet barbecue sauce

20–22 10-inch flour tortillas

20 buttery crackers

long-grain rice

½ cup chopped walnuts

½ cup raisins

biscuit baking mix

pickled Italian hot peppers,
 optional

chopped olives, *optional*

salsa, *optional*

dried oregano

dried parsley

dried basil

dried thyme

celery seed

salt

pepper

seasoning salt

garlic powder

sugar

cornstarch

baking soda

flour

½ cup rye flour

½ cup yellow cornmeal

½ cup whole wheat flour

⅓ cup molasses

soy sauce

low-sodium soy sauce

Worcestershire sauce

sesame oil

oil of your choice

olive oil

4 cloves garlic

hot sauce, *optional*

**DO YOU HAVE THESE ON
HAND?**

pumpkin pie spice

Italian Chicken Fajita Wraps

Phyllis Good, Lancaster, PA

Makes 6–8 servings

Prep. Time: 20 minutes
Cooking Time: 2–4 hours
Chilling Time: 4–8 hours or
*   overnight*
Ideal slow-cooker size: 3-qt.

3 lbs. boneless, skinless
    chicken breasts
4 cloves garlic, sliced thinly
4 Tbsp. dried oregano
2 Tbsp. dried parsley
2 tsp. dried basil
1 tsp. dried thyme
½ tsp. celery seed
2 Tbsp. sugar
1 tsp. salt
1 tsp. freshly ground pepper
2 16-oz. bottles Italian salad
    dressing
2 cups salsa
2 green bell peppers, sliced
    in ribs
2 red bell peppers, sliced in
    ribs
1 large onion, sliced in rings
10 10-inch-flour tortillas

**Toppings (choose all or
some):**
freshly grated Parmesan
    cheese
fresh mozzarella cheese
    slices
hot sauce, or pickled Italian
    hot peppers
chopped olives
lemon wedges
shredded lettuce
chopped tomatoes
chopped fresh basil

1. Cut chicken into thin strips. Place in large mixing bowl.
2. Add garlic, herbs, sugar, salt, pepper, salad dressing, and salsa. Mix well. Cover and marinate 4–8 hours or overnight in the fridge.

3. Pour chicken and marinade into slow cooker. Cook on Low for 2–4 hours, until chicken is white through the middle and tender.
4. Spoon the chicken with its sauce into an ovenproof serving dish or rimmed baking sheet. Add the

vegetables. Slide it under the broiler for a few minutes until browned spots appear on the chicken and vegetables.

5. Serve with tortillas and toppings and lots of napkins.

Apple and Onion Beef Pot Roast

Betty K. Drescher,
Quakertown, PA

Makes 8–10 servings

Prep. Time: 20 minutes
Cooking Time: 5–6 hours
Ideal slow-cooker size: 4-qt.

3-lb. boneless beef roast, cut
  in half
oil of your choice
1 cup water
1 tsp. seasoning salt
½ tsp. soy sauce
½ tsp. Worcestershire sauce
¼ tsp. garlic powder
1 large tart apple, quartered
1 large onion, sliced
2 Tbsp. cornstarch
2 Tbsp. water

1. Brown roast on all sides in oil in skillet. Transfer roast to slow cooker.

2. Add water to skillet. Stir with wooden spoon to loosen browned bits. Pour over roast.

3. Sprinkle with seasoning salt, soy sauce, Worcestershire sauce, and garlic powder.

4. Top with apple and onion.

5. Cover. Cook on Low 5–6 hours.

6. Remove roast, apple pieces, and onion. Let stand 15 minutes.

7. To make gravy, pour juices from roast into saucepan and simmer until reduced to 2 cups.

8. Combine cornstarch and water until smooth in small bowl.

9. Stir into beef broth. Bring to boil. Cook and stir 2 minutes, or until thickened.

10. Slice pot roast and serve with gravy.

Italian Chicken Quesadillas

Hope Comerford,
Clinton Township, MI

Makes 4–6 servings

Prep. Time: 5 minutes
Cooking Time: 5 minutes

10–12 10-inch flour tortillas
leftover chicken
8 oz. shredded cheddar
  cheese

Toppings:
chopped onion
chopped green or black olives
shredded lettuce
diced tomatoes
diced cucumbers
sour cream
guacamole
salsa

1. Warm the leftover chicken.

2. In a skillet or on a griddle, place a tortilla and then add some chicken and any other toppings of your choice. Finish with more cheese so the two sides sick together and top with another tortilla.

3. Flip the quesadilla when the first side is barely toasted. Cook on the second side until all the cheese is melted.

4. Serve with any additional toppings you choose.

Creamy Vegetable Beef Stew

Lorna Rodes, Port Republic, VA

Makes 6–8 servings

Prep. Time: 20 minutes
Cooking Time: 5–7 hours
Ideal slow-cooker size: 4-qt.

4 cups tomato juice
½ cup chopped onion
1 cup diced potatoes
1 cup diced carrots
¼ tsp. pepper
½ tsp. dried basil
2 tsp. salt
2–3 cups leftover shredded
　pot roast

White Sauce:
2 Tbsp. butter
2 Tbsp. flour
1⅓ cups milk

1. Place tomato juice, onion, potatoes, carrots, pepper, basil, and salt in slow cooker.

2. Cover and cook on Low 4–6 hours. 1 hour before serving, stir in leftover pot roast. Then, make white sauce.

3. In saucepan, melt butter. Whisk in flour and cook, stirring, until flour and butter are bubbly.

4. Pour in milk gradually, whisking, and whisk until smooth. Stir over low heat until sauce thickens.

5. Pour white sauce into soup, stirring. Cook an additional hour on Low.

Sweet and Saucy Pork Tenderloins

Hope Comerford,
Clinton Township, MI

Makes 4–6 servings

Prep. Time: 5 minutes
Cooking Time: 7–8 hours
Ideal slow-cooker size: 3-qt.

4–5 lb. pork tenderloin
salt and pepper, to taste
21-oz. can apple pie filling
½ cup sweet barbecue sauce

1. Place the pork tenderloin in the bottom of your crock and sprinkle with salt and pepper.

2. Cover your tenderloin with the apple pie filling and pour the barbecue sauce on top of that.

3. Cover and cook on Low for 7–8 hours.

Chili Rellenos Casserole

Darla Sathre, Baxter, MN
Becky Harder, Monument, CO

Makes 6 servings

Prep. Time: 10 minutes
Cooking Time: 1½–1¾ hours
Ideal slow-cooker size: 4-qt.

6 eggs, beaten slightly
1½ cups low-fat cottage cheese
20 buttery crackers, crushed
4-oz. can chopped green chilies
¾ cup shredded cheddar cheese, *divided*
¾ cup shredded Monterey Jack cheese, *divided*

1. Grease interior of slow-cooker crock.

2. In a bowl, mix together eggs, cottage cheese, crackers, chilies, and half the cheddar and Monterey Jack cheeses.

3. Cover. Cook on High for 1¼ hours. Check to see if mixture is set. If not, cook another 15 minutes and check again.

4. Uncover and sprinkle dish with remaining cheese.

5. Cook, uncovered, until cheese melts.

6. Let stand 5 minutes before serving.

Pork Fried Rice

Hope Comerford,
Clinton Township, MI

Makes 4 servings

Prep. Time: 10 minutes
Cooking Time: 10 minutes

1 cup leftover pork, diced
2 Tbsp. olive oil, *divided*
2 eggs, beaten
4 cups cooked rice
½ tsp. sesame oil
2 green onions, chopped
2 Tbsp. low-sodium soy sauce
½ tsp. salt

1. In a wok or a skillet, add ½ Tbsp. of the olive oil and warm up the pork. Set it aside in a bowl.

2. Heat another ½ Tbsp. of olive oil and scramble the eggs. Place these in the bowl with the pork.

3. Heat the rest of your oils and heat up your rice, stirring it around and breaking up any clumps. Do this until it's heated through.

4. Add in the green onions and let them heat for a moment.

5. Add in the soy sauce and heated pork and scrambled eggs and salt. Stir until everything is coated and heated through.

Boston Brown Bread

Jean Butzer, Batavia, NY

Makes 3 loaves

Prep. Time: 15–20 minutes
Cooking Time: 4 hours
Ideal slow-cooker size: large enough to hold 3 cans upright, with the cooker lid on

3 15½-oz., or 16-oz., vegetable cans, cleaned and emptied
½ cup rye flour
½ cup yellow cornmeal
½ cup whole wheat flour
3 Tbsp. sugar
1 tsp. baking soda
¾ tsp. salt
½ cup chopped walnuts
½ cup raisins
1 cup buttermilk
⅓ cup molasses

1. Spray insides of vegetable cans, and one side of three 6-inch-square pieces of foil, with nonstick cooking spray. Set aside.
2. Combine rye flour, cornmeal, whole wheat flour, sugar, baking soda, and salt in a large bowl.
3. Stir in walnuts and raisins.
4. Whisk together buttermilk and molasses in a separate bowl. Add to dry ingredients. Stir until well mixed. Spoon into prepared cans.
5. Place one piece of foil, greased side down, on top of each can. Secure foil with rubber bands or cotton string. Place upright in slow cooker.
6. Pour boiling water into slow cooker to come halfway up sides of cans. (Make sure foil tops do not touch boiling water.)
7. Cover cooker. Cook on Low 4 hours, or until skewer inserted in center of bread comes out clean.
8. To remove bread, lay cans on their sides. Roll and tap gently on all sides until bread releases. Cool completely on wire racks.

Serving Suggestion: Serve with butter or cream cheese.

Tip: To substitute for buttermilk, pour 1 Tbsp. lemon juice into a 1-cup measure. Add enough milk to fill the cup. Let stand 5 minutes before mixing with molasses.

Pumpkin Pie Pudding

Orpha Herr, Andover, NY

Makes 6–8 servings

Prep. Time: 10 minutes
Cooking Time: 5–7 hours
Ideal slow-cooker size: 3-qt.

15-oz. can solid-pack pumpkin
12-oz. can evaporated milk
¾ cup sugar
½ cup biscuit baking mix
2 eggs, beaten
2 Tbsp. butter, melted
2½ tsp. pumpkin pie spice
vanilla whipped cream or ice cream, for serving

1. In large bowl, combine all ingredients (except for whipped cream or ice cream).
2. Transfer to lightly greased slow cooker.
3. Cover and cook on Low for 5–7 hours or until set and a cooking thermometer reads 160°F.
4. Serve in bowls with whipped cream or ice cream.

FALL

Week 6

THIS WEEK'S
Menu

Sunday: "Eye-Popping" Ribs
Monday: Slow Cooker Spaghetti Sauce
Tuesday: Dawn's Sausage and Peppers
Wednesday: Spicy Chili
Thursday: Turkey Thighs, Acorn Squash, and Apples
Friday: Brunswick Soup Mix
Saturday: Tuna Noodle Casserole

Recommended Side Dish: Stuffed Acorn Squash
Special Dessert: Apple Caramel Dessert

Shopping List

PROTEIN
2 lbs. boneless country ribs
3 lbs. sweet Italian sausage
½ lb. ground beef
4 turkey thighs

FROZEN
2 cups frozen, cubed hash browns
2 cups frozen peas

DAIRY and REFRIGERATED
½ cup shredded Swiss, or sharp cheddar, cheese
1 Tbsp. butter
3 Tbsp. orange juice
1 cup apple juice, or cider

PRODUCE
4 apples
6 medium Granny Smith apples

5 medium onions
½ cup chopped onions
1 shallot or 1 small onion
2 lbs. acorn squash
3 small carnival, or acorn, squash
1 sweet red bell pepper
1 sweet green bell pepper
1 sweet yellow bell pepper
3 Tbsp. diced celery
½ lb. fresh mushrooms
⅛ cup chopped celery
3 Tbsp. diced celery
⅛ cup chopped green bell pepper

CANNED/DRY GOODS
28-oz. can chopped tomatoes
3 14-oz. cans diced tomatoes

Download this shopping list to your smartphone!
(x.co/ShopList)

3 6-oz. cans tomato paste	pepper
6-oz. can tomato sauce	dried basil
16-oz. can tomato juice	dried thyme
15¼-oz. can corn	crushed red pepper flakes
15¼-oz. can lima beans	ground cinnamon
6- or 12-oz. can tuna	ground allspice
10¾-oz. can cream of	ground or dried sage
mushroom soup	ground cardamom
1 cup salsa	brown sugar
2½ cups dry noodles	sugar
8 oz. spaghetti	oil of your choice
instant brown rice	8 cloves garlic
dried cranberries	Worcestershire sauce
7 oz. caramels, unwrapped	4 cups chicken broth
	vanilla extract

DO YOU HAVE THESE ON HAND?

creamy peanut butter

¼ cup almonds, *optional*

garlic powder

onion powder

SPIRITS

bay leaf

2 cups Leelanau Cellars Witches Brew, or other red wine

dried oregano

dried minced onion

salt

apple brandy

"Eye-Popping" Ribs

Hope Comerford,
Clinton Township, MI

Makes 6 servings

Prep. Time: 10 minutes
Cooking Time: 8 hours
Ideal slow-cooker size: 4-qt.

2 lbs. boneless country ribs
¼ cup brown sugar
1 Tbsp. garlic powder
1 Tbsp. onion powder
2 apples, "eyeballs" cut out
   with a melon baller
2 cups Leelanau Cellars
   Witches Brew, or other red
   wine

1. Place the ribs into the crock.
2. Add the brown sugar, garlic powder, and onion powder and top with the apple "eyeballs"
3. Lastly, pour the Witches Brew over the ribs and apple "eyeballs."
4. Cook on Low for 8 hours.

Slow Cooker Spaghetti Sauce

Lucille Amos, Greensboro, NC
Julia Lapp, New Holland, PA

Makes 6–8 servings

Prep. Time: 15 minutes
Cooking Time: 7 hours
Ideal slow-cooker size: 4-qt.

1 medium onion, chopped
2 14-oz. cans diced tomatoes,
   with juice

6-oz. can tomato paste
8-oz. can tomato sauce
1 bay leaf
4 cloves garlic, minced
2 tsp. dried oregano
1 tsp. salt
2 tsp. dried basil
1 Tbsp. brown sugar
½–1 tsp. dried thyme
leftover rib meat, shredded or
   diced
cooked spaghetti

1. Add all ingredients to the slow cooker except the rib meat and pasta.
2. Cover. Cook on Low 7 hours. The last hour of cooking, add in the leftover rib meat. If the sauce seems too runny, keep the lid off during last hour of cooking.
3. Serve over spaghetti.

Dawn's Sausage and Peppers

Dawn Day, Westminster, CA

Makes 8–10 servings

Prep. Time: 25–30 minutes
Cooking Time: 6 hours
Ideal slow-cooker size: 5-qt.

3 medium onions, sliced
1 sweet red bell pepper, sliced

1 sweet green bell pepper,
  sliced
1 sweet yellow bell pepper,
  sliced
4 cloves garlic, minced
1 Tbsp. oil of your choice
28-oz. can chopped tomatoes
1 tsp. salt
½ tsp. crushed red pepper
  flakes
3 lbs. sweet Italian sausage,
  cut into 3-inch pieces

1. Sauté onions, peppers, and garlic in oil in skillet.

When just softened, place in slow cooker. (Or skip this step, but check that the vegetables are cooked to your liking at the end of the 6-hour cooking time.)

2. Add tomatoes, salt, and crushed red pepper. Mix well.

3. Add sausage pieces.

4. Cover. Cook on Low 6 hours.

Serving Suggestion: Serve on rolls, or over pasta or baked potatoes.

Spicy Chili

Deborah Swartz, Grottoes, VA

Makes 4–6 servings

Prep. Time: 20 minutes
Cooking Time: 4–6 hours
Ideal slow-cooker size: 3½-qt.

½ lb. ground beef
½ cup chopped onions
½ lb. fresh mushrooms, sliced
⅛ cup chopped celery
⅛ cup chopped green bell
  peppers
1 cup salsa
16-oz. can tomato juice
6-oz. can tomato paste
½ tsp. sugar
½ tsp. salt
½ tsp. dried oregano
½ tsp. Worcestershire sauce
¼ tsp. dried basil
¼ tsp. pepper
leftover sausage, cut into bite-
  sized pieces

1. Brown ground beef and onions in skillet. Stir frequently to break up clumps of meat.

2. During last 3 minutes of browning, add mushrooms, celery, and green peppers. Continue cooking; then drain off drippings.

3. Spoon meat and sautéed vegetables into cooker. Stir in remaining ingredients except the leftover sausage.

4. Cover. Cook on Low 4–6 hours. The last hour of cooking, add in the leftover sausage.

Slow Cooker Spaghetti Sauce (page 268)

Turkey Thighs, Acorn Squash, and Apples

Mary E. Wheatley, Mashpee, MA

Makes 6–8 servings

Prep. Time: 35 minutes
Cooking Time: 6–8 hours
Ideal slow-cooker size: 6-qt.

2 lbs. acorn squash, peeled, seeded, and cut into 1-inch-thick rings
6 medium Granny Smith, or other tart, apples, cored and cut into ½-inch-thick rings
4 turkey thighs, skin and excess fat removed
salt and pepper, to taste
1 shallot, or small onion, chopped
½ cup apple juice, or cider
1 Tbsp. apple brandy
3 Tbsp. brown sugar
1 tsp. ground cinnamon
½ tsp. ground allspice

1. Spray inside of slow cooker with nonstick spray. Layer in squash, followed by apple rings.
2. Place turkey thighs on top. Sprinkle with salt, pepper, and onion or shallot.
3. In a small bowl, combine apple juice, brandy, brown sugar, cinnamon, and allspice. Pour over turkey.
4. Cover. Cook on Low 6–8 hours, or just until turkey and squash are tender.

Brunswick Soup Mix

Joyce B. Suiter, Garysburg, NC

Makes 7 servings

Prep. Time: 10–15 minutes
Cooking Time: 7 hours
Ideal slow-cooker size: 5-qt.

1 medium onion, chopped
2 cups frozen, cubed, hash browns, thawed
14½-oz. can diced tomatoes
6-oz. can tomato sauce
15¼-oz. can corn
15¼-oz. can lima beans, drained
4 cups chicken broth
½ tsp. salt
½ tsp. pepper
¼ tsp. Worcestershire sauce
⅛ cup sugar
leftover turkey, chopped up

1. Combine all ingredients except the turkey in large slow cooker.
2. Cover. Cook on Low 7 hours. The last hour of cooking, add in leftover turkey.
3. Serve when turkey is heated through.

Tuna Noodle Casserole

Ruth Hofstetter, Versailles, MO

Makes 8 servings

Prep. Time: 5–10 minutes
Cooking Time: 2–4 hours
Ideal slow-cooker size: 3-qt.

2½ cups dry noodles
1 tsp. salt
½ cup finely chopped onion
6- or 12-oz. can tuna, according to your taste preference
10¾-oz. can cream of mushroom soup
half a soup can of water
¼ cup almonds, *optional*
½ cup shredded Swiss, or sharp cheddar, cheese
1 cup frozen peas

1. Combine all ingredients in slow cooker, except peas.
2. Cover. Cook on High 2–3 hours or on Low 4 hours, stirring occasionally.
3. Twenty minutes before end of cooking time, stir in peas and reduce heat to Low if cooking on High.

Stuffed Acorn Squash

Jean Butzer, Batavia, NY

Makes 6 servings

Prep. Time: 15 minutes
Cooking Time: 2½ hours
Ideal slow-cooker size: 5- to 6-qt.

3 small carnival, or acorn, squash
5 Tbsp. instant brown rice, uncooked
3 Tbsp. dried cranberries
3 Tbsp. diced celery
3 Tbsp. dried minced onion
pinch of ground, or dried, sage
1 Tbsp. butter, *divided*
3 Tbsp. orange juice
½ cup water

1. Slice off points on bottoms of squash so they will stand in slow cooker. Slice off tops and discard. Scoop out seeds. Place squash side by side in slow cooker.

2. Combine rice, cranberries, celery, onion, and sage in bowl. Stuff into squash centers.

3. Dot with butter.

4. Pour 1 Tbsp. orange juice into each squash center.

5. Pour water into bottom of slow cooker.

6. Cover. Cook on Low 2½ hours.

Apple Caramel Dessert

Jeanette Oberholtzer, Manheim, PA

Makes 7 servings

Prep. Time: 15 minutes
Cooking Time: 6 hours
Ideal slow-cooker size: 2-qt.

½ cup apple juice
7 oz. caramels, unwrapped

1 tsp. vanilla extract
⅛ tsp. ground cardamom
½ tsp. ground cinnamon
⅓ cup creamy peanut butter
2 medium apples, peeled, cored, and cut in wedges

1. Combine apple juice, caramels, vanilla, and spices in slow cooker.

2. Drop peanut butter, 1 Tbsp. at a time, into slow cooker. Stir well after each addition.

3. Gently stir in apple wedges.

4. Cover. Cook on Low 5 hours.

5. Stir well.

6. Cover. Then cook 1 more hour on Low.

Serving Suggestion: Serve about ⅓ cup warm mixture over each slice of angel food cake, and then top each with ice cream.

Week 7

THIS WEEK'S
Menu

Sunday: Spanish Beef

Monday: Hot Spanish Beef and Gravy Open-Faced Sandwiches

Tuesday: Cozy Kielbasa

Wednesday: Easy Veggie-Beef Soup

Thursday: Mix-It-and-Rub Chicken

Friday: Sauerkraut-Sausage Bean Soup

Saturday: Scalloped Chicken

Recommended Side Dish: Seasoned Mashed Potatoes

Special Dessert: Easy Autumn Cake

Shopping List

PROTEIN

3–4 lb. boneless beef chuck roast

3 lbs. smoked kielbasa

8 boneless, skinless chicken breast halves

FROZEN

1 lb. frozen green beans

1 cup frozen peas

DAIRY and REFRIGERATED

2 eggs

1½ cups milk

8 oz. cream cheese

2 cups buttermilk

1 stick butter

PRODUCE

2 large onions

3 medium onions

2 cups sliced carrots

1 lb. potatoes

CANNED/DRY GOODS

2 4-oz. cans chopped green chilies

2 16-oz. cans sliced apples (not pie filling)

14½-oz. can corn, or 16-oz. bag frozen corn

28-oz. can diced tomatoes

10¾-oz. can cream of celery soup

2 10¾-oz. cans cream of mushroom soup

2 15-oz. cans cut green beans

3 15-oz. can white beans

16-oz. can sauerkraut

18¼-oz. pkg. spice cake mix

2 cups salsa

Download this shopping list to your smartphone!
(x.co/ShopList)

½ cup pecans   dry mustard

½–1 loaf bread   garlic powder

2 cups unsweetened   dried minced onion

  applesauce   seasoning salt

1 box stuffing mix for   4 beef bouillon cubes

  chicken   3 tsp. instant beef bouillon

1 cup dry milk   cornstarch or flour

1 envelope dry ranch   sugar

  dressing mix   brown sugar

  ½ cup ketchup

DO YOU HAVE THESE ON   3 cups beef or vegetable

HAND?   broth

salt   soy sauce

pepper   Worcestershire sauce

Spanish Beef

Phyllis Good, Lancaster, PA

Makes 10–12 servings

Prep. Time: 10 minutes
Cooking Time: 10–12 hours
Ideal slow-cooker size: 4-qt.

3–4 lb. boneless beef chuck roast
2 large onions, sliced thin
2 4-oz. can chopped green chilies, undrained
4 beef bouillon cubes
1 Tbsp. dry mustard
1 tsp. garlic powder
2 tsp. seasoning salt
1 tsp. pepper
water
2 cup salsa, as mild or as hot as you like

1. Combine all ingredients except salsa in slow cooker. Add just enough water to cover the meat.
2. Cover cooker and cook on Low 10–12 hours, or until beef is tender but not dry. Lift meat out of cooker into bowl. Reserve liquid in cooker.
3. Shred beef using two forks to pull it apart.
4. Combine beef, salsa, and enough of the reserved liquid to have the consistency you want. Save the rest of the liquid for making gravy tomorrow.

Serving Suggestion: Use as filling for burritos, chalupas, quesadillas, or tacos.

Hot Spanish Beef and Gravy Open-Faced Sandwiches

Hope Comerford, Clinton Township, MI

Makes: 4–8 servings

Prep. Time: 5 minutes
Cooking Time: 10 minutes

cooking liquid from Spanish beef
½ tsp. soy sauce
½ tsp. Worcestershire sauce
¼ tsp. salt
⅛ tsp. pepper
cornstarch or flour
1 lb. leftover beef, shredded
bread

1. To make the gravy, heat the cooking liquid from the Spanish beef, soy sauce,

Seasoned Mashed Potatoes

Elena Yoder, Carlsbad, NM

Makes 12 servings

Prep. Time: 30 minutes
Cooking Time: 3–4 hours
Ideal slow-cooker size: 4-qt.

1 lb. potatoes (enough to fill a 4-qt. slow cooker), peeled and cut into chunks
boiling water to cover potatoes
8-oz. pkg. cream cheese, softened
2 cups buttermilk
1 cup dry milk
1 envelope dry ranch dressing mix

1. Place potatoes in slow cooker. Cover with boiling water.

2. Cover and cook on High 3–4 hours, or until very tender.

3. Drain, reserving liquid.

4. Mash potatoes.

5. Beat in cream cheese.

6. Beat in buttermilk, dry milk, and ranch dressing mix.

7. If needed, beat in as much reserved potato water as you want until potatoes reach desired consistency.

Easy Autumn Cake

Janice Muller, Derwood, MD

Makes 8 servings

Prep. Time: 15 minutes
Cooking Time: 3–5 hours
Ideal slow-cooker size: 3½- to 4-qt.

2 16-oz. cans sliced apples (not pie filling), undrained
18¼-oz. pkg. spice cake mix
1 stick butter, melted
½ cup pecans, chopped

1. Spray interior of slow cooker with nonstick cooking spray.

2. Spoon apples and their juice into slow cooker, spreading evenly over the bottom.

3. Sprinkle with dry spice cake mix.

4. Pour melted butter over dry mix. Top with chopped pecans.

5. Cook on Low 3–5 hours, or until a toothpick inserted into topping comes out dry.

6. Serve warm from cooker.

FALL

Week 8

THIS WEEK'S
Menu

Sunday: Apple Corned Beef and Cabbage
Monday: Autumn Harvest Loin
Tuesday: Reuben Casserole
Wednesday: Kale and Friends Soup
Thursday: Cheesy Macaronis
Friday: Peppercorn Roast Beef
Saturday: Vegetable Beef Borscht

Recommended Side Dish: Dressed-Up Acorn Squash
Special Dessert: Carrot Cake

Shopping List

PROTEIN

5-lb. corned beef brisket

3-lb. pork loin

3–4-lb. chuck roast

DAIRY and REFRIGERATED

4 cups pure apple juice

1 cup apple cider, or juice

½ cup shredded, or 8 slices, Swiss cheese

2 lbs. Velveeta or shredded sharp cheddar

3 cups milk

5⅓ Tbsp. (⅓ cup) butter

2 Tbsp. orange juice

2 eggs

sour cream, *optional*

PRODUCE

2 small heads cabbage

6–7 medium potatoes

2–3 cups baby carrots

4 carrots

½ cup grated carrots

2 whole butternut squash

2 acorn squash

½ bunch kale

2 large Granny Smith apples

1 large onion

1 cup diced tomatoes

1 cup green beans

1 cup corn

CANNED/DRY GOODS

15-oz. can sauerkraut

15-oz. can cannellini beans

12-oz. can evaporated milk

¼ cup Thousand Island dressing

4 cups dry packaged stuffing mix

1 lb. dry macaroni

Download this shopping list to your smartphone!
(x.co/ShopList)

2 cups tomato juice

⅔ cup cracker crumbs

½ cup coarsely chopped
  pecans

½ cup raisins, or chopped
  dates

**DO YOU HAVE THESE ON
HAND?**

salt

pepper

ground cinnamon

dried thyme

dried sage

dried basil

dried rosemary

garlic powder

bay leaf

peppercorns

dill seed

ground nutmeg

ground allspice

ground cloves

brown sugar

flour

sugar

baking powder

3–4 cups chicken broth

2 cups beef broth

½ cup soy sauce

vegetable oil

½ cup chopped nuts

Apple Corned Beef and Cabbage

Donna Treloar, Hartford City, IN

Makes 6–8 servings

Prep. Time: 15 minutes
Cooking Time: 8–10 hours
Ideal slow-cooker size: 5-qt.

5-lb. corned beef brisket (not in a brine), cut into 6–8 pieces
1 small head of cabbage, cut in thin wedges
3–4 medium potatoes, cut in chunks
2–3 cups baby carrots, or sliced full-sized carrots, *optional*
1 qt. pure apple juice
1 cup brown sugar

1. Place corned beef in slow cooker.
2. Place vegetables around and on top of meat.
3. Pour apple juice over everything. Sprinkle with brown sugar.
4. Cover and cook on Low 8–10 hours, or until meat and vegetables are tender but not overcooked.

Autumn Harvest Loin

Phyllis Good, Lancaster, PA

Makes 4–6 servings

Prep. Time: 30 minutes
Cooking Time: 4½–5½ hours
Standing Time: 10–15 minutes
Ideal slow-cooker size: 5-qt.

1½ whole butternut squash, peeled and cubed
1 cup cider, or apple juice
3-lb. pork loin
salt
pepper
2 large Granny Smith apples, peeled and quartered
⅓ cup brown sugar
¼ tsp. ground cinnamon
¼ tsp. dried thyme
¼ tsp. dried sage

1. Put peeled and cubed squash into slow cooker. Pour in cider. Cover and cook on Low 1½ hours.
2. Sprinkle pork loin with salt and pepper on all sides. Settle into slow cooker on top of the squash.
3. Lay apple quarters around the meat.

4. Sprinkle everything with brown sugar, cinnamon, thyme, and sage.

5. Cover. Cook on Low 3–4 hours. Stick your instant-read thermometer into the center of the loin. The meat is done the minute the thermometer reads 140°F.

6. Remove pork from cooker. Cover with foil to keep warm. Continue cooking the squash and apples if they're not as tender as you like them.

7. You can cut the loin into ½-inch-thick slices after it has stood 10–15 minutes. Keep covered until ready to serve.

8. Serve topped with apples and squash. Pass the cooking juices in a small bowl to spoon over the meat, squash, and apples.

Reuben Casserole

Melanie Thrower, McPherson, KS

Makes 4 servings

Prep. Time: 10 minutes
Cooking Time: 2–4 hours
Ideal slow-cooker size: 2-qt.

2 cups leftover corned beef, chopped up, *divided*
15-oz. can sauerkraut, drained, *divided*
½ cup shredded, or 8 slices, Swiss cheese, *divided*
¼ cup Thousand Island salad dressing, *divided*
4 cups dry packaged stuffing mix, *divided*

1. Spray slow cooker with nonstick cooking spray.

2. Layer half of each ingredient in the order listed.

3. Repeat layers.

4. Cover and cook on Low 2–4 hours, until casserole is cooked through and cheese has melted.

Kale and Friends Soup

Bob Coffey, New Windsor, NY

Makes 6 servings

Prep. Time: 20 minutes
Cooking Time: 8 hours
Ideal slow-cooker size: 5½-qt.

½ bunch kale, torn into bite-sized pieces
½ butternut squash, peeled and cubed
15-oz. can cannellini beans, drained and rinsed
½ cup diced, leftover cooked pork
3–4 cups chicken broth
½ tsp. dried basil
¼ tsp. dried rosemary
¼ tsp. dried thyme
salt and pepper, to taste

1. Combine all ingredients in slow cooker.

2. Cover and cook on Low 8 hours.

3. Taste to correct seasonings. Add more broth if too thick or you're trying to stretch the soup.

Cheesy Macaronis

Renee Suydam, Lancaster, PA
Patricia Fleischer, Carlisle, PA
Ruth Zendt, Mifflintown, PA

Makes 10–12 servings

Prep. Time: 30 minutes
Cooking Time: 3 hours
Ideal slow-cooker size: 6-qt.

1 lb. dry macaroni
12-oz. can evaporated milk
3 cups milk
2 lbs. Velveeta cheese,
  cubed, or sharp cheese,
  shredded

1. Cook macaroni according to package directions. Drain.
2. Put both milks in slow cooker. Add cheese to milk.
3. Stir in cooked macaroni.
4. Cover and cook on Low 3 hours.

Peppercorn Roast Beef

Stacie Skelly, Millersville, PA

Makes 6–8 servings

Prep. Time: 10–15 minutes
Cooking Time: 8–10 hours
Ideal slow-cooker size: 4-qt.

3–4-lb. chuck roast
½ cup soy sauce
1 tsp. garlic powder
1 bay leaf
3–4 peppercorns
2 cups water

Optional Ingredients:
1 tsp. thyme
½ cup flour
½ cup water

1. Place roast in slow cooker.
2. In a mixing bowl, combine all other ingredients and pour over roast.
3. Cover and cook on Low 8–10 hours.
4. Remove meat to a platter and allow to rest before slicing or shredding.

Vegetable Beef Borscht

Jeanne Heyerly, Chenoa, IL

Makes 6–8 servings

Prep. Time: 20 minutes
Cooking Time: 6–8 hours
Ideal slow-cooker size: 5-qt.

half a small head of cabbage,
  sliced thin
3 medium potatoes, diced
4 carrots, sliced
1 large onion, diced
1 cup diced tomatoes
1 cup corn
1 cup green beans
2 cups beef broth
2 cups tomato juice
¼ tsp. garlic powder
¼ tsp. dill seed
2 tsp. salt
½ tsp. pepper
water
leftover roast beef, cut
  into bite-sized pieces or
  shredded
sour cream, *optional*

1. Grease interior of slow-cooker crock.
2. Mix together all ingredients except water, sour cream, and leftover roast beef. Add water to fill slow cooker three-quarters full.
3. Cover. Cook on Low 6–8 hours, or until vegetables are as soft as you like them. The last hour of cooking add in the leftover roast beef.
4. Pass sour cream around the table so individuals can add a dollop to their bowls if they wish.

Dressed-Up Acorn Squash

Dale Peterson, Rapid City, SD

Makes 4 servings

Prep. Time: 15 minutes
Cooking Time: 6–8 hours
Ideal slow-cooker size: 5- or 6-qt.,
 or 2 4- or 6-qt., depending on
 size of squash

2 acorn squash
⅔ cup cracker crumbs
½ cup coarsely chopped
  pecans
5⅓ Tbsp. (⅓ cup) butter,
  melted
4 Tbsp. brown sugar
½ tsp. salt
¼ tsp. ground nutmeg
2 Tbsp. orange juice

1. Grease interior of slow-cooker crock.
2. Cut squash in half through the middle. Remove seeds.
3. Combine remaining ingredients in a bowl. Spoon into squash halves.
4. Place squash halves in slow cooker side by side.
5. Cover. Cook on Low 6–8 hours, or until squash is tender.

Carrot Cake

Colleen Heatwole, Burton, MI

Makes 6–8 servings

Prep. Time: 20 minutes
Cooking Time: 3–4 hours
Ideal slow-cooker size: large
 enough to hold your baking
 insert or a bread pan

½ cup vegetable oil
2 eggs
1 Tbsp. hot water
½ cup grated raw carrots
¾ cup flour plus 2 Tbsp. flour,
  divided
¾ cup sugar
½ tsp. baking powder
⅛ tsp. salt
¼ tsp. ground allspice
½ tsp. ground cinnamon
⅛ tsp. ground cloves
½ cup chopped nuts
½ cup raisins, or chopped
  dates

1. In large bowl, beat oil, eggs, and hot water for 1 minute.
2. Add carrots. Mix well.
3. In a separate bowl, stir together ¾ cup flour, sugar, baking powder, salt, allspice, cinnamon, and cloves. Add to creamed mixture.
4. Toss nuts and raisins in bowl with 2 Tbsp. flour. Add to creamed mixture. Mix well.
5. Pour into greased and floured baking dish or bread pan that fits into your slow cooker. Place baking dish or bread pan in slow cooker.
6. Cover insert with its lid, or cover with 8 paper towels, folded down over edge of slow cooker to absorb moisture. Cover paper towels with cooker lid.
7. Cook on High 3–4 hours, or until toothpick inserted in center of cake comes out clean.
8. Remove can or insert from cooker and allow to cool on rack for 10 minutes. Run knife around edge of cake. Invert onto serving plate.

FALL

Week 9

THIS WEEK'S
Menu

Sunday: French Chicken

Monday: Chicken Cordon Bleu Casserole

Tuesday: Lotsa-Beans Chili

Wednesday: Seven-Layer Casserole

Thursday: Apple Cider Sausage

Friday: Sweet Pepper Burritos

Saturday: Ruth's Split Pea Soup

Recommended Side Dish: Green Bean Tomato Sauté

Special Dessert: Raisin Nut-Stuffed Apples

Shopping List

PROTEIN

4 lbs. skinless, bone-in
  chicken thighs
1 lb. chipped ham
2 lbs. ground beef
2 lbs. bacon
10 sweet Italian sausage
  links

FROZEN

1 qt. frozen green beans

DAIRY and REFRIGERATED

½ lb. grated Swiss cheese
1½ cups shredded cheddar
  cheese
3 oz. cream cheese
2¼ cups milk
5 Tbsp. butter
2 eggs
¾ cup apple cider

PRODUCE

1 lb. baby carrots
1 small onion
4 medium onions
1 large onion
¾ cup chopped onion
1 red onion
2 ribs celery
1½ cups diced celery
2 Tbsp. chopped fresh
  parsley
2 apples
6 baking apples
2 medium sweet red bell
  peppers
1 medium sweet yellow bell
  pepper
1 medium sweet green bell
  pepper
¼ cup chopped green bell
  pepper

Download this shopping list to your
smartphone!
(x.co/ShopList)

2 medium potatoes	1 bag (2¼ cups) dry split
2 cups fresh sliced	peas
mushrooms	salsa

CANNED/DRY GOODS	DO YOU HAVE THESE ON
10¾-oz. can cream of	HAND?
chicken soup	salt
2 15-oz. cans green beans	pepper
2 14½-oz. cans baked beans	dried basil
2 15-oz. cans butter beans	dried marjoram
2 16-oz. cans kidney beans	dry mustard
12-oz. can whole kernel corn	ground cumin
8-oz. can tomato sauce	dried thyme
14½-oz. can diced tomatoes	4 cloves garlic
4-oz. can chopped green	½ cup white cooking wine,
chilies	or chicken stock
1-oz. envelope dry ranch	¾ cup brown sugar
dressing mix	½ cup sugar
8 cups cubed bread	½ cup ketchup
½ cup uncooked rice	maple syrup
¾ cup uncooked brown rice	olive oil
hot dog buns	liquid smoke
6 6-inch whole wheat	raisins
tortillas	3 Tbsp. chopped walnuts

French Chicken

Phyllis Good, Lancaster, PA

Makes 4–6 servings

Prep. Time: 15 minutes
Cooking Time: 4½–5½ hours
Ideal slow-cooker size: 5-qt.

1 lb. baby carrots
2 medium onions, sliced
2 ribs celery, diced
4 cloves garlic, peeled
4 lbs. skinless, bone-in
   chicken thighs
½ cup white cooking wine, or
   chicken stock
1½ tsp. salt
½ tsp. black pepper
1 tsp. dried basil
½ tsp. dried marjoram
2 Tbsp. chopped fresh parsley

1. Place carrots, onions, celery, and garlic in bottom of slow cooker.

2. Lay chicken thighs on top. Pour wine or broth over chicken.

3. Sprinkle with salt, pepper, basil, and marjoram.

4. Cover. Cook on Low 4½–5½ hours, until chicken registers 165°F on a meat thermometer and carrots are tender.

5. Sprinkle with fresh parsley before serving.

Chicken Cordon Bleu Casserole

Marcia S. Myer, Manheim, PA
Rachel King, Castile, NY

Makes 20–24 servings

Prep. Time: 30 minutes
Baking Time: 1 hour

Filling:
8 cups cubed bread
3 Tbsp. butter
1½ cups diced celery
1 small onion, chopped
2 eggs
1¾ cups milk
½ tsp. salt

¼ tsp. pepper
1 lb. chipped ham
½ lb. grated Swiss cheese
2–3 cups cooked, diced
   leftover chicken
10¾-oz. can cream of chicken
   soup
½ cup milk

1. Prepare filling by sautéing celery and onion in butter in saucepan until soft.

2. Place cubed bread in large mixing bowl.

3. Pour sautéed vegetables, eggs, 1¾ cups milk, salt, and pepper over bread.

4. Grease 2 9×13-inch baking pans.

5. Layer half of ham, cheese, and filling into each pan.

6. Layer half of chicken into each pan, distributing evenly over top of filling mixture.

7. In mixing bowl, blend soup and ½ cup milk together.

8. Pour soup mixture over top of chicken.

9. Bake at 350°F for 60 minutes.

Lotsa-Beans Chili

Jean Weller, State College, PA

Makes 12–15 servings

Prep. Time: 25 minutes
Cooking Time: 8–9 hours
Ideal slow-cooker size: 5-qt.

2 lbs. ground beef
1½ lbs. bacon, diced
½ cup chopped onion
½ cup brown sugar
½ cup sugar
½ cup ketchup
2 tsp. dry mustard
1 tsp. salt
½ tsp. pepper
2 15-oz. cans green beans, drained
2 14½-oz. cans baked beans
2 15-oz. cans butter beans, drained
2 16-oz. cans kidney beans, rinsed and drained

1. Brown ground beef and bacon in skillet. Drain.

Reserve 1 lb. of the browned beef in the refrigerator.

2. Combine all ingredients in slow cooker.

3. Cover. Cook on High 1 hour. Reduce heat to Low and cook 8–9 hours.

Seven-Layer Casserole

Phyllis Good, Lancaster, PA

Makes 6–8 servings

Prep. Time: 20 minutes
Cooking Time: 4–6 hours
Ideal slow-cooker size: 4-qt.

½ cup uncooked rice
12-oz. can whole kernel corn, undrained
8-oz. can tomato sauce, *divided*
½ cup water, *divided*
¼ cup chopped onion
¼ cup chopped green bell pepper
1 lbs. leftover browned ground beef
½ tsp. salt
⅛–¼ tsp. pepper, as you like
6–8 slices lean bacon (½ lb.)

1. Grease your slow cooker well. Spread the uncooked rice over the bottom of the cooker. Spoon the corn over top of the rice, including the juice from the corn.

2. In a bowl, mix together 1 can of tomato sauce with ½ cup water. Spoon over the corn. Sprinkle with the onion and green pepper.

3. Place the browned ground beef over the vegetables.

4. Combine the remaining can of tomato sauce with ½ cup water. Stir in the salt and pepper. Spoon over the meat.

5. Cut the bacon slices into fourths and arrange over top.

6. Cover. Cook on Low 4–6 hours, or until the vegetables are as tender as you like them. Uncover the cooker during the last 15 minutes so that the bacon gets a bit crispy.

Apple Cider Sausage

Hope Comerford, Clinton Township, MI

Makes 6–8 servings

Prep. Time: 5 minutes
Cooking Time: 6 hours
Ideal slow-cooker size: 3- to 4-qt.

10 sweet Italian sausage links
2 apples, peeled and cut into wedges
1 red onion, quartered
¾ cup apple cider
1 tsp. maple syrup
hot dog buns

1. Place the sausage links into the crock.

2. Add in the apples and onions, then pour the apple cider and maple syrup over the top.

3. Cover and cook on Low for 6 hours.

4. Serve in hot dog buns.

Sweet Pepper Burritos

Anita King, Bellefontaine, OH

Makes 6 servings

Prep. Time: 35 minutes
Cooking Time: 2–2¼ hours
Baking Time: 10–15 minutes
Ideal slow-cooker size: 5-qt.

¾ cup uncooked brown rice
1¼ cups water
1 medium onion, chopped
2 tsp. ground cumin
½ tsp. black pepper
2 medium sweet red bell peppers, diced
1 medium sweet yellow bell pepper, diced
1 medium sweet green bell pepper, diced
1½ cups cheddar cheese, shredded
3-oz. pkg. cream cheese, cubed
6 whole wheat tortillas, about 6-inch in diameter
salsa, as mild or hot as you like, *optional*

1. Grease interior of slow-cooker crock.
2. Place raw brown rice, water, onion, cumin, and black pepper in crock. Stir until well mixed.
3. Cover. Cook on High for 1¾ hours, or until rice is nearly tender.
4. Stir in diced sweet bell peppers at end of cooking time, along with cheddar and cream cheeses.
5. Cover. Continue cooking on High 30 more minutes, or until rice and peppers are as tender as you like them.
6. Spoon ⅔ cup rice-pepper-cheese mixture onto lower half of each tortilla. Fold in the sides. Then bring up the bottom and roll up.
7. Place each burrito, seam side down, in greased 9x13-inch baking pan.
8. Cover. Bake at 425°F 10–15 minutes.
9. Let stand 4 minutes. Serve with salsa if you wish.

Ruth's Split Pea Soup

Ruth Conrad Liechty, Goshen, IN

Makes 6–8 servings

Prep. Time: 15 minutes
Cooking Time: 6–12 hours
Ideal slow-cooker size: 4-qt.

1 bag (2¼ cups) dry split peas
6 cups water
2 medium potatoes, diced
1 medium onion, chopped
½ tsp. dried marjoram, or thyme
½ tsp. pepper

Green Bean Tomato Sauté (page 295)

leftover Italian sausage, cut
into bite-sized pieces

1. Wash and sort dried peas,
removing any stones. Then
combine all ingredients except
the sausage in slow cooker.
2. Cover. Cook on Low 12
hours or High for 6. The last
hour of cooking, add in the
Italian sausage.

Green Bean Tomato Sauté

Becky S. Frey, Lebanon, PA

Makes 4–6 servings

Prep. Time: 20–30 minutes
Cooking Time: 30 minutes

1–2 Tbsp. olive oil
1 large onion, coarsely
    chopped
2 cups sliced fresh
    mushrooms
14½-oz. can diced tomatoes
1 qt. frozen green beans
4-oz. can green chilies,
    chopped
1-oz. envelope dry ranch
    dressing mix
1 Tbsp. liquid smoke, or to
    taste

1. Pour olive oil into skillet
and sauté onion over low
heat, covered, until onion is
caramelized. Stir occasionally.
2. Add mushrooms. Increase
heat to medium and stir
continually until they begin to
give up their moisture.
3. Add tomatoes, green
beans, chilies, ranch dressing,
and liquid smoke.

4. Cook until beans are as
tender as you like them.

Raisin Nut-Stuffed Apples

Margaret Rich, North Newton, KS

Makes 6 servings

Prep. Time: 15 minutes
Cooking Time: 6–8 hours
Ideal slow-cooker size: 5-qt.

6 baking apples, cored
2 Tbsp. butter, or margarine,
    melted
¼ cup packed brown sugar
¾ cup raisins
3 Tbsp. chopped walnuts
½ cup water

1. Peel a strip around each
apple about one-third of the
way below the stem end to
prevent splitting.
2. Mix together butter and
brown sugar. Stir in raisins
and walnuts. Stuff into apple
cavities.
3. Place apples in slow
cooker. Add water.
4. Cover and cook on Low
6–8 hours.

Week 10

THIS WEEK'S

Menu

Sunday: Easy and Elegant Ham
Monday: Schnitz und Knepp
Tuesday: Ham and Broccoli
Wednesday: Pasta Bean Pot
Thursday: Turkey Slow Cooker
Friday: Turkey Cacciatore
Saturday: Turkey Frame Soup

Recommended Side Dish: Old-Fashioned Stuffing
Special Dessert: Slow-Cooker Pumpkin Pie

Shopping List

PROTEIN

6-lb. fully cooked boneless ham

6-lb. turkey breast

FROZEN

whipped topping

DAIRY and REFRIGERATED

5 eggs

1 stick, plus 5 Tbsp. butter

4½ cups milk

PRODUCE

¾ lb. fresh broccoli, or frozen

1 rib, plus 1½ cups chopped, celery

1 small onion

1½ medium onions

1 green bell pepper

1–2 Tbsp. fresh chopped parsley

3 cups fresh chopped vegetables of your choice

CANNED/DRY GOODS

2 20-oz. cans sliced pineapple

6-oz. jar maraschino cherries

12-oz. jar orange marmalade

10¾-oz. can cream of mushroom soup

8-oz. jar cheese sauce

8-oz. can water chestnuts

14-oz. can stewed or diced tomatoes

15-oz. can whole tomatoes

8-oz. can chopped tomatoes

½ 12-oz. can cannellini beans

Download this shopping list to your smartphone!

(x.co/ShopList)

½ 12-oz. can kidney beans

16-oz. can whole cranberry
  sauce

4-oz. can sliced mushrooms

15-oz. can solid-pack
  pumpkin

12-oz. can evaporated milk

¾–1 lb. dried sweet apples

1¼ cups uncooked long-
  grain rice

4 oz. uncooked elbow
  macaroni

1½ cups uncooked noodles

12-oz. pkg. bread cubes, or
  about 15 slices stale bread

½ cup low-fat buttermilk
  baking mix

1-oz. envelope dry onion
  soup mix

**DO YOU HAVE THESE ON
HAND?**
salt

pepper

paprika

dried oregano

dried parsley

red pepper

dried onion flakes

bay leaf

dried thyme

ground cinnamon

ground ginger

ground nutmeg

cinnamon stick

brown sugar

¾ cup sugar

2 cups flour

baking powder

olive oil

2 cloves garlic

vinegar of your choice

6 oz. chicken broth

2 qts. turkey broth

1 Tbsp. chicken bouillon
  granules

2 Tbsp. finely chopped
  pimentos

2 tsp. tomato paste

Easy and Elegant Ham

Lorraine Pflederer, Goshen, IN

Makes 18–20 servings

Prep. Time: 10 minutes
Cooking Time: 6–7 hours
Standing Time: 10–15 minutes
Ideal slow-cooker size: 5-qt.

2 20-oz. cans sliced
  pineapple, *divided*
6-lb. fully cooked boneless
  ham (about 6 lbs.), halved
6-oz. jar maraschino cherries,
  well drained
12-oz. jar orange marmalade

1. Drain pineapple,
reserving juice. Set juice
aside.
2. Place half of pineapple in
ungreased slow cooker.
3. Top with ham. Add
cherries, remaining
pineapple, and reserved juice.
4. Spoon marmalade over
ham.
5. Cover. Cook on Low
6–7 hours or until heated
through. Remove to serving
platter and let stand for 10–15
minutes before slicing.
6. Serve pineapple and
cherries over sliced ham.

Schnitz und Knepp

Jean Robinson, Cinnaminson, NJ

Makes 6 servings

Prep. Time: 20 minutes
Soaking Time: 2–3 hours
Cooking Time: 5¼ hours
Ideal slow-cooker size: 4-qt.

Schnitz:
¾–1 lb. dried sweet apples
  (also known as "schnitz")
3 lbs. ham slices, cut into
  2-inch cubes, from leftovers
2 Tbsp. brown sugar
1 cinnamon stick

Knepp (dumplings):
2 cups flour
4 tsp. baking powder
1 egg, well beaten
3 Tbsp. butter, melted
scant ½ cup milk
1 tsp. salt
¼ tsp. pepper

1. Cover apples with water
in large bowl and let soak for
a few hours.
2. Place ham cubes in slow
cooker. Cover with water.
3. Cover cooker. Cook on
High 2 hours.
4. Add apples and water
in which they have been
soaking.
5. Add brown sugar and
cinnamon stick. Mix until
sugar dissolves.
6. Cover. Cook on Low 3
hours.
7. Combine dumpling
ingredients in bowl. Drop
into hot liquid in cooker by
tablespoonfuls.

8. Turn cooker to High.
Cover. Do not lift lid for 15
minutes.
9. Serve piping hot on a
large platter

Ham and Broccoli

Dede Peterson, Rapid City, SD

Makes 6–8 servings

Prep. Time: 20 minutes
Cooking Time: 3¼–4¼ hours
Ideal slow-cooker size: 5-qt.

¾ lb. fresh broccoli, chopped,
  or 10-oz. pkg. frozen
  chopped broccoli
10¾-oz. can cream of
  mushroom soup
8-oz. jar cheese sauce
2½ cups milk
1¼ cups uncooked long-grain
  rice
1 rib celery, sliced
⅛ tsp. pepper
3 cups leftover cooked ham,
  cubed
8-oz. can water chestnuts,
  drained and sliced
½ tsp. paprika

1. Combine all ingredients
except ham, water chestnuts,
and paprika in slow cooker.
2. Cover. Cook on High 3–4
hours.
3. Stir in ham and water
chestnuts. Cook 15–20
minutes, or until heated
through. Let stand 10
minutes before serving.
4. Sprinkle with paprika
just before serving.

Pasta Bean Pot

Donna Conto, Saylorsburg, PA

Makes 4–6 servings

Prep. Time: 10–15 minutes
Cooking Time: 4–5 hours
Ideal slow-cooker size: 4-qt.

½ Tbsp. olive oil
½ medium onion, chopped
1 garlic clove, minced
½ tsp. vinegar of your choice
4 oz. uncooked elbow
    macaroni
14-oz. can stewed, or diced,
    tomatoes
½ of a 12-oz. can cannellini
    beans, undrained
½ of a 12-oz. can kidney
    beans, undrained
6 oz. chicken broth
½ tsp. dried oregano
½ tsp. dried parsley
dash red pepper

1. Put all ingredients in
slow cooker. Mix well.
2. Cover. Cook on Low 4–5
hours, or until macaroni are
tender but not mushy.

Turkey Slow Cooker

Arlene Leaman Kliewer,
Lakewood, CO

Makes 10–12 servings

Prep. Time: 5 minutes
Cooking Time: 8 hours
Ideal slow-cooker size: 7-qt.

6-lb. turkey breast
1 envelope dry onion soup
    mix
16-oz. can whole berry
    cranberry sauce

1. Place turkey in slow
cooker.
2. Combine soup mix and
cranberry sauce in bowl.
Spread over turkey.
3. Cover. Cook on Low 8
hours.

Turkey Cacciatore

Dorothy M. Van Deest,
Memphis, TN

Makes 6 servings

Prep. Time: 20 minutes
Cooking Time: 4 hours
Ideal slow-cooker size: 4-qt.

2½ cups cut-up leftover
    cooked turkey
1 tsp. salt
dash of pepper
1 Tbsp. dried onion flakes
1 green bell pepper, seeded
    and finely chopped
1 clove garlic, finely chopped
15-oz. can whole tomatoes,
    mashed
4-oz. can sliced mushrooms,
    drained
2 tsp. tomato paste
1 bay leaf
¼ tsp. dried thyme
2 Tbsp. finely chopped
    pimento

1. Combine all ingredients
well in slow cooker.
2. Cover. Cook on Low 4
hours.

Serving Suggestion: Serve
over rice or pasta. Or drain off
most liquid and serve in taco
shells.

Turkey Frame Soup

Joyce Zuercher, Hesston, KS

Makes 6 servings

Prep. Time: 40 minutes
Cooking Time: 3¼–4½ hours
Ideal slow-cooker size: 6-qt.

2 cups cooked leftover turkey, diced
2 qts. turkey broth
1 medium onion, diced
½–¾ tsp. salt, or to taste
8-oz. can chopped tomatoes
1 Tbsp. chicken bouillon granules
1 tsp. dried thyme
⅛ tsp. pepper
1½ tsp. dried oregano
3 cups chopped fresh vegetables (any combination of sliced celery, carrots, onions, rutabaga, broccoli, cauliflower, mushrooms, and more)
1½ cups uncooked noodles

1. Place turkey, broth, onion, salt, tomatoes, bouillon granules, thyme, pepper, oregano, and vegetables into slow cooker. Stir.
2. Cover. Cook on Low 3–4 hours, or until vegetables are nearly done.
3. About 15 to 30 minutes before serving time, stir in noodles. Cover. Cook on Low. If noodles are thin and small, they'll cook in 15 minutes or less. If heavier, they may need 30 minutes to become tender.
4. Stir well before serving.

Old-Fashioned Stuffing

Elaine Rineer, Lancaster, PA
Rhonda Freed, Croghan, NY

Makes 6 servings

Prep. Time: 20–30 minutes
Cooking Time: 5 hours
Ideal slow-cooker size: 4-qt.

1 stick (8 Tbsp.) butter
1½ cups chopped celery
1 small onion, chopped
12-oz. pkg. bread cubes, or about 15 slices stale bread
½–¾ tsp. salt
⅛ tsp. pepper
1–2 Tbsp. fresh parsley, chopped
2 eggs
1½ cups milk

1. Melt butter in skillet. Sauté celery and onion in it.
2. Meanwhile, spray interior of slow cooker with nonstick cooking spray. Place bread cubes, salt, pepper, and parsley in cooker.
3. Pour in sautéed vegetables, eggs, and milk. Stir together gently until well mixed.
4. Cover. Cook on High 1 hour. Stir.
5. Cover. Cook on High 4 more hours.

Slow-Cooker Pumpkin Pie

Colleen Heatwole, Burton, MI

Makes 5–6 servings

Prep. Time: 10 minutes
Cooking Time: 3–4 hours
Cooling Time: 2–4 hours
Ideal slow-cooker size: 3-qt.

15-oz. can solid-pack pumpkin
12-oz. can evaporated milk
¾ cup sugar
½ cup low-fat buttermilk baking mix
2 eggs, beaten
¼ stick (2 Tbsp.) butter, melted
1½ tsp. cinnamon
¾ tsp. ground ginger
¼ tsp. ground nutmeg
whipped topping

1. Spray slow cooker with cooking spray.
2. Mix all ingredients together in slow cooker, except whipped topping.
3. Cover. Cook on Low 3–4 hours, or until a toothpick inserted in center comes out clean.
4. Allow to cool to warm, or chill, before serving with whipped topping.

FALL

Week 11

THIS WEEK'S
Menu

Sunday: Butter and Sage Cornish Hens
Monday: Chicken Corn Soup
Tuesday: Zucchini Torte
Wednesday: Dilled Pot Roast
Thursday: Spicy Scrumptious Sausage
Friday: Chorizo and Beef Enchilada Casserole
Saturday: Sausage Tortellini

Recommended Side Dish: Potato Cheese Puff
Special Dessert: Apple Caramel Pie

Shopping List

PROTEIN

4–6 Cornish game hens

3–3½ lb. beef pot roast

8 spicy Italian sausage links

12 oz. chorizo

DAIRY and REFRIGERATED

10–14 Tbsp. butter

6 eggs

1 cup sour cream

1 cup milk

2-crust pkg. refrigerated pie dough

½ cup grated Parmesan cheese

2 cups shredded Mexican-blend cheese

2¼ cups Velveeta

16-oz. package tortellini

PRODUCE

3 medium onions

1 cup chopped onion

1 small onion

2 carrots

1 cup grated carrots

1 cup thinly sliced carrots

2 ribs celery

14 medium potatoes

½ cup chopped fresh Italian parsley

5 cups diced zucchini

¾ cup sliced zucchini, *optional*

3 Tbsp. chopped fresh parsley

2 cups diced fresh tomatoes

CANNED/DRY GOODS

12-oz. can cream-style corn

Download this shopping list to your smartphone!
(x.co/ShopList)

14-oz. can whole kernel corn	pepper
16-oz. can kidney beans	garlic powder
16-oz. can chili beans	dried sage
4-oz. can mild or hot diced green chilies	mixed dried herbs
	dried marjoram
3 14-oz. cans diced tomatoes	dried dill weed
16-oz. can tomato sauce	dried basil
10-oz. can mild green enchilada sauce	dried oregano
	ground cinnamon
10-oz. can mild red enchilada sauce	olive oil
	3 cloves garlic
1½ cup biscuit baking mix	vinegar of your choice
2 22-oz. cans apple pie filling	flour
⅓ cup tomato sauce	5 cups chicken or beef stock
long-grain rice	3 cups chicken stock
9 small flour tortillas	
12 caramels	**SPIRITS**
	½–1 cup white wine, or chicken broth
DO YOU HAVE THESE ON HAND?	
	¾ cup red wine
salt	

Butter and Sage Cornish Hens

Hope Comerford,
Clinton Township, MI

Makes 4–6 servings

Prep. Time: 10 minutes
Cooking Time: 7–8 hours
Ideal slow-cooker size: 6- to 7-qt.
(or use 2 5- to 7-qts. if they
don't fit in 1 slow cooker)

2–4 Tbsp. olive oil
salt and pepper, to taste
4–6 Cornish game hens
½–1 cup white wine, or
   chicken broth
4–8 Tbsp. butter, cut into
   pieces
2–4 Tbsp. olive oil
garlic powder and sage, to
   taste

1. Warm the olive oil in a skillet.

2. Meanwhile, salt and pepper all sides of the Cornish hens.

3. Place the Cornish hens breasts down in the skillet and brown them a bit. Turn and brown the underside as well.

4. Pour the wine or chicken broth into the bottom of your crock, then place the hens in the crock as well.

5. Season them with the sage and garlic powder. Place the pieces of butter on top of your Cornish hens as well.

6. Cover and cook on Low for 7–8 hours.

Chicken Corn Soup

Eleanor Larson, Glen Lyon, PA

Makes 4–6 servings

Prep. Time: 15 minutes
Cooking Time: 8–9 hours
Ideal slow-cooker size: 4-qt.

1 medium onion, chopped
1 garlic clove, minced
2 carrots, sliced
2 ribs celery, chopped
2 medium potatoes, cubed
1 tsp. mixed dried herbs
⅓ cup tomato sauce
12-oz. can cream-style corn
14-oz. can whole kernel corn
3 cups chicken stock
leftover diced Cornish hen
   meat
¼ cup chopped fresh Italian
   parsley

Zucchini Torte (page 309)

1 tsp. salt
¼ tsp. pepper

1. Combine all ingredients except parsley, salt, and pepper in slow cooker.
2. Cover. Cook on Low 8–9 hours, or until chicken is tender.
3. Add parsley and seasonings 30 minutes before serving.

Zucchini Torte

Mary Clair Wenger,
Kimmswick, MO

Makes 8 servings

Prep. Time: 25 minutes
Cooking Time: 4–5 hours
Ideal slow-cooker size: 4-qt.

5 cups diced zucchini
1 cup grated carrots
1 small onion, diced finely
1½ cups biscuit baking mix
½ cup grated Parmesan cheese
4 eggs, beaten
¼ cup olive oil
2 tsp. dried marjoram
½ tsp. salt
pepper, to taste

1. Grease interior of slow-cooker crock.
2. Mix together all ingredients. Pour into greased slow cooker.
3. Cover and cook on Low for 4–5 hours, until set. Remove lid last 30 minutes to allow excess moisture to evaporate.
4. Serve hot or at room temperature.

Dilled Pot Roast

C. J. Slagle, Roann, IN

Makes 6 servings

Prep. Time: 5 minutes
Cooking Time: 7¼–9¼ hours
Ideal slow-cooker size: 4- to 5-qt.

3–3½-lb. beef pot roast
1 tsp. salt
¼ tsp. pepper
2 tsp. dried dill weed, *divided*
¼ cup water
1 Tbsp. vinegar of your choice
3 Tbsp. flour
½ cup water
1 cup sour cream

1. Sprinkle both sides of meat with salt, pepper, and 1 tsp. dill. Place in slow cooker. Add water and vinegar.
2. Cover. Cook on Low 7–9 hours, or until tender. Remove meat from pot. Turn to High.
3. Dissolve flour in water. Stir into meat drippings. Stir in additional 1 tsp. dill. Cook on High 5 minutes. Stir in sour cream. Cook on High another 5 minutes.

Spicy Scrumptious Sausage

Hope Comerford,
Clinton Township, MI

Makes 8 servings

Prep. Time: 5 minutes
Cooking Time: 6 hours
Ideal slow-cooker size: 4-qt.

8 spicy Italian sausage links
16-oz. can red kidney beans, drained, rinsed
16-oz. can chili beans
4-oz. can mild or hot diced green chilies
14-oz. can diced tomatoes
1 medium-onion, chopped
1 tsp. salt
⅛ tsp. pepper
long-grain rice

1. Place all ingredients into the crock except the rice.
2. Cook on Low for 6 hours.
3. Serve over cooked rice.

Chorizo and Beef Enchilada Casserole

Hope Comerford,
Clinton Township, MI

Makes 8 servings

Prep. Time: 10 minutes
Cooking Time: 4–6 hours
Ideal slow-cooker size: 6-qt.

9 small flour tortillas
2 cups leftover pot roast
1 medium onion, chopped
2 cups diced fresh tomato
12 oz. chorizo, browned
10-oz. can mild red enchilada sauce
2 cups shredded Mexican-blend cheese
10-oz. can mild green enchilada sauce

1. Spray your crock liberally with nonstick spray.

2. Place 3 tortillas into the bottom of your crock. You may need to cut them to make them fit.

3. Layer in half of the pot roast, half of the onions, half of the tomatoes, and half of the chorizo.

Pour half of the red enchilada sauce over the top. Top it with ½ cup of the shredded cheese.

4. Do this whole process once more, then top it with another layer of tortillas, the entire can of green enchilada sauce, and the remaining cup of shredded cheese.

5. Cover and cook on Low for 4–6 hours.

Sausage Tortellini

Christie Detamore-Hunsberger,
Harrisonburg, VA

Makes 8 servings

Prep. Time: 25–30 minutes
Cooking Time: 1½–2½ hours
Ideal slow-cooker size: 6-qt.

leftover sausage
1 cup chopped onions
2 cloves garlic, minced
5 cups beef or chicken broth
¾ cup water
¾ cup red wine
2 14¾-oz. cans diced tomatoes, undrained
1 cup thinly sliced carrots
¾ tsp. dried basil
¾ tsp. dried oregano
16-oz. can tomato sauce
¾ cup sliced zucchini, *optional*
16-oz. pkg. tortellini
3 Tbsp. chopped fresh parsley

1. Add leftover sausage, onions, garlic, broth, water, wine, tomatoes, carrots, basil, oregano, and tomato sauce to crock. Stir together well.

2. Add zucchini if you wish, and tortellini.

3. Cover. Cook on High 1½–2½ hours, or until pasta is as tender as you like it, but not mushy.

4. Stir in parsley and serve.

Potato Cheese Puff

Mary Sommerfeld, Lancaster, PA

Makes 10 servings

Prep. Time: 45 minutes
Cooking Time: 2½–4 hours
Ideal slow-cooker size: 4- to 5-qt.

12 medium potatoes, boiled
   and mashed
1 cup milk
6 Tbsp. butter
¾ tsp. salt
2¼ cups Velveeta, cubed
2 eggs, beaten

1. Combine all ingredients. Pour into slow cooker.

2. Cover. Cook on High 2½ hours, or on Low 3–4 hours.

Apple Caramel Pie

Sue Hamilton, Minooka, IL

Makes 8–10 servings

Prep. Time: 5 minutes
Cooking Time: 3 hours
Ideal slow-cooker size: 4- to 5-qt.

2-crust pkg. refrigerated pie
   dough
2 22-oz. cans apple pie filling
1 tsp. ground cinnamon
12 caramels

1. Press one crust into half the bottom of a greased cold slow cooker, and an inch or so up half its interior side. Overlap by ¼ inch the second crust with the first crust in center of slow cooker bottom. Press remainder of second crust an inch or so up the remaining side of the cooker. Press seams flat where two crusts meet.

2. Cover. Cook on High 1½ hours.

3. In a bowl, mix together pie filling, cinnamon, and caramels.

4. Pour mixture into hot crust.

5. Cover. Cook on High an additional 1½ hours.

FALL

Week 12

THIS WEEK'S
Menu

Sunday: Balsamic-Glazed Pork Ribs
Monday: Enchilada Quinoa Casserole
Tuesday: Easy Ranch Chicken
Wednesday: White Chicken Chili
Thursday: Coney Dogs
Friday: Pasta à la Carbonara
Saturday: Coney Fries

Recommended Side Dish: Baked Stuffed Tomatoes
Special Dessert: Bay Pound Cake

Shopping List

PROTEIN
3 lbs. pork ribs
3 lbs. frozen boneless, skinless chicken breasts
2 lbs. ground beef
2 lbs. hot dogs, or fresh smoked sausage
1½ pkgs. thick-cut bacon

FROZEN
30-oz. bag frozen fries (whatever cut you prefer)

DAIRY and REFRIGERATED
4 oz. cottage cheese
1 stick plus 3 Tbsp. butter
½ cup milk
2–4 cups shredded cheese, your choice of flavor
1 cup shredded Mexican-blend cheese
1¼ cup grated Parmesan cheese
8-oz. block pepper jack cheese
8-oz. block Monterey Jack cheese
2 eggs plus 2 egg yolks
sour cream, *optional*

PRODUCE
1 large onion
1 medium onion
2 cups diced onions
2 green onions
6 medium tomatoes
½ cup plus 2 tsp. flat-leaf parsley
2 tsp. chopped fresh basil
2 tsp. chopped fresh oregano
avocado, *optional*

Download this shopping list to your smartphone!
(x.co/ShopList)

diced tomatoes, *optional*	pepper
chopped fresh cilantro,	crushed red pepper
optional	kosher salt
	dried rosemary
CANNED/DRY GOODS	fennel seeds
30 oz. red enchilada sauce	dried sage
15-oz. can black beans	dried thyme
15-oz. can corn	paprika
14-oz. can diced tomatoes	ground coriander
with green chilies	ground allspice
16-oz. jar salsa	ground cumin
16-oz. can tomato sauce	chili powder
1 cup uncooked quinoa	garlic powder
1 lb. rotini pasta, uncooked	bay leaves
1 pkg. dry ranch dressing	4 cloves garlic
mix	olive oil
1 cup dry navy beans	balsamic vinegar
hot dog rolls	½ cup chicken broth
¾ cup fine bread crumbs	1 chicken bouillon cube
tortilla chips, *optional*	prepared mustard
	¾ cup sugar
DO YOU HAVE THESE ON	1 cup all-purpose flour
HAND?	½ cup whole wheat flour
salt	baking powder

Balsamic-Glazed Pork Ribs

Phyllis Good, Lancaster, PA

Makes 6–8 servings

Prep. Time: 30 minutes
Cooking Time: 4–6 hours
Standing Time: 2–12 hours
Ideal slow-cooker size: 6-qt.

2 Tbsp. olive oil
½ tsp. dried rosemary
1 Tbsp. kosher salt
1 Tbsp. fennel seeds
1 tsp. freshly ground pepper
½ tsp. dried sage
¼ tsp. dried thyme
1 tsp. paprika
pinch–1 tsp. crushed red
  pepper, depending on the
  heat you like
½ tsp. ground coriander
¼ tsp. ground allspice
3 lbs. pork ribs
3 Tbsp. balsamic vinegar

1. In a small bowl, combine olive oil, rosemary, salt, fennel seeds, pepper, sage, thyme, paprika, red pepper, coriander, and allspice.

2. Rub spice paste all over ribs and let stand at room temperature for 2 hours, or refrigerate overnight.

3. Place ribs in slow cooker, cutting if needed to fit.

4. Cook on Low for 4–6 hours, until tender.

5. Remove ribs from slow cooker and place on rimmed baking sheet. Preheat broiler. Brush meaty side of ribs with balsamic vinegar and broil 6 inches from heat until browned, about 2 minutes.

6. Let stand for 5 minutes, then cut between ribs, or serve in slabs.

Enchilada Quinoa Casserole

Hope Comerford,
Clinton Township, MI

Makes 4–6 servings

Prep. Time: 5 minutes
Cooking Time: 4 hours
Ideal slow-cooker size: 3-qt.

30 oz. red enchilada sauce,
  divided

15-oz. can black beans,
  drained and rinsed
15-oz. can corn, drained
14-oz. can diced tomatoes
  with green chilies
1 cup uncooked quinoa
leftover pork, chopped into
  bite-sized pieces
4 oz. cottage cheese (blended
  until smooth)
1 tsp. salt
⅛ tsp. pepper
1 cup shredded Mexican-
  blend cheese

Optional Toppings:
avocado
diced tomatoes
chopped fresh cilantro
sour cream

1. Add half of the enchilada sauce, the beans, corn, diced tomatoes, quinoa, pork, blended cottage cheese, salt, and pepper to a greased slow cooker and stir.

2. Pour the remaining enchilada sauce over the top. Top with the shredded cheese.

3. Cover and cook on Low for 4 hours.

4. Serve with any of the optional toppings you desire.

Easy Ranch Chicken

Hope Comerford,
Clinton Township, MI

Makes 8 servings

Prep. Time: 5 minutes
Cooking Time: 6–7 hours
Ideal slow-cooker size: 4-qt.

1 medium onion, cut in half and then sliced into half rings
3 lb. frozen boneless, skinless chicken breasts
1 pkg. dry ranch dressing mix
1½ cups warm water

1. Place the onion into the slow cooker, put the chicken on top, then sprinkle with the ranch dressing.

2. Pour the cup of warm water over the top, being careful not to wash off the dressing.

3. Cook on Low for 6–7 hours.

White Chicken Chili

Hope Comerford,
Clinton Township, MI

Makes 4 servings

Prep. Time: 10 minutes
Soaking Time: overnight
Cooking Time: 7–9 hours
Ideal slow-cooker size: 4- to 6-qt.

1 cup dry navy beans
4 cups water
½ cup chicken broth
16-oz. jar salsa
1 large onion, chopped
1 Tbsp. ground cumin
½ tsp. salt
½ tsp. pepper
8 oz. pepper jack cheese, cut into chunks
8 oz. Monterey Jack cheese, cut into chunks
leftover chicken, chopped into bite-sized pieces
tortilla chips, *optional*

1. Soak the navy beans in a large bowl or pot overnight. Make sure to cover them with about 4 inches of water. In the morning, drain and rinse the beans.

2. Pour the beans and 4 cups of water into your slow cooker. Add the chicken broth, salsa, onion, cumin, salt, and pepper to crock pot. Stir.

3. Cook on Low for 6–8 hours.

4. The last hour, add the chicken Monterey Jack and pepper jack cheese and stir.

5. Switch your slow cooker to High for 1 hour.

6. Stir and serve with crushed tortilla chips on top or on the side if you wish.

Coney Dogs

Anita Troyer, Fairview, MI

Makes 8–10 servings

Prep. Time: 30 minutes
Cooking Time: 3 hours
Ideal slow-cooker size: 4-qt.

2 lbs. ground beef
2 cups diced onions
2 cloves garlic, crushed
2 lbs. hot dogs, or fresh or smoked sausage, cut into 5-inch lengths
2 Tbsp. chili powder
1½ Tbsp. prepared mustard
16-oz. can tomato sauce
¾ cup water
hot dog rolls

1. Grease interior of slow-cooker crock.

2. If you have time, brown beef, onion, and garlic together in a skillet.

3. When browned, place in crock.

4. If you're using fresh sausage, brown in drippings in skillet. Place in crock.

5. Stir chili powder, mustard, tomato sauce, and water into meat in crock. Mix well.

6. Cover. Cook on Low for 2 hours.

7. Stir in hot dogs or fresh sausage. Cook on Low another hour, uncovered so sauce can reduce.

8. Serve in rolls.

Pasta à la Carbonara

Hope Comerford,
Clinton Township, MI

Makes 8 servings

Prep. Time: 10 minutes
Cooking Time: 8 hours
Ideal slow-cooker size: 4- to 6-qt.

1 pkg. thick-cut bacon, sliced
into bite-sized pieces
1 chicken bouillon cube
2 tsp. garlic powder
1 tsp. (or less depending on
the level of heat you prefer)
crushed red pepper flakes
1 lb. rotini pasta
¼ cup of pasta water (the
water you cook the pasta in)
2 egg yolks
½ tsp. pepper
¼ cup grated Parmesan
cheese
½ cup flat-leaf parsley,
chopped

1. Place the cut-up bacon in
the bottom of your crock. Try
to separate it as much as you
can so the pieces are not all
completely stuck together. Cover
and cook on Low for 7 hours.
2. The last 30–45 minutes
of cooking, turn your slow
cooker up to High and add
your bouillon cube, garlic
powder, and crushed red
pepper flakes. Give it a stir.
3. Cook your pasta according
to the package instructions.
When your pasta is done,
reserve ¼ cup of water.
4. In a bowl, mix together
the egg yolks, pepper, and
Parmesan cheese. Next, whisk

in the ¼ cup pasta water to
temper your egg yolks.
5. Pour your pasta into the
slow cooker, pour the egg/
Parmesan mixture over the
top, and toss in the parsley.
Mix all together.

Coney Fries

Hope Comerford,
Clinton Township, MI

Makes 6 servings

Prep. Time: 10 minutes
Cooking Time: 30 minutes

30-oz. bag of frozen fries
(whatever cut/style you like)
leftover chili
2–4 cups shredded cheese,
your choice of flavor
6 slices bacon, cooked and
chopped
2 green onions, chopped

1. Cook the fries according
to the package instructions.
2. Meanwhile, warm the
leftover chili.
3. When the fries are
cooked, top them with the
chili and shredded cheese. Put
them into a 400°F oven for
10–15 minutes, or until the
cheese is all melted.
4. Top them with the bacon
pieces and green onions.

Baked Stuffed Tomatoes

Leslie Scott, Troy, NY

Makes 6 servings

Prep. Time: 30 minutes
Cooking Time: 3–4 hours
Ideal slow-cooker size: 5-qt.

6 medium tomatoes
3 Tbsp. butter, melted
2 tsp. chopped fresh basil
2 tsp. chopped fresh oregano
2 tsp. chopped fresh flat-leaf parsley
2 cloves garlic, minced
1 cup grated Parmesan cheese
¾ cup fine bread crumbs
salt and pepper, to taste

1. Remove cores from tomatoes, and cut away an additional inch or so underneath to make a little cavity in each tomato.
2. Mix together butter, herbs, garlic, Parmesan, bread crumbs, and salt and pepper.
3. Gently stuff each tomato with mixture.
4. Set tomatoes in lightly greased slow cooker.
5. Cover and cook on Low for 3–4 hours, until tomatoes are soft and hot through.

Bay Pound Cake

Nancy J. Reppert,
Mechanicsburg, PA

Makes 12 servings

Prep. Time: 30 minutes
Cooking Time: 3–4 hours
Ideal slow-cooker size: 6-qt.

4 bay leaves
½ cup milk
1 stick butter, softened
¾ cup sugar
2 eggs, room temperature
1 cup all-purpose flour
½ cup whole wheat flour
¼ tsp. salt
1 tsp. baking powder

1. Mix together bay leaves and milk in saucepan. Heat until milk is steaming hot, stirring occasionally. Set aside to cool to room temperature.
2. When milk is cooled, beat butter until fluffy.
3. Add sugar and beat again. Add eggs and beat again.
4. Separately, stir together flours, salt, and baking powder. Stir gently into butter mixture until just barely blended.
5. Strain bay leaves from milk. Add milk to batter, stirring until just mixed. Do not overmix.
6. Prepare an 8x4-inch loaf pan by greasing and flouring. It should fit into your slow cooker without touching the sides. Place a jar lid or ring or trivet on the floor of the crock so the loaf pan will not sit directly on the floor of the crock.
7. Pour batter into prepared pan. Place pan on jar lid/ring/trivet.
8. Cover slow cooker and prop the lid open at one end with a wooden chopstick or wooden spoon handle.
9. Cook on High for 3–4 hours, until tester inserted in middle of cake comes out clean.
10. Wearing oven gloves to protect your knuckles, remove hot pan from cooker. Allow to cool 10 minutes before running a knife around the edge and turning cake out onto a cooling rack. Serve warm or room temperature, plain or with saucy fruit.

Week 13

THIS WEEK'S
Menu

Sunday: Sausage Breakfast Casserole
Monday: Tarragon Chicken
Tuesday: Italian Wedding Soup
Wednesday: BBQ Meat Loaf
Thursday: Chicken Alfredo
Friday: BBQ Burgers
Saturday: Black Bean Burritos

Recommended Side Dish: Polenta in a Crock
Special Dessert: Chocolate Nut Clusters from the Crock

Shopping List

PROTEIN

1 lb. bulk sausage

1½ lbs. lean ground pork

½ lb. spicy pork sausage

8 boneless, skinless chicken
   thighs

3 lbs. lean ground beef

½ lb. ground beef or turkey

FROZEN

32-oz. pkg. frozen shredded
   hash brown potatoes

DAIRY and REFRIGERATED

3½ cups shredded cheese,
   your choice of flavor

¼–½ cups plus 2 Tbsp.
   grated Parmesan cheese

16 eggs

1½ sticks butter

½ cup milk

3 cups heavy cream

cheese slices, *optional*

PRODUCE

6 green onions

¼ cup diced red bell pepper

2 medium onions

1 Tbsp. fresh chopped
   tarragon

¼–½ cup fresh chopped
   parsley

1 cup chopped spinach

hot chilies

chopped lettuce

chopped tomatoes

lettuce, *optional*

CANNED/DRY GOODS

14-oz. can diced tomatoes

½ cup bread crumbs

⅔ cup uncooked pasta

Download this shopping list to your
smartphone!
(x.co/ShopList)

dry pasta	red pepper flakes
hamburger buns	garlic powder
2 cups dried black beans	dried oregano
⅓ cup salsa	chili powder
6–8 flour tortillas	12 cloves garlic
1½ lbs. pkg. almond bark	flour
4-oz. pkg. German chocolate bar	½–¾ cup almond flour or all-purpose flour
8 oz. dark chocolate chips	cornstarch
8 oz. peanut butter chips	1 cup coarsely ground cornmeal
1 lb. salted peanuts	
1 lb. unsalted peanuts	92 oz. chicken broth
relish, sweet or dill, *optional*	2 cups barbecue sauce
pickles, sweet or dill, *optional*	ketchup, *optional*
	mustard, *optional*
DO YOU HAVE THESE ON HAND?	mayonnaise, *optional*
salt	**SPIRITS**
pepper	½ cup dry white wine
dried tarragon	

Sausage Breakfast Casserole

Shelia Heil, Lancaster, PA

Makes 8–10 servings

Prep. Time: 20 minutes
Cooking Time: 4–8 hours
Ideal slow-cooker size: 6-qt.

32-oz. pkg. frozen shredded hash brown potatoes
1 lb. bulk sausage, cooked and drained
2 cups shredded cheese of your choice
14-oz. can diced tomatoes, drained
6 green onions, sliced
¼ cup diced red bell pepper
12 eggs
½ cup milk
½ tsp. salt
¼ tsp. ground black pepper

1. Place half of potatoes in lightly greased slow cooker.
2. Top with half the sausage, half the cheese, half the tomatoes, half the green onions, and half the bell pepper.
3. Repeat layers.
4. Beat eggs, milk, salt, and pepper in mixing bowl until well combined.
5. Pour evenly over potato-sausage mixture.
6. Cover and cook on Low for 6–8 hours or on High for 4 hours, until eggs have set and casserole is firm in the middle.

Tarragon Chicken

Cassius L. Chapman, Tucker, GA

Makes 6 servings

Prep. Time: 15–20 minutes
Cooking Time: 4 hours
Ideal slow-cooker size: 5-qt.

8 boneless, skinless chicken thighs
¾ tsp. salt, *divided*
½ tsp. black pepper, coarsely ground
1 tsp. dried tarragon
2 Tbsp. chopped onion
½ cup dry white wine
2 Tbsp. butter
2 Tbsp. flour
1 cup heavy cream
1 Tbsp. chopped fresh tarragon

1. Grease interior of slow-cooker crock.

2. Place thighs in cooker. If you need to create a second layer, stagger the pieces so they don't directly overlap each other.

3. In a small bowl, mix together ½ tsp. salt, pepper, dried tarragon, chopped onion, and wine.

4. Spoon over thighs, making sure to top those on both levels with the sauce.

5. Cover. Cook on Low for 4 hours, or until instant-read meat thermometer registers 160–165°F when stuck in the thighs.

6. Close to end of cooking time, melt butter in skillet or small saucepan with the cooking juices. Blend in flour and ¼ tsp. salt. Cook, stirring continuously over heat for 1–2 minutes to take the raw flour taste away.

7. Gradually pour in cream, stirring continuously over medium heat until sauce thickens.

8. To serve, place thighs on platter. Spoon sauce over. Sprinkle with chopped fresh tarragon leaves.

Italian Wedding Soup

Janie Steele, Moore, OK

Makes 6 servings

Prep. Time: 30 minutes
Cooking Time: 3–7 hours
Ideal slow-cooker size: 3- to 4-qt.

2 eggs
½ cup bread crumbs
¼ cup chopped fresh parsley
2 Tbsp. grated Parmesan cheese
3 cloves garlic, minced
¼ tsp. red pepper flakes
½ lb. ground beef or turkey
½ lb. spicy pork sausage, casings removed
2 32-oz. cartons chicken broth
salt and pepper, to taste
⅔ cup uncooked pasta
1 cup chopped fresh spinach

1. Mix eggs, bread crumbs, parsley, Parmesan, garlic, red pepper flakes, ground meat, and sausage.

2. Form mixture into 1-inch meatballs. Brown in skillet or oven.

3. Transfer meatballs to slow cooker. Add chicken broth, salt, pepper, and pasta.

4. Cook on High for 3–4 hours or Low 6–7, adding spinach 30 minutes before end of cooking.

BBQ Meat Loaf

Marjorie Nolt, Denver, PA

Makes 10 servings

Prep. Time: 30 minutes
Cooking Time: 5–6 hours
Ideal slow-cooker size: 6-qt. oval

3 lbs. lean ground beef
1½ lbs. lean ground pork
¾ cup finely chopped onion
½–¾ cup almond, or all-
    purpose, flour
1½ tsp. salt
1 tsp. black pepper
2 tsp. garlic powder
2 large eggs
1 cup of your favorite
    barbecue sauce

1. Grease interior of slow-cooker crock.

2. Make a tinfoil sling for your slow cooker so you can lift the cooked meat loaf out easily. Begin by folding a strip of tinfoil accordion-fashion so that it's about 1½–2 inches wide, and long enough to fit from the top edge of the crock, down inside and up the other side, plus a 2-inch overhang on each side of the cooker. Make a second strip exactly like the first.

3. Place the one strip in the crock, running from end to end. Place the second strip in the crock, running from side to side. The 2 strips should form a cross in the bottom of the crock.

4. In a large bowl, mix all ingredients together, except barbecue sauce. Mix well with your hands until fully combined. Set aside half of the mixture for later this week.

5. Form the remaining meat mixture into a loaf and place into your crock, centering it where the 2 foil strips cross.

6. Cover. Cook on Low 3–4 hours.

7. Thirty minutes before end of cooking time, brush top and sides of loaf with about ⅓ cup barbecue sauce.

8. Use foil handles to lift meat loaf out of the crock and onto a serving platter. Let stand 10–15 minutes to allow meat to gather its juices.

9. Slice and serve with remaining barbecue sauce.

Chicken Alfredo

Hope Comerford,
Clinton Township, MI

Makes 24 servings

Prep. Time: 5 minutes
Cooking Time: 4–6 hours
Ideal slow-cooker size: 2- to 3-qt.

3½ cups chicken broth
2 cups heavy cream
1 stick butter, unsalted
6 cloves garlic, minced
½ cup flour or cornstarch
1 cup grated Parmesan
    cheese or Parmesan/
    Romano blend
leftover chicken, chopped into
    bite-sized pieces
pasta
fresh chopped parsley,
    optional

1. Spray the inside of your crock with nonstick spray, then add the chicken broth, cream, butter, and garlic.

2. Cook on Low for 4–6 hours.

3. Briskly whisk in the flour or cornstarch a very little at a time until it is thickened.

4. Add the chicken and cook for an additional 30–40 minutes, or until the chicken is warmed through.

5. Serve over cooked pasta. Garnish with fresh parsley if you wish.

Tip: Freeze the rest of this sauce to use another time.

BBQ Burgers

Hope Comerford,
Clinton Township, MI

*Makes 6–8 burgers, depending on
the size you make them*

Prep. Time: 5 minutes
Cooking Time: 4–5 hours
Ideal slow-cooker size: 6-qt.

extra meat loaf mixture from
    earlier this week
hamburger buns
1 cup barbecue sauce
    (whatever your favorite is)

Optional Toppings:
onions, sliced into rings
relish, sweet or dill
pickles, sweet or dill
ketchup
mustard
mayonnaise
cheese slices
lettuce

1. In the bottom of your crock, crumble up some foil.

This will prop the burgers off the bottom of the crock so they're not sitting in grease.

2. Form the meat loaf mixture into 6–8 hamburger patties.

3. Place them into the crock. You may have to make 2 layers depending on the shape/size of your crock. If so, make some foil strips and place them across the other burgers, then put the remaining patties on top of those.

4. Cover. Cook on Low for 4–5 hours.

5. Serve on buns with the barbecue sauce and your favorite toppings.

Black Bean Burritos

Esther Nafziger, La Junta, CO

Makes 6–8 servings

Prep. Time: 20 minutes
Cooking Time: 7–12 hours
Ideal slow-cooker size: 5-qt.

2 cups dried black beans
7 cups water
hot chilies, diced, to taste
½ cup chopped onion
⅓ cup salsa, as hot or mild as you like
3 cloves garlic, minced
1 tsp. dried oregano
1 tsp. chili powder
2 tsp. salt
½ tsp. black pepper

6–8 flour tortillas
chopped lettuce
fresh tomatoes, chopped, or salsa
1½ cups shredded cheese of your choice

1. Grease interior of slow-cooker crock.

2. Sort and rinse dried beans.

3. Place in crock. Add water.

4. Cover. Cook on Low 9–10 hours, or on High 6–7 hours, or until beans are as tender as you like them.

5. Drain off any cooking liquid.

6. Stir hot chilies, onion, salsa, garlic, oregano, chili powder, salt, and pepper into cooked beans in crock.

7. Cover. Cook on High 1 hour, or on Low 2 hours, or until veggies are as tender as you want.

8. Spoon filling down center of each tortilla. Top with lettuce, tomatoes or salsa, and cheese.

9. Fold top and bottom of each tortilla over filling. Roll up to serve.

Polenta in a Crock

Carolyn Spohn, Shawnee, KS

Makes 4 servings

Prep. Time: 10–15 minutes
Cooking Time: 2–5 hours
Ideal slow-cooker size: 2-qt.

1 cup coarsely ground cornmeal
3 cups boiling water
½–1 tsp. salt
1 Tbsp. butter or olive oil
¼–½ cup grated Parmesan cheese

1. Grease interior of slow-cooker crock.

2. Place cornmeal, boiling water, and salt in crock. Stir together well until there are no lumps.

3. Cover. Cook on High 2–3 hours, or on Low 4–5 hours.

4. When cornmeal is cooked and thick, stir in butter or oil and grated cheese.

Chocolate Nut Clusters from the Crock

A. Catherine Boshart,
Lebanon, PA

Makes 24 servings

Prep. Time: 15 minutes
Cooking Time: 2 hours
Chilling Time: 45 minutes
Ideal slow-cooker size: 4-qt.

1½-lb. pkg. almond bark
4-oz. pkg. sweet German
   chocolate bar
8 oz. dark chocolate chips
8 oz. peanut butter chips
1 lb. salted peanuts
1 lb. unsalted peanuts

1. Layer ingredients into slow cooker in order as listed.
2. Cover. Cook on Low for 2 hours. Do not stir or lift lid during cooking time.
3. At end of 2 hours, stir and mix well.
4. Drop by teaspoonfuls or tablespoonfuls on wax paper or parchment paper.
5. Refrigerate for 45 minutes until hard.
6. Store in tight container in cool place.

WINTER

Week 1

THIS WEEK'S
Menu

Sunday: Raspberry-Glazed Ham
Monday: Ham 'n' Cabbage Stew
Tuesday: Creamy Ham Topping (for baked potatoes)
Wednesday: Herby Beef Sandwiches
Thursday: Beef Dumpling Soup
Friday: Turkey Breast with Orange Sauce
Saturday: Zucchini and Turkey Dish

Recommended Side Dish: Christmas Potatoes with Cheese
Special Dessert: Holiday Apple Date Pudding

Shopping List

PROTEIN

8–10-lb. boneless ham, fully cooked

3–4-lb. boneless beef chuck roast

4–5-lb. boneless, skinless turkey breast

1 cup shredded Swiss cheese

sliced cheese of your choice, *optional*

shredded cheese of your choice

sour cream

DAIRY and REFRIGERATED

¼ cup apple juice

1½ cups orange juice

1½ sticks butter

5 cups plus 6 Tbsp. milk

1 egg

¼ cup half-and-half

¼ cup grated Romano cheese

¼ cup grated Parmesan cheese

½ cup shredded provolone cheese

PRODUCE

3 small onions

1 large onion

4 cups shredded cabbage

5–6 carrots

1 cup sliced mushrooms

1 rib celery

3 cups sliced zucchini

2 Tbsp. chopped fresh parsley

3 Tbsp. fresh basil, or dried

3 Tbsp. fresh oregano, or dried

Download this shopping list to your smartphone!

(x.co/ShopList)

3 tomatoes

6 medium potatoes

baking potatoes (enough for your family)

4–5 apples

CANNED/DRY GOODS

4-oz. can sliced mushrooms

4-oz. jar sliced pimento

⅓ cup seedless raspberry jam

2 envelopes dry onion soup mix

1 cup buttermilk biscuit mix

¾ cup dry stuffing mix

1½ cups soft bread crumbs

½ cup chopped dates

½ cup toasted, chopped pecans

sandwich rolls

DO YOU HAVE THESE ON HAND?

ground cinnamon

salt

pepper

caraway seeds

Italian seasoning

dried rosemary

dry mustard

dried basil

dried oregano

4 cloves garlic

cornstarch

sugar

flour

baking powder

lemon juice

Worcestershire sauce

1 Tbsp. chicken bouillon granules

⅔ cup beef broth

Raspberry-Glazed Ham

Gloria Frey, Lebanon, PA

Makes 16–20 servings

Prep. Time: 10–15 minutes
Cooking Time: 4 hours
Ideal slow-cooker size: 6-qt.

8–10-lb. boneless ham, fully cooked
¼ cup apple juice
2 Tbsp. lemon juice
2 tsp. cornstarch
⅓ cup seedless raspberry jam, *divided*
1 Tbsp. butter

1. Place ham in slow cooker. Cover. Cook on Low 2 hours.
2. While ham is cooking, blend apple juice, lemon juice, and cornstarch together in saucepan.
3. Stir in about half of jam after liquid is well blended.
4. Cook and stir until hot and bubbly. Add butter. Stir in remaining jam.
5. Spoon glaze over ham after it has cooked 2 hours.
6. Cover. Cook 2 more hours on Low.
7. Slice ham and serve.

Ham 'n' Cabbage Stew

Dede Peterson, Rapid City, SD

Makes 4–5 servings

Prep. Time: 25–30 minutes
Cooking Time: 4–6 hours
Ideal slow-cooker size: 4-qt.

½ lb. leftover ham, cubed
½ cup diced onions
1 garlic clove, minced
4-oz. can sliced mushrooms, undrained
4 cups shredded cabbage
2 cups sliced carrots
¼ tsp. pepper
¼ tsp. caraway seeds
⅔ cup beef broth
1 Tbsp. cornstarch
2 Tbsp. water

1. Combine all ingredients except cornstarch and water in slow cooker.

2. Cover. Cook on Low 4–6 hours, or until vegetables are cooked as you like them.

3. In a small bowl, mix cornstarch into water until smooth. Stir into slow cooker during last hour to thicken stew slightly.

Creamy Ham Topping (for baked potatoes)

Judy Buller, Bluffton, OH

Makes 6 servings

Prep. Time: 15 minutes
Cooking Time: 1–2 hours
Ideal slow-cooker size: 3½-qt.

½ stick (4 Tbsp.) butter
¼ cup flour
2 cups milk
¼ cup half-and-half
1 Tbsp. chopped fresh parsley
1 Tbsp. chicken bouillon granules
½ tsp. Italian seasoning
2 cups diced leftover ham
¼ cup Romano cheese, grated
1 cup sliced mushrooms
baking potatoes (enough to feed your family)
shredded cheese of your choice
sour cream

1. Melt butter in saucepan over medium heat. Stir in flour. Add milk and half-and-half.

2. Continue stirring until sauce thickens and becomes smooth.

3. Stir in remaining ingredients (except potatoes, shredded cheese, and sour cream). Pour into slow cooker.

4. Cover. Cook on Low 1–2 hours. Meanwhile, bake potatoes.

5. Serve topping over baked potatoes. Top with shredded cheese and sour cream.

Herby Beef Sandwiches

Jean A. Shaner, York, PA

Makes 10–12 servings

Prep. Time: 5 minutes
Cooking Time: 7–8 hours
Ideal slow-cooker size: 4-qt.

3–4-lb. boneless beef chuck roast
3 Tbsp. fresh basil, or 1 Tbsp. dried basil
3 Tbsp. fresh oregano, or 1 Tbsp. dried oregano
1½ cups water
1 pkg. dry onion soup mix
sandwich rolls
sliced cheese of your choice, optional

1. Place roast in slow cooker.

2. Combine basil, oregano, and water in a bowl. Pour over roast.

3. Sprinkle with onion soup mix.

4. Cover. Cook on Low 7–8 hours.

5. Shred meat with fork. Stir sauce through shredded meat.

6. Serve the shredded Herby Beef on sandwich rolls alone or with melted cheese.

Beef Dumpling Soup

Barbara Walker, Sturgis, SD

Makes 5–6 servings

Prep. Time: 10–15 minutes
Cooking Time: 4½–6½ hours
Ideal slow-cooker size: 4-qt.

2 carrots, peeled and shredded
1 rib celery, finely chopped
1 tomato, peeled and chopped
1 envelope dry onion soup mix
6 cups hot water
1 cup buttermilk biscuit mix
1 Tbsp. finely chopped parsley
6 Tbsp. milk
leftover shredded beef

1. Add carrots, celery, and tomato, onion soup mix, and water to slow cooker.

2. Cover. Cook on Low 4–5 hours, or until the vegetables are as tender as you like them. Add the leftover shredded beef and continue to cook for 1 hour.

3. Combine biscuit mix and parsley in bowl. Stir in milk with fork until moistened. Drop dumplings by teaspoonfuls into cooker.

4. Cover. Cook on High 30 minutes.

Turkey Breast with Orange Sauce

Jean Butzer, Batavia, NY

Makes 6–8 servings

Prep. Time: 10 minutes
Cooking Time: 7–8 hours
Ideal slow-cooker size: 7-qt.

1 large onion, chopped
3 cloves garlic, minced
1 tsp. dried rosemary
½ tsp. pepper
4–5-lb. boneless, skinless turkey breast
1½ cups orange juice

1. Place onions in slow cooker.
2. Combine garlic, rosemary, and pepper in a small bowl.
3. Make gashes in turkey, about ¾ of the way through, at 2-inch intervals. Stuff with herb mixture. Place turkey in slow cooker.
4. Pour juice over turkey.
5. Cover. Cook on Low 7–8 hours, or until turkey is no longer pink in center.

Zucchini and Turkey Dish

Dolores Kratz, Souderton, PA

Makes 6 servings

Prep. Time: 15 minutes
Cooking Time: 4–5 hours
Ideal slow-cooker size: 4-qt.

3 cups sliced zucchini
1 small onion, chopped
¼ tsp. salt
1 cup cubed leftover turkey
2 fresh tomatoes, sliced, or 14½-oz. can diced tomatoes
½ tsp. dried oregano
1 tsp. dried basil
¼ cup grated Parmesan cheese
½ cup shredded provolone cheese
¾ cup dry stuffing mix

1. Combine zucchini, onion, salt, turkey, tomatoes, oregano, and basil in slow cooker. Mix well.
2. Top with cheeses and stuffing.
3. Cover. Cook on Low 4–5 hours.

Christmas Potatoes with Cheese

Jean Turner, Williams Lake, BC

Makes 6 servings

Prep. Time: 30 minutes
Cooking Time: 3–7 hours
Ideal slow-cooker size: 2½-qt.

5 Tbsp. butter, *divided*
2 Tbsp. flour
½ tsp. dry mustard
½ tsp. Worcestershire sauce
1½ tsp. salt
⅛ tsp. pepper
3 cups milk
1 cup shredded Swiss cheese
6 medium potatoes, peeled
  and thinly sliced (6 cups)
4-oz. jar sliced pimento,
  chopped and drained
¼ cup finely chopped onion
1½ cups soft bread crumbs

1. Melt 3 Tbsp. butter in saucepan. Blend in flour, mustard, Worcestershire sauce, salt, pepper, and milk. Cook and stir until thickened and bubbly. (I do this in the microwave.)

2. Add cheese. Stir to melt.

3. Place potatoes, pimento, and onion in slow cooker. Stir in cheesy sauce and blend well.

4. Cover. Cook on Low 5½–6½ hours or on High 2½–3½ hours, or until potatoes are as soft as you wish.

5. Melt remaining butter in saucepan. Toss with bread crumbs. Sprinkle over potatoes. Cook 30 minutes more, uncovered.

Holiday Apple Date Pudding

Colleen Heatwole, Burton, MI

Makes 8 servings

Prep. Time: 30 minutes
Cooking Time: 3–4 hours
Ideal slow-cooker size: 2-qt.

4–5 apples, peeled, cored,
  and diced
½ cup sugar
½ cup chopped dates
½ cup toasted, chopped
  pecans
1 Tbsp. flour
1 tsp. baking powder
⅛ tsp. salt
½ tsp. cinnamon
2 Tbsp. butter, melted
1 beaten egg

1. In a greased slow cooker, mix together apples, sugar, dates, and pecans.

2. In a separate bowl, mix together flour, baking powder, salt, and cinnamon. Stir into apple mixture.

3. Drizzle melted butter over batter and stir.

4. Stir in egg.

5. Cover. Cook on Low 3–4 hours. Serve warm.

WINTER

Week 2

THIS WEEK'S

Menu

Sunday: Bavarian Beef
Monday: Tempting Beef Stew
Tuesday: Spicy Sweet Chicken
Wednesday: Chicken Rice Special
Thursday: Cranberry Pork
Friday: Macaroni and Cheddar/Parmesan Cheese
Saturday: Pork on Sweet Potatoes

Recommended Side Dish: Creamy Green Bean Casserole
Special Dessert: Holiday Cherry Cobbler

Shopping List

PROTEIN
4–4½-lb. boneless beef
  chuck roast
6 lbs. chicken breasts,
  thighs, and/or legs
1 lb. pork, or turkey, sausage
3–4-lb. boneless rolled pork
  loin roast

FROZEN
1-lb. bag frozen peas with
  onions
1-lb. bag frozen green beans

DAIRY and REFRIGERATED
1 cup fat-free milk
3 large eggs
4 cups grated fat-free sharp
  cheddar cheese
¼ cup grated fat-free
  Parmesan cheese

1 cup Colby cheese,
  shredded

PRODUCE
1½ carrots
3 cups sliced carrots
1 small onion
1 medium onion
3 cups sliced onions
4 ribs celery
1 cup sliced celery
1 large sweet green bell
  pepper
2 medium sweet potatoes
2 apples

CANNED/DRY GOODS
8-oz. can whole, or stewed,
  tomatoes
16-oz. can whole berry
  cranberry sauce

Download this shopping list to your
smartphone!
(x.co/ShopList)

14-oz. can whole berry cranberry sauce	**DO YOU HAVE THESE ON HAND?**
13-oz. can evaporated milk	seasoned salt
3 Tbsp. evaporated milk	ground cinnamon
15-oz. can sauerkraut	white pepper
6 14-oz. cans green beans	black pepper
2 10¾-oz. cans cream of mushroom soup	salt
	bay leaves
3-oz. can french-fried onions	ground cloves
16-oz. can cherry pie filling (light or regular)	dry mustard
	oil of your choice
2-oz. jar pimentos	canola oil
instant tapioca	2 large kosher dill pickles
¼ cup bread crumbs	¼ cup beef broth
1 cup uncooked rice	4 cups chicken broth
¼ cup spicy sweet Catalina dressing	German-style mustard
	flour
2 Tbsp. dry onion soup mix	brown sugar
2-oz. pkg. dry noodle-soup mix	sugar
	cornstarch
½ cup sliced almonds	
½ cup chopped walnuts	**SPIRITS**
8-oz. pkg. elbow macaroni	½ cup red wine, or beef broth
1 pkg. cake mix for 1 layer white or yellow cake	
	¼ cup white wine
¾ cup cranberry juice	

Bavarian Beef

Naomi E. Fast, Hesston, KS

Makes 6–8 servings

Prep. Time: 15 minutes
Cooking Time: 6½–7½ hours
Ideal slow-cooker size: 6-qt.

4–4½-lb. boneless beef chuck
    roast
oil of your choice
3 cups sliced carrots
3 cups sliced onions
2 large kosher dill pickles,
    chopped
1 cup sliced celery
½ cup dry red wine, or beef
    broth
⅓ cup German-style mustard
2 tsp. coarsely ground black
    pepper
2 bay leaves
¼ tsp. ground cloves
⅓ cup flour
1 cup water

1. Brown roast on both
sides in oil in skillet. Transfer
to slow cooker.

2. Distribute carrots,
onions, pickles, and celery
around roast in slow cooker.

3. Combine wine, mustard,
pepper, bay leaves, and
cloves in a bowl. Pour over
ingredients in slow cooker.

4. Cover. Cook on Low
6–7 hours, or until meat and
vegetables are tender but not
dry or mushy.

5. Remove meat and
vegetables to large platter.
Cover to keep warm.

6. Mix flour with 1 cup
water in bowl until smooth.
Turn cooker to High. Stir in
flour-water paste, stirring
continually until broth is
smooth and thickened. Serve
with broth alongside.

Serving Suggestion: Try
serving this over noodles or
spaetzli.

Tempting Beef Stew

Patricia Howard,
Albuquerque, NM

Makes 5–6 servings

Prep. Time: 10 minutes
Cooking Time: 7–8 hours
Ideal slow-cooker size: 5-qt.

1½ carrots, sliced thin
½ of a 1-lb. pkg. frozen green
    peas with onions
½ of a 1-lb. pkg. frozen green
    beans
8-oz. can whole, or stewed,
    tomatoes
¼ cup beef broth
¼ cup white wine
¼ cup brown sugar
2 Tbsp. instant tapioca
¼ cup bread crumbs
1 tsp. salt
1 bay leaf
pepper to taste
leftover beef

1. Combine all ingredients
except the leftover beef in
slow cooker.

2. Cover. Cook on Low 7–8
hours, or until the vegetables
are as tender as you wish.
Add the leftover beef in the
last hour.

Spicy Sweet Chicken

Carolyn Baer, Conrath, WI

Makes 8 servings

Prep. Time: 25 minutes
Cooking Time: 4–7¾ hours
Ideal slow-cooker size: 6-qt.

6 lbs. chicken breasts, thighs, and/or legs, skinned
1 Tbsp. oil of your choice
16-oz. can whole berry cranberry sauce, *divided*
¼ cup spicy-sweet Catalina salad dressing
2 Tbsp. dry onion soup mix
1 Tbsp. cornstarch

1. Rinse chicken. Pat dry. Brown in hot oil in skillet. Arrange in slow cooker.
2. In a bowl, combine half of cranberry sauce and all of salad dressing and soup mix. Pour over chicken.
3. Cover. Cook on Low 7 hours or on High 3½ hours.
4. Stir cornstarch into remaining cranberry sauce in bowl. Stir into chicken mixture.
5. Turn slow cooker to High. Cover and cook 30–45 minutes more, or until thickened and bubbly.

Serving Suggestion: Serve over cooked noodles or rice.

Chicken Rice Special

Jeanne Allen, Rye, CO

Makes 6–8 servings

Prep. Time: 40 minutes
Cooking Time: 4–6 hours
Ideal slow-cooker size: 4-qt.

1 lb. pork, or turkey, sausage
leftover chicken, chopped
4 cups chicken broth
half a large sweet green bell pepper, chopped
1 medium onion, chopped
4 ribs celery, chopped
1 cup uncooked rice
2-oz. pkg. dry noodle-soup mix
½ cup sliced almonds
2-oz. jar pimentos, chopped

1. Brown sausage in skillet. Drain off any drippings. Place meat in slow cooker.
2. Add all other ingredients, except almonds and pimentos, to slow cooker. Stir well.
3. Top with almonds and pimentos.
4. Cover. Cook on High 4–6 hours, or until rice is done and liquid has been absorbed.
5. Stir well 1 hour before serving.

Cranberry Pork

Barbara Walker, Sturgis, SD
Donna Treloar, Muncie, IN

Makes 9–12 servings

Prep. Time: 15 minutes
Cooking Time: 6¼–8¼ hours
Ideal slow-cooker size: 5-qt.

3–4-lb. boneless rolled pork
  loin roast
2 Tbsp. canola oil
14-oz. can whole berry
  cranberry sauce
¾ cup sugar
¾ cup cranberry juice
1 tsp. dry mustard
1 tsp. pepper
¼ tsp. ground cloves
¼ cup cornstarch
¼ cup cold water
salt, to taste

1. In Dutch oven, brown roast in oil on all sides over medium-high heat. You may need to cut roast in half to fit into your Dutch oven and/or your slow cooker.

2. Place browned roast in slow cooker.

3. In a medium-sized bowl, combine cranberry sauce, sugar, cranberry juice, mustard, pepper, and cloves. Pour over roast.

4. Cover. Cook on Low 6–8 hours, or until a meat thermometer reads 160°F in center of roast. Remove roast and keep warm. Keep sauce on Low in slow cooker.

5. In a small bowl, combine cornstarch, water, and salt until smooth.

6. Turn cooker to High. Stir cornstarch-water mixture into cooking juices. Bring to a boil. Cook and stir until sauce thickens. Serve with slices of pork roast.

Macaroni and Cheddar/ Parmesan Cheese

Sherry L. Lapp, Lancaster, PA

Makes 8 servings

Prep. Time: 15 minutes
Cooking Time: 3 hours
Ideal slow-cooker size: 4-qt.

8-oz. pkg. elbow macaroni,
  cooked al dente
13-oz. can fat-free evaporated
  milk
1 cup fat-free milk
2 large eggs, slightly beaten
4 cups grated fat-free sharp
  cheddar cheese, *divided*
¼ tsp. salt
⅛ tsp. white pepper
¼ cup grated fat-free
  Parmesan cheese

1. Spray inside of cooker with nonfat cooking spray. Then, in cooker, combine lightly cooked macaroni, evaporated milk, milk, eggs,

3 cups cheddar cheese, salt, and pepper.

2. Top with remaining cheddar and Parmesan cheeses.

3. Cover. Cook on Low 3 hours.

Pork on Sweet Potatoes

Dottie Schmidt, Kansas City, MO

Makes 5 servings

Prep. Time: 15–20 minutes
Cooking Time: 2–5 hours
Ideal slow-cooker size: 6- to 7-qt. oval

2 medium sweet potatoes, peeled and cut into ½-inch-thick slices
1 small onion, chopped
2 apples, cored, peeled or not, and sliced
1 Tbsp. brown sugar
¼ tsp. ground cinnamon
¼ tsp. salt
⅛ tsp. coarsely ground black pepper
leftover pork
15-oz. can sauerkraut, drained

1. Grease interior of slow-cooker crock.

2. Arrange sweet potato slices over bottom of slow cooker.

3. Sprinkle chopped onion over potatoes.

4. Cover with apple slices.

5. In a small bowl, stir together brown sugar, cinnamon, salt, and pepper. Sprinkle over apple slices.

6. Top with leftover pork. If you must make a second layer, stagger the pieces so they don't directly overlap each other.

7. Spoon drained sauerkraut over top of the leftover pork, including any on the bottom layer.

8. Cover. Cook on Low 4½–5 hours or on High 2–3 hours.

Creamy Green Bean Casserole

Jena Hammond, Traverse City, MI

Makes 10 servings

Prep. Time: 10 minutes
Cooking Time: 3 hours
Ideal slow-cooker size: 5- to 6-qt.

3 qts., or 6 14½-oz. cans, green beans
2 10¾-oz. cans cream of mushroom soup
1 tsp. black pepper
1 tsp. seasoned salt

Toppings:
3-oz. can french-fried onions
1 cup Colby cheese, shredded

1. Drain half of liquid off green beans. (Find another use for it or discard.)

2. Mix beans, soup, pepper, and seasoned salt together in the slow cooker.

3. Cover. Cook on Low 3 hours.

4. Twenty minutes before serving, top beans with french-fried onions and shredded cheese.

Holiday Cherry Cobbler

Colleen Heatwole, Burton, MI

Makes 5–6 servings

Prep. Time: 15 minutes
Cooking Time: 2½–3½ hours
Ideal slow-cooker size: 4-qt.

16-oz. can cherry filling (light or regular)
1 pkg. cake mix for 1 layer white, or yellow, cake
1 egg
3 Tbsp. evaporated milk
½ tsp. cinnamon
½ cup walnuts, chopped

1. Spray slow cooker with cooking spray.

2. Spread pie filling in bottom of cooker.

3. Cover. Cook on High 30 minutes.

4. Meanwhile, in a medium-sized mixing bowl, mix together cake mix, egg, evaporated milk, cinnamon, and walnuts.

5. Spoon over hot pie filling. Do not stir.

6. Cover. Cook on Low 2–3 hours, or until toothpick inserted in cake layer comes out clean.

WINTER

Week 3

THIS WEEK'S
Menu

Sunday: Succulent Steak
Monday: Garlic Beef Stroganoff
Tuesday: Chicken and Dumplings
Wednesday: Chianti-Braised Short Ribs
Thursday: Chicken and Rice Casserole
Friday: Hearty Beef and Cabbage Soup
Saturday: Fully-Loaded Baked Potato Soup

Recommended Side Dish: Vegetable Medley
Special Dessert: Cinnamon Raisin Bread Pudding

Shopping List

PROTEIN
3-lb. round steak
3 lbs. boneless, skinless chicken breasts
5 lbs. meaty beef short ribs on bone

FROZEN
1 lb. frozen vegetable of your choice
16-oz. bag frozen broccoli
1½ cups frozen whole kernel corn

DAIRY and REFRIGERATED
6 oz. fat-free cream cheese
1 Tbsp. butter
1½ cups milk
1 cup fat-free, cholesterol-free egg product
1 cup grated, fat-free cheddar cheese
shredded cheese of your choice, for garnish
sour cream, for garnish

PRODUCE
1 large onion
5 medium onions
½ cup chopped onions
1 small onion or 4 scallions
6 medium tomatoes
½ cup chopped celery
2 cups thinly sliced cabbage
3 large potatoes
4 cups peeled and diced potatoes
1 cup sliced carrots
chopped fresh parsley, for garnish

Download this shopping list to your smartphone!
(x.co/ShopList)

CANNED/DRY GOODS

4-oz. can sliced mushrooms

2 4½-oz. jars sliced
 mushrooms

10¾-oz. can 98% fat-free,
 reduced-sodium cream of
 mushroom soup

10¾-oz. can 98% fat-free,
 reduced-sodium cream of
 chicken soup

28-oz. can crushed tomatoes

15-oz. can crushed tomatoes

15-oz. can kidney beans

16-oz. can fat-free
 sweetened condensed milk

low-fat buttermilk biscuit
 mix

1 cup long-grain rice

noodles

10 slices cinnamon raisin
 bread

1 cup raisins

paprika

garlic powder

onion salt

chili powder

dried basil

dried dill weed

dried rosemary

ground cinnamon

3 cups vegetable broth

½ cup beef broth

24 oz. fat-free low-sodium
 chicken broth

2 tsp. sodium-free beef
 bouillon granules

2 tsp. low-sodium chicken
 bouillon granules

4 cloves garlic

vegetable oil

flour

sugar

vanilla extract

1 tsp. tomato paste

Worcestershire sauce

DO YOU HAVE THESE ON HAND?

salt

pepper

SPIRITS

2 cups Chianti wine

Succulent Steak

Betty B. Dennison, Grove City, PA

Makes 8 servings

Prep. Time: 20 minutes
Cooking Time: 8¼–9¼ hours
Ideal slow-cooker size: 4-qt.

¼ cup plus 2 Tbsp. flour, *divided*
1 tsp. salt
½ tsp. pepper
½ tsp. paprika
3-lb. round steak, trimmed of fat
2 medium onions, sliced
4-oz. can sliced mushrooms, drained
½ cup beef broth
2 tsp. Worcestershire sauce
3 Tbsp. water

1. Mix together ¼ cup flour, salt, pepper, and paprika.
2. Cut steak into 5–6½–¾-inch-thick pieces. Dredge steak pieces in seasoned flour until lightly coated.
3. Layer half of onions, half of steak, and half of mushrooms into cooker. Repeat.
4. Combine beef broth and Worcestershire sauce. Pour over mixture in slow cooker.
5. Cover. Cook on Low 8–10 hours.
6. Remove steak to serving platter and keep warm. Mix together 2 Tbsp. flour and water. Stir into drippings and cook on High until thickened, about 10 minutes. Pour over steak and serve.

Garlic Beef Stroganoff

Sharon Miller, Holmesville, OH

Makes 6 servings

Prep. Time: 20 minutes
Cooking Time: 5–6 hours
Ideal slow-cooker size: 4- or 5-qt.

2 tsp. sodium-free beef bouillon granules
2 4½-oz. jars sliced mushrooms, drained, with juice reserved
mushroom juice, with boiling water added to make a full cup
10¾-oz. can 98% fat-free, reduced-sodium cream of mushroom soup
1 large onion, chopped
3 cloves garlic, minced
1 Tbsp. Worcestershire sauce
leftover steak, chopped up
noodles
6-oz. fat-free cream cheese, cubed and softened

1. Dissolve bouillon in mushroom juice and water in slow cooker.
2. Add soup, mushrooms, onion, garlic, and Worcestershire sauce.
3. Cover. Cook on Low 4–5 hours. Add the leftover steak and cook 1 more hour.

4. Turn off heat.

5. Stir in cream cheese until smooth.

6. Serve over noodles.

Chicken and Dumplings

Annabelle Unternahrer,
Shipshewana, IN

Makes 6 servings

Prep. Time: 25 minutes
Cooking Time: 2½–3½ hours
Ideal slow-cooker size: 3- or 4-qt.

3 lbs. boneless, skinless chicken breasts, cut in 1-inch cubes
1 lb. frozen vegetables of your choice
1 medium onion, diced
24 oz. fat-free low-sodium chicken broth, *divided*
1½ cups low-fat buttermilk biscuit mix

1. Combine chicken, vegetables, onion, and chicken broth (reserve ½ cup, plus 1 Tbsp., broth) in slow cooker.

2. Cover. Cook on High 2–3 hours.

3. Mix biscuit mix with reserved broth until moistened. Drop by tablespoonfuls over hot chicken and vegetables.

4. Cover. Cook on High 10 minutes.

5. Uncover. Cook on High 20 minutes more.

Chianti-Braised Short Ribs

Veronica Sabo, Shelton, CT

Makes 8 servings

Prep. Time: 30–40 minutes
Cooking Time: 6 hours
Ideal slow-cooker size: 5- or 6-qt.

5 lbs. meaty beef short ribs on bone
salt, to taste
pepper, to taste
1 Tbsp. vegetable oil
1 medium onion, finely chopped
2 cups Chianti wine
2 tomatoes, seeded and chopped
1 tsp. tomato paste, or to taste

1. Season ribs with salt and pepper.

2. Add vegetable oil to large skillet. Brown half the ribs 7–10 minutes, turning to brown all sides. Drain and remove to slow cooker.

3. Repeat browning with second half of ribs. Drain and transfer to slow cooker.

4. Pour off all but one tablespoon drippings from skillet.

5. Sauté onion in skillet, scraping up any browned bits, until slightly softened, about 4 minutes.

6. Add wine and tomatoes to skillet. Bring to a boil.

7. Carefully pour hot mixture into slow cooker.

8. Cover. Cook on Low 6 hours, or until ribs are tender.

9. Transfer ribs to serving plate and cover to keep warm.

10. Strain cooking liquid from slow cooker into a measuring cup. Skim off as much fat as possible.

11. Pour remaining juice into skillet used to brown ribs. Boil sauce until reduced to one cup.

12. Stir in tomato paste until smooth. Season to taste with salt and pepper.

13. Serve sauce over ribs or on the side.

Chicken and Rice Casserole

Wanda Roth, Napoleon, OH

Makes 8 servings

Prep. Time: 20 minutes
Cooking Time: 2–6 hours
Ideal slow-cooker size: 6-qt.

1 cup uncooked long-grain rice
3 cups water
2 tsp. low-sodium chicken bouillon granules
10¾-oz. can fat-free, low-sodium cream of chicken soup
leftover chicken (it's okay that it's covered in sauce—it will add to the flavor of this dish)
¼ tsp. garlic powder
1 tsp. onion salt
1 cup grated, fat-free cheddar cheese
16-oz. bag frozen broccoli, thawed

1. Combine all ingredients except broccoli in slow cooker.

2. One hour before end of cooking time, stir in broccoli.

3. Cook on High a total of 2–3 hours or on Low a total of 4–6 hours.

Hearty Beef and Cabbage Soup

Carolyn Mathias,
Williamsville, NY

Makes 8 servings

Prep. Time: 15 minutes
Cooking Time: 4 hours
Ideal slow-cooker size: 5-qt.

1 medium onion, chopped
28-oz. can crushed tomatoes
15-oz. can crushed tomatoes
2 cups water
15-oz. can kidney beans
1 tsp. salt
½ tsp. pepper
1 Tbsp. chili powder
½ cup chopped celery
2 cups thinly sliced cabbage
leftover ribs meat, off the
    bone and chopped up

1. Combine all ingredients except cabbage and leftover rib meat in slow cooker.

2. Cover. Cook on Low 3 hours.

3. Add cabbage and leftover rib meat. Cook on High 60 minutes longer.

Fully-Loaded Baked Potato Soup

Beverly Hummel, Fleetwood, PA
Penny Blosser, Beavercreek, OH

Makes 6 servings

Prep. Time: 20 minutes
Cooking Time: 3 hours
Ideal slow-cooker size: 4-qt.

3 large potatoes, baked
1 Tbsp. butter
1 small onion, chopped, or 4
    scallions, sliced
1 clove garlic, minced
3 Tbsp. all-purpose flour
1 tsp. salt
1 tsp. dried basil
½ tsp. pepper
3 cups vegetable broth
1½ cups milk
shredded cheese of your
    choice, for garnish
chopped fresh parsley, for
    garnish
sour cream, for garnish

1. Peel the baked potatoes if you wish. Cube the baked potatoes. Place in slow cooker.

2. In a skillet, melt butter and sauté onion and garlic.

3. Stir in flour, salt, basil, and pepper. Add broth, whisking continuously. Heat and stir until hot.

4. Pour over potatoes in slow cooker.

5. Cook on Low for 2 hours.

6. Add milk. Cook an additional 30–40 minutes on Low.

7. Garnish with cheese, parsley, and sour cream.

Vegetable Medley

Deborah Santiago, Lancaster, PA
Judi Manos, West Islip, NY

Makes 8 servings

Prep. Time: 25 minutes
Cooking Time: 5–6 hours
Ideal slow-cooker size: 4-qt.

4 cups peeled and diced potatoes
1½ cups frozen whole kernel corn
4 medium tomatoes, seeded and diced
1 cup sliced carrots
½ cup chopped onions
¾ tsp. salt
½ tsp. sugar
¾ tsp. dill weed
¼ tsp. black pepper
½ tsp. dried basil
¼ tsp. dried rosemary

1. Combine all ingredients in slow cooker.

2. Cover. Cook on Low 5–6 hours, or until vegetables are tender.

Cinnamon Raisin Bread Pudding

Penny Blosser, Beavercreek, OH

Makes 8 servings

Prep. Time: 15 minutes
Cooking Time: 2½–3 hours
Ideal slow-cooker size: 4-qt.

10 slices cinnamon bread, cut into cubes
1 cup raisins
1 cup fat-free, cholesterol-free egg product
1½ cups warm water
1 tsp. vanilla extract
½ tsp. ground cinnamon
16-oz. can fat-free sweetened condensed milk

1. Place bread cubes and raisins in greased slow cooker. Mix together gently.

2. Mix remaining ingredients together and pour over top.

3. Cover. Cook on High 30 minutes, then on Low 2–2½ hours.

Week 4

THIS WEEK'S
Menu

Sunday: CC Roast (Company's Coming)
Monday: Cowtown Favorite
Tuesday: Chicken in a Pot
Wednesday: Sauerkraut and Kielbasa
Thursday: Barley and Chicken Soup
Friday: Wanda's Chicken and Rice Casserole
Saturday: Election Lunch

Recommended Side Dish: Garlic Mushrooms
Special Dessert: Chocolate Rice Pudding

Shopping List

PROTEIN

3-lb. boneless pot roast

6–8 lbs. chicken pieces

2 lbs. reduced-fat turkey
   kielbasa

FROZEN

16-oz. bag frozen broccoli

DAIRY and REFRIGERATED

1 cup grated cheddar
   cheese

7 Tbsp. butter

PRODUCE

4 medium potatoes

3 large potatoes

7 medium onions

1 large onion

4 scallions

7–8 carrots

3 cups sliced carrots

7–8 ribs of celery

2 cups green beans

1 lb. mushrooms

1½ lb. fresh sauerkraut, or
   canned

fresh parsley, as desired

fresh basil, as desired

CANNED/DRY GOODS

2 14-oz. cans low-sodium
   stewed tomatoes

2 12-oz. cans evaporated milk

10¾-oz. can low-sodium
   tomato soup

10¾-oz. can cream of
   chicken soup

10-oz. can tomatoes with
   green chili peppers

16-oz. can lima or butter
   beans

Download this shopping list to your
smartphone!

(x.co/ShopList)

16-oz. can red kidney beans	cocoa powder
16-oz. can garbanzo beans	2 cloves garlic
2 Tbsp. instant tapioca	vanilla extract
½ lb. dry barley	flour
1 cup long-grain rice	sugar
1⅓ cups white rice	1 cup chicken broth, water, or white cooking wine
DO YOU HAVE THESE ON HAND?	chicken bouillon granules
	¼ cup honey
salt	lemon juice
black pepper	prepared mustard
dried basil	chili sauce
garlic powder	Worcestershire sauce
onion salt	apple cider vinegar
dry mustard	

CC Roast (Company's Coming)

Anne Townsend,
Albuquerque, NM

Makes 8 servings

Prep. Time: 20 minutes
Cooking Time: 6–8 hours
Ideal slow-cooker size: 4- or 5-qt.

3-lb. boneless pot roast
2 Tbsp. flour
1 Tbsp. prepared mustard
1 Tbsp. chili sauce
1 Tbsp. Worcestershire sauce
1 tsp. apple cider vinegar
1 tsp. sugar
4 medium potatoes, sliced
2 medium onions, sliced

1. Place pot roast in slow cooker.
2. Make a paste with the flour, mustard, chili sauce, Worcestershire sauce, vinegar, and sugar. Spread over roast.
3. Top with potatoes and then the onions.
4. Cover. Cook on Low 6–8 hours.

Cowtown Favorite

Jean Harris Robinson,
Cinnaminson, NJ

Makes 5 servings

Prep. Time: 25 minutes
Cooking Time: 3–5 hours
Ideal slow-cooker size: 4-qt.

1 medium onion, sliced thin
3 large potatoes, peeled and chopped
3 cups carrots cut in ½-inch slices
1 rib celery, chopped
2 cups green beans, cut in 1-inch pieces
2 14-oz. cans low-sodium stewed tomatoes, undrained
10¾-oz. can low-sodium tomato soup
2 Tbsp. instant tapioca
leftover roast, chopped

1. Place onions, potatoes, carrots, celery, and green beans into the slow cooker.
2. Mix tomatoes, soup, and tapioca together. Pour over the vegetables.
3. Cover. Cook on High 3 hours or on Low 4–5 hours.
4. Add in the leftover roast the last hour of cooking.

Chicken in a Pot

Carolyn Baer, Conrath, WI
Evie Hershey, Atglen, PA
Judy Koczo, Plano, IL
Mary Puskar, Forest Hill, MD
Mary E. Wheatley, Mashpee, MA

Makes 12 servings

Prep. Time: 10 minutes
Cooking Time: 3½–10 hours
Ideal slow-cooker size: 5-qt.

6 carrots, sliced
4 medium onions, sliced
4 ribs celery, cut in 1-inch
  pieces
6–8 lb. chicken pieces
2 tsp. salt
½ tsp. coarse black pepper
1 tsp. dried basil
1 cup chicken broth, water, or
  white cooking wine

1. Place vegetables in bottom of slow cooker. Place chicken on top of vegetables. Add seasonings and water.
2. Cover. Cook on Low 8–10 hours, or on High 3½–5 hours (use 1½ cups liquid if cooking on High).

Sauerkraut and Kielbasa

Colleen Heatwole, Burton, MI

Makes 4 servings

Prep. Time: 5–10 minutes
Cooking Time: 5–6 hours
Ideal slow-cooker size: 4½- or 5-qt.

1½ lbs. fresh or canned
  sauerkraut, drained and
  rinsed

2 lbs. reduced-fat turkey
  kielbasa, cut in 1-inch slices

1. Combine sauerkraut and turkey kielbasa in slow cooker.
2. Cover. Cook on Low 5–6 hours.
3. Stir before serving.

Barley and Chicken Soup

Millie Schellenburg,
Washington, NJ

Makes 5 servings

Prep. Time: 15–20 minutes
Cooking Time: 4 hours
Ideal slow-cooker size: 5- or 6-qt.

½ lb. dry barley
fresh celery, as desired
fresh parsley, as desired

fresh basil, as desired
carrots, as desired
7–8 cups water
2 cups leftover chicken, diced

1. Combine all ingredients in slow cooker except chicken.
2. Cover. Cook on Low for 4 hours. Add in leftover chicken the last hour of cooking.
3. Continue cooking until barley is soft and chicken is heated through.

Wanda's Chicken and Rice Casserole

Wanda Roth, Napoleon, OH

Makes 6–8 servings

Prep. Time: 10 minutes
Cooking Time: 3–4 hours
Ideal slow-cooker size: 4-qt.

1 cup long-grain rice, uncooked
3 cups water
2 tsp. chicken bouillon granules
10¾-oz can cream of chicken soup
16-oz. bag frozen broccoli
2 cups chopped leftover chicken
¼ tsp. garlic powder
1 tsp. onion salt
1 cup grated cheddar cheese

1. Combine all ingredients in slow cooker.
2. Cook on High 3–4 hours.

Tip: If casserole is too runny, remove lid from slow cooker for 15 minutes while continuing to cook on High.

Election Lunch

Alix Nancy Botsford, Seminole, OK

Makes 6–12 servings

Prep. Time: 30 minutes
Cooking Time: 2–4 hours
Ideal slow-cooker size: 6-qt., or 2 4-qt. cookers

1 large onion, chopped
1 rib celery, sliced
1 Tbsp. Worcestershire sauce
1½ tsp. dry mustard
¼ cup honey
10-oz. can tomatoes with green chili peppers
16-oz. can lima, or butter, beans, drained, with liquid reserved
16-oz. can red kidney beans, drained, with liquid reserved
16-oz. can garbanzo beans, drained, with liquid reserved
leftover sausage, chopped into bite-sized pieces

1. Place all ingredients into slow cooker, combining well. Add reserved juice from lima, kidney, and garbanzo beans if there's enough room in the cooker(s).
2. Cover. Cook on Low 2–4 hours.

Garlic Mushrooms

Lizzie Ann Yoder, Hartville, OH

Makes 4 servings

Prep. Time: 20 minutes
Cooking Time: 15–20 minutes

½ stick (4 Tbsp.) butter
2 cloves garlic, minced
1 lb. mushrooms, sliced
4 scallions, chopped
1 tsp. lemon juice

1. In a skillet, melt the butter and sauté the garlic briefly.
2. Add mushrooms, scallions, and lemon juice and cook, stirring, about 10 minutes.

Chocolate Rice Pudding

Michele Ruvola, Selden, NY

Makes 4 servings

Prep. Time: 10 minutes
Cooking Time: 2½–3½ hours
Chilling Time: 2–5 hours
Ideal slow-cooker size: 3-qt.

4 cups cooked white rice
¾ cup sugar
¼ cup baking cocoa powder
3 Tbsp. butter, melted
1 tsp. vanilla extract
2 12-oz. cans evaporated milk

1. Combine all ingredients in greased slow cooker.
2. Cover. Cook on Low 2½–3½ hours, or until liquid is absorbed.
3. Chill for 2–5 hours before serving.

WINTER

Week 5

THIS WEEK'S
Menu

Sunday: Chicken Tikki Masala
Monday: Indian Chicken Curry
Tuesday: Three-Cheese Broccoli Soup
Wednesday: Saucy Round Steak Supper
Thursday: Saucy Round Steak Sandwiches
Friday: Rosemary Pork Loin
Saturday: Creamy Pork and Potato Soup

Recommended Side Dish: Glazed Carrots
Special Dessert: Baked Custard

Shopping List

PROTEIN

4 lbs. boneless, skinless
   chicken thighs

3-lb. round steak

4–5 lb. pork loin

FROZEN

2 10-oz. bags frozen broccoli
   florets

16-oz. pkg. frozen baby
   carrots

DAIRY and REFRIGERATED

¾ cup plain Greek yogurt

½ cup cream

2 cups whole milk

3½ cups 2% milk

3 eggs

½ cup sour cream

3 cups three different
   cheeses, such as Jarlsberg,
Gruyère, and sharp
   cheddar

6–8 Swiss cheese slices

½ lb. cheese of your choice,
   shredded

2¼ cups apple cider

PRODUCE

½ cup very finely diced
   white onion

2 medium onions

¾ cup chopped onion

fresh ginger

1 green or red bell pepper

1 cups sliced carrots

½ cup chopped carrots

1 cups sliced celery

1 cup chopped celery

1 sweet potato

3 cups chopped potatoes

Download this shopping list to your
smartphone!
(x.co/ShopList)

¾ tsp. chopped fresh
  oregano, or dried

1 Tbsp. fresh rosemary
  leaves, or dried

CANNED/DRY GOODS

29-oz. can pureed tomatoes

14-oz. can coconut milk

15-oz. can garbanzo beans

8-oz. can mushrooms,
  stems, and pieces

⅓ cup French dressing

¼ cup apple jelly

bread or rolls, of your choice

horseradish sauce

DO YOU HAVE THESE ON HAND?

ground cumin

paprika

cinnamon stick

salt

cayenne pepper

bay leaves

curry powder

ground coriander

garam masala

black pepper

kosher salt

ground nutmeg

onion salt

dried parsley

ground cinnamon

4 cups chicken or vegetable
  broth

2 chicken or vegetable
  bouillon cubes

flour

Dijon mustard

sugar

vanilla extract

Worcestershire sauce

8 cloves garlic

olive oil

cornstarch

Tabasco sauce

1 Tbsp. tomato paste or
  ketchup

Chicken Tikki Masala

Susan Kasting, Jenks, OK

Makes 6–8 servings

Prep. Time: 20 minutes
Cooking Time: 4¼ hours
Ideal slow-cooker size: 6-qt.

4 lbs. boneless, skinless chicken thighs
1 medium onion, chopped
3 cloves garlic, minced
1½ Tbsp. grated ginger
29-oz. can pureed tomatoes
1 Tbsp. olive oil
1 Tbsp. garam masala
½ tsp ground cumin
½ tsp. paprika
1 cinnamon stick
1 tsp. salt
1–1½ tsp. cayenne pepper, depending on how much heat you like
2 bay leaves
¾ cup plain Greek yogurt
½ cup cream
1½ tsp. cornstarch

1. Grease interior of slow-cooker crock.

2. Lay thighs in crock. If you need to make a second layer, stagger pieces so they don't directly overlap each other.

3. In a good-sized bowl, mix together onion, garlic, ginger, tomatoes, olive oil, garam masala, cumin, paprika, cinnamon stick, salt, cayenne pepper, and bay leaves.

4. Cover. Cook 4 hours on Low, or until instant-read meat thermometer registers 165°F when inserted in center of thigh.

5. Remove thighs and keep warm on platter or bowl.

6. Mix Greek yogurt into sauce in cooker.

7. In a small bowl, combine cream and cornstarch until smooth. Mix into sauce in cooker.

8. Return chicken to cooker.

9. Cover. Cook an additional 15–20 minutes, or until sauce has thickened.

Tip: Serve over rice.

Indian Chicken Curry

Judy Buller, Bluffton, OH

Makes 4 servings

Prep. Time: 35 minutes
Cooking Time: 5–6 hours
Ideal slow-cooker size: 6-qt. oval

2 Tbsp. curry powder
1 tsp. ground coriander
1 tsp. ground cumin
3 cloves garlic, minced
14-oz. can coconut milk

½ tsp. Tabasco sauce

1 Tbsp. tomato paste or ketchup

15-oz. can garbanzo beans, drained

1 medium onion, chopped

1 green or red bell pepper, chopped

1 cup sliced carrots

1 cup sliced celery

1 sweet potato, peeled and chopped

leftover chicken, chopped

1. Grease interior of slow-cooker crock.

2. In the crock, combine curry powder, coriander, cumin, minced garlic, coconut milk, Tabasco, and tomato paste. Blend well.

3. Add in the beans, onion, bell pepper, carrots, celery, and sweet potato.

4. Cover. Cook on Low 5–6 hours, or until the vegetables are as tender as you like them. Add the leftover chicken in the last hour of cooking. Stir well.

Tip: Serve over cooked rice.

Three-Cheese Broccoli Soup

Deb Kepiro, Strasburg, PA

Makes 8 servings

Prep. Time: 15 minutes
Cooking Time: 2–6
Ideal slow-cooker size: 4- to 5-qt.

4 cups chicken or vegetable broth

2 cups 2% milk

2 10-oz. bags frozen broccoli florets

½ cup very finely diced white onion

½ tsp. black pepper

½ tsp. kosher salt

½ tsp. ground nutmeg

3 cups three different grated cheeses, preferably Jarlsberg, Gruyère, and sharp cheddar

1. In slow cooker, combine broth, milk, broccoli, onion, pepper, salt, and nutmeg.

2. Cook on Low for 5–6 hours or High for 2–3, until onion is soft.

3. Add cheese 20 minutes before serving. Cheese may be stringy and stick to broccoli—that's fine.

Saucy Round Steak Supper

Shirley Sears, Tiskilwa, IL

Makes 8–10 servings

Prep. Time: 10–15 minutes
Cooking Time: 8–9 hours
Ideal slow-cooker size: 4-qt.

3 lbs. round steak, sliced
  diagonally into ⅛-inch strips
  (reserve meat bone)
½ cup chopped onion
½ cup chopped celery
8-oz. can mushrooms,
  stems and pieces, drained
  (reserve liquid)
⅓ cup French dressing
½ cup sour cream
1 tsp. Worcestershire sauce

1. Place steak and bone in slow cooker. Add onion, celery, and mushrooms.

2. Combine dressing, sour cream, Worcestershire sauce, and mushroom liquid. Pour over mixture in slow cooker.

3. Cover. Cook on Low 8–9 hours.

Serving Suggestion: Serve over noodles.

Saucy Round Steak Sandwiches

Hope Comerford,
Clinton Township, MI

Makes 4–6 sandwiches

Prep. Time: 5 minutes
Cooking Time: 15 minutes

leftover saucy round steak
bread or rolls of your choice
6–8 Swiss cheese slices
horseradish sauce

1. Warm the leftover saucy round steak.

2. Preheat the oven to 400°F. Place the bread on a baking sheet and top with the warmed round steak. Place a slice or two of Swiss cheese over the top. Bake until the cheese is melted, about 8–10 minutes.

3. Before serving, top each sandwich with some horseradish sauce.

Rosemary Pork Loin

Phyllis Good, Lancaster, PA

Makes 8–10 servings

Prep. Time: 5–10 minutes
Cooking Time: 3½–4 hours
Chilling Time: 8 hours or overnight
Ideal slow-cooker size: 5-qt.

4–5-lb. pork loin
2 cups apple cider
2 cloves garlic, minced
1 tsp. onion salt
¾ tsp. chopped fresh
  oregano, or ¼ tsp. dried
1 Tbsp. fresh rosemary
  leaves, or 1 tsp. dried
1 bay leaf

1. Place pork loin in baking pan.

2. Mix together remaining ingredients in a bowl. Pour over roast.

3. Cover. Refrigerate for at least 8 hours. When you think of it, spoon some of the marinade over the roast.

4. Place roast in slow cooker. Pour marinade over roast.

5. Cover. Cook on Low 3½–4 hours, or until meat registers 140–145°F on an instant-read thermometer when it's stuck into the center of the roast.

6. When the meat is finished cooking, lift out of cooker onto a platter. Cover with foil to keep it warm. Let stand 15 minutes before slicing.

7. Slice and serve topped with marinade. (Fish out the bay leaf before serving.)

Creamy Pork and Potato Soup

Janeen Troyer, Fairview, MI

Makes 4–6 servings

Prep. Time: 30 minutes
Cooking Time: 3¼–3½ hours
Ideal slow-cooker size: 4-qt.

3 cups chopped potatoes,
  peeled or unpeeled
1 cup water
½ cup chopped celery
½ cup chopped carrots
¼ cup chopped onions
2 cubes chicken, or
  vegetable, bouillon
1 tsp. dried parsley
½ tsp. salt
¼ tsp. pepper
1½ cups 2% milk
2 Tbsp. flour
leftover pork
½ lb. cheese of your choice,
  shredded

1. Combine potatoes, water, celery, carrots, onion, bouillon, parsley, salt, and pepper in slow cooker.

2. Cover. Cook on High 3 hours, or until vegetables are tender.

3. In a jar with a tight-fitting lid, add milk to flour. Cover tightly and shake until flour dissolves in milk. When smooth, add mixture to vegetables in cooker. Stir well.

4. Add in the leftover pork and stir again. Cover. Cook on High another 15–30 minutes, or until soup is thickened and smooth and pork is heated through. Stir occasionally to prevent lumps from forming.

5. Add cheese. Stir until melted.

Glazed Carrots

Gloria Frey, Lebanon, PA

Makes 4 servings

Prep. Time: 10–15 minutes
Cooking Time: 2½–3½ hours
Ideal slow-cooker size: 2-qt.

16-oz. pkg. frozen baby
   carrots
¼ cup apple cider, or apple
   juice
¼ cup apple jelly
1½ tsp. Dijon mustard

1. Put carrots and apple juice in slow cooker.

2. Cover and cook on High 2–3 hours, until carrots are tender.

3. Blend jelly and mustard together in a small bowl.

4. After carrots are tender, stir in blended apple jelly and

mustard. Continue to heat until steaming hot.

Baked Custard

Barbara Smith, Bedford, PA

Makes 5–6 servings

Prep. Time: 10–15 minutes
Cooking Time: 2–3 hours
Ideal slow-cooker size: 4- to 5-qt.

2 cups whole milk
3 eggs, slightly beaten
⅓ cup, plus ½ tsp., sugar,
   divided
1 tsp. vanilla extract
¼ tsp. ground cinnamon

1. Heat milk in a small uncovered saucepan until a skin forms on top. Remove from heat and let cool slightly.

2. Meanwhile, in a large mixing bowl combine eggs, ⅓ cup sugar, and vanilla.

3. Slowly stir cooled milk into egg-sugar mixture.

4. Pour into a greased 1-qt. baking dish that will fit into your slow cooker, or into a baking insert designed for your slow cooker.

5. Mix cinnamon and ½ tsp. reserved sugar in a small bowl. Sprinkle over custard mixture.

6. Cover baking dish or insert with foil. Set container on a metal rack or trivet in slow cooker. Pour hot water around dish to a depth of 1 inch.

7. Cover cooker. Cook on High 2–3 hours, or until custard is set. (When blade of a knife inserted in center of custard comes out clean, custard is set.)

8. Serve warm from baking dish or insert.

WINTER

Week 6

THIS WEEK'S

Menu

Sunday: Taters 'n Beef
Monday: Another Chicken in a Pot
Tuesday: Green Chili Stew
Wednesday: Pasta with Tomatoes, Olives, and Two Cheeses
Thursday: Tangy Pork Chops
Friday: Asian Pork Soup
Saturday: Meatless Mexican Lasagna

Recommended Side Dish: Golden Cauliflower
Special Dessert: Cranberry Pudding

Shopping List

PROTEIN

2½ lbs. ground beef

4-lb. whole chicken

6–7 ½-inch-thick pork chops

4 slices bacon

FROZEN

3 cups frozen corn

2 10-oz. pkgs. frozen cauliflower

DAIRY and REFRIGERATED

1 cup milk

½ cup fat-free half-and-half

4 Tbsp. light, soft tub margarine

2½ cups Havarti cheese

⅓ cup grated Parmesan cheese

1½ cups shredded Mexican-blend cheese

6 Tbsp. sour cream

PRODUCE

1¾ cups chopped onion

3 medium onions

1 small onion

7 green onions

11 potatoes

1-lb. bag baby carrots

2 medium carrots

¾ cup chopped green chilies

¼ cup finely chopped fresh basil

2 ribs celery

1 large green bell pepper

fresh ginger

1 cup sliced mushrooms

1 cup bean sprouts

2 cups whole cranberries

CANNED/DRY GOODS

1 cup canned tomato soup

14½-oz. can green beans

Download this shopping list to your smartphone!

(x.co/ShopList)

1 medium onion, sliced
salt and pepper, to taste
¾ cup chopped green chilies

Optional Ingredients:
1 tsp. garlic powder
1 beef bouillon cube

1. Add all ingredients to slow cooker. Stir together thoroughly.
2. Cover and cook on Low 6–8 hours, or until the vegetables are tender.

Pasta with Tomatoes, Olives, and Two Cheeses

Diane Clement, Rogers, AR

Makes 6–8 servings

Prep. Time: 30 minutes
Cooking Time: 3 hours
Ideal slow-cooker size: 5- or 6-qt.

leftover chopped chicken
1½ cups chopped onion
1 tsp. minced garlic
3 28-oz. cans Italian plum tomatoes, drained
2 tsp. dried basil
¼–½ tsp. red pepper flakes, according to the amount of heat you like
2 cups chicken broth
salt and black pepper, to taste
1 lb. uncooked penne or rigatoni
3 Tbsp. olive oil
2½ cups Havarti cheese

⅓ cup sliced, pitted, brine-cured olives (such as Kalamata)
⅓ cup grated Parmesan cheese
¼ cup finely chopped fresh basil

1. Grease interior of slow-cooker crock.
2. Place chicken, onion, garlic, tomatoes, dried basil, and red pepper flakes in crock. Stir together well, breaking up tomatoes with back of spoon.
3. Stir in chicken broth.
4. Season with salt and pepper.
5. Cover. Cook on High 2 hours.

6. Uncover. Continue cooking on High 1 hour, or until sauce is reduced to the consistency you like.
7. During last 30 minutes of cooking, prepare pasta according to package directions in a large stockpot until al dente.
8. Drain pasta and stir in olive oil. Cover and keep warm.
9. When sauce is done cooking, pour over pasta and toss to blend.
10. Stir in Havarti cheese and allow to melt.
11. Spoon into serving bowl. Top with olives and Parmesan cheese.
12. Sprinkle with fresh basil, then serve immediately.

Tangy Pork Chops

Tracy Clark, Mt. Crawford, VA
Lois M. Martin, Lititz, PA
Becky Oswald, Broadway, PA

Makes 4–6 servings

Prep. Time: 15 minutes
Cooking Time: 5½–6½ hours
Ideal slow-cooker size: 4-qt.

6–7½-inch-thick pork chops
½ tsp. salt
⅛ tsp. pepper
2 medium onions, chopped
2 ribs celery, chopped
1 large green bell pepper,
  sliced
14½-oz. can stewed tomatoes
½ cup ketchup
2 Tbsp. apple cider vinegar
2 Tbsp. brown sugar
2 Tbsp. Worcestershire sauce
1 Tbsp. lemon juice
1 beef bouillon cube
2 Tbsp. cornstarch
2 Tbsp. water

1. Place chops in slow cooker. Sprinkle with salt and pepper.
2. Add onions, celery, pepper, and tomatoes.
3. Combine ketchup, vinegar, brown sugar, Worcestershire sauce, lemon juice, and bouillon. Pour over vegetables.
4. Cover. Cook on Low 5–6 hours.
5. Combine cornstarch and water until smooth. Stir into slow cooker.
6. Cover. Cook on High 30 minutes, or until thickened.

Asian Pork Soup

Judi Manos, West Islip, NY

Makes 8 servings

Prep. Time: 25 minutes
Cooking Time: 4–10 hours
Ideal slow-cooker size: 5-qt.

2 cloves garlic, minced
2 medium carrots, cut into
  matchsticks
4 green onions, cut into 1-inch
  pieces
2 Tbsp. light soy sauce
½ tsp. fresh ginger, chopped
⅛ tsp. pepper
2 14½-oz. cans chicken broth
2½ tsp. sodium-free chicken
  bouillon granules
2½ cups water
leftover pork, chopped
1 cup sliced mushrooms
1 cup bean sprouts

1. Combine all ingredients except leftover pork, mushrooms, and sprouts in slow cooker.
2. Cover. Cook on Low 7–9 hours or High 3–4 hours.
3. Stir in leftover pork, mushrooms, and bean sprouts.
4. Cover. Cook on Low 1 hour.

Meatless Mexican Lasagna

Mabel Shirk, Mt. Crawford, VA

Makes 6 servings

Prep. Time: 15 minutes
Cooking Time: 2 hours
Ideal slow-cooker size: 5-qt.

3 cups frozen corn, thawed
15-oz. can black beans,
  rinsed and drained
14½-oz. can diced tomatoes
  with basil, oregano, and
  garlic, undrained
4-oz. can chopped green
  chilies
3 green onions, sliced
2 tsp. dried oregano
2 tsp. ground cumin
4 6-inch corn tortillas, *divided*
1½ cups shredded Mexican-
  blend cheese, *divided*
6 Tbsp. sour cream

1. In a bowl, combine, corn, beans, tomatoes, green chilies, onions, oregano, and cumin.
2. Grease 5-qt. slow cooker. Place 2 tortillas in crock.
3. Spread tortillas with half of the bean mixture.
4. Sprinkle with cheese.
5. Repeat the layers.
6. Cook on High 2 hours or until heated through.
7. Let stand for 5 minutes.
8. Garnish with sour cream.

Golden Cauliflower

Carol Peachey, Lancaster, PA

Makes 4–6 servings

Prep. Time: 10 minutes
Cooking Time: 3½–5 hours
Ideal slow-cooker size: 3-qt.

2 10-oz. pkgs. frozen
  cauliflower, chopped,
  thawed
8-oz. jar cheese sauce
4 slices bacon, crisply
  browned and crumbled

1. Place cauliflower in slow cooker.
2. Pour cheese over top. Top with bacon.
3. Cover. Cook on High 1½ hours and then reduce to Low for an additional 2 hours. Or cook only on Low 4–5 hours.

Cranberry Pudding

Margaret Wheeler,
North Bend, OR

Makes 12 servings

Prep. Time: 35 minutes
Cooking Time: 3½–4½ hours
Ideal slow-cooker size: 4- or 5-qt.

Pudding:
1⅓ cups flour
½ tsp. salt
2 tsp. baking soda
⅓ cup boiling water
6 Tbsp. dark molasses
2 cups whole cranberries
½ cup chopped walnuts
½ cup water

Butter Sauce:
1 cup confectioners' sugar
½ cup fat-free half-and-half
4 Tbsp. light, soft tub
  margarine
1 tsp. vanilla extract

1. Mix together flour and salt.
2. Dissolve baking soda in boiling water. Add to flour and salt.
3. Stir in molasses. Blend well.
4. Fold in cranberries and nuts.
5. Pour into well-greased and floured bread or cake pan that will sit in your cooker. Cover with greased tinfoil.
6. Pour ½ cup water into cooker. Place foil-covered pan in cooker. Cover with cooker lid and steam on High 3 to 4 hours, or until pudding tests done with a wooden pick.
7. Remove pan and uncover. Let stand 5 minutes, then unmold.
8. To make butter sauce, mix together all ingredients in saucepan. Cook, stirring over medium heat, until sugar dissolves.
9. Serve warm butter sauce over warm cranberry pudding.

WINTER

Week 7

THIS WEEK'S
Menu

Sunday: Beer Braised Chicken
Monday: Tasty Pork Tacos
Tuesday: White Chicken Chili
Wednesday: Mexican Rice and Beans
Thursday: Hearty Pork and Veggie Soup
Friday: Barbecued Ham Steaks
Saturday: Macaroni and Cheese with Ham and Peas

Recommended Side Dish: Potluck Baked Corn
Special Dessert: Toffee Treasure Cake

Shopping List

PROTEIN

6-lb. whole chicken

6-lb. boneless pork butt
  roast

3–4 lbs. ham steaks

FROZEN

10-oz. pkg. frozen whole-
  kernel corn

1 cup frozen peas

8 cups frozen corn

DAIRY and REFRIGERATED

2½ sticks butter

6 eggs

1 cup shredded cheese of
  your choice

¼ lb. your favorite creamy
  cheese

12 oz. sour cream

4¼ cups 2% or whole milk

¾ cup shredded cheddar
  cheese

PRODUCE

1 medium onion

1 small onion

½ cup chopped onion

3 limes

1 cup fresh chopped cilantro

2 tomatoes

lettuce

jalapeño peppers

¼ cup chopped bell pepper

2 cups diced potatoes

3 cups chopped mixed
  vegetables, or 1-lb. pkg.
  frozen mixed vegetables

CANNED/DRY GOODS

2 14½-oz. cans cannellini
  beans

Download this shopping list to your smartphone!
(x.co/ShopList)

14½-oz. can garbanzo beans	**DO YOU HAVE THESE ON HAND?**
15-oz. can black beans	
2 16-oz. jars thick and chunky salsa	salt
	pepper
2 10¾-oz. cans cream of celery or mushroom soup	dried basil
	garlic powder
1½ cups vegetable or tomato juice	ground cumin
	dried oregano
7 oz. bottle 7up, Sprite, or ginger ale	cayenne pepper
	dry mustard
tortillas (enough for your family)	ground cinnamon
	whole cloves
minced garlic	sugar
sliced black olives	flour
1 cup long-grain brown rice	baking powder
2 cups uncooked elbow macaroni	baking soda
	vanilla extract
2 slices bread	confectioners' sugar, *optional*
½ of a 1.8-oz. pkg. dry beef-flavored soup mix	2 cups chicken broth
	ketchup
½ of a 1.8 oz. pkg. dry tomato flavored soup mix	¼ cup chopped nuts
6 5/8 oz. ("fun-sized") chocolate-toffee candy bars	**SPIRITS**
	12 oz. beer

Beer Braised Chicken

Hope Comerford,
Clinton Township, MI

Makes 6–8 Servings

Prep. Time: 8–10 minutes
Cooking Time: 8–9 hours
Ideal slow-cooker Size: 6½- to 7-qt.

6-lb. whole chicken
½ stick butter, cut up
12 oz. beer
1 medium onion, quartered

Rub:
½ tsp. salt
⅛ tsp. pepper
1 tsp. dried basil
1 Tbsp. garlic powder

1. Take the giblets out of your chicken breast; rinse the chicken and dry it. Place the chicken breast side down in your slow cooker insert.
2. Stuff it with your onion pieces and place some butter under the skin and around the chicken.
3. Pour the beer over the top. Combine the rub ingredients and sprinkle over the top.
4. Cover and cook on Low for 8–9 hours.

Tasty Pork Tacos

Donna Suter, Pandora, OH

Makes 10–12 servings

Prep. Time: 20 minutes
Cooking Time: 6 hours
Ideal slow-cooker size: 4-qt.

6-lb. boneless pork butt roast
juice and zest of 3 limes
1 tsp. garlic powder
1 tsp. minced garlic
1 tsp. salt
1–2 tsp. ground cumin
1 cup fresh chopped cilantro, *divided*
tortillas

Toppings:
salsa
chopped onions
chopped fresh tomatoes
sliced black olives
torn lettuce
shredded cheese, your choice of flavor
chopped jalapeño peppers
sour cream

1. Grease interior of slow-cooker crock.
2. Place pork in crock.
3. In a bowl, mix together juice and zest of limes, garlic powder, salt, cumin, and ½ cup chopped cilantro.

4. Pour sauce over roast.

5. Cover. Cook on Low 6 hours, or until instant-read meat thermometer registers 145°–150°F when inserted in center of roast.

6. Remove roast from crock and place in good-sized bowl. Shred, using 2 forks.

7. Stir shredded meat back into crock. Add remainder of chopped cilantro.

8. Fill tortillas with shredded meat and add your favorite toppings

White Chicken Chili

Lucille Hollinger, Richland, PA

Makes 8 servings

Prep. Time: 10 minutes
Cooking Time: 5–6 hours
Ideal slow-cooker size: 3-qt.

leftover chicken, chopped
2 cups chicken broth
2 14½-oz. cans cannellini
 beans
14½-oz. can garbanzo beans
¼ cup chopped onion
¼ cup chopped bell pepper
2 tsp. ground cumin
½ tsp. dried oregano
¼ tsp. cayenne pepper
¼ tsp. salt

1. Combine all ingredients in slow cooker.

2. Cover and cook on Low for 5–6 hours.

Tip: Serve with sour cream, shredded cheese, and tortilla chips.

Mexican Rice and Beans

Helen Schlabach, Winesburg, OH

Makes 6–8 servings

Prep. Time: 10 minutes
Cooking Time: 2–3 hours
Ideal slow-cooker size: 4-qt.

1 cup leftover shredded pork
15-oz. can black beans,
 rinsed and drained
10-oz. pkg. frozen whole-
 kernel corn
1 cup long-grain brown rice,
 uncooked
16-oz. jar thick and chunky
 mild or medium salsa
1½ cups vegetable or tomato
 juice
½ tsp. ground cumin
½ tsp. dried oregano
½ tsp. salt
¼ tsp. black pepper
¾ cup shredded cheddar
 cheese

1. Grease interior of slow-cooker crock.

2. Combine all ingredients, except cheese, in crock.

3. Cover. Cook on High 2–3 hours, until rice is tender, stirring once halfway through.

4. Scatter cheese over rice and beans.

5. Allow to stand, uncovered, until cheese melts.

Hearty Pork and Veggie Soup

Sara Harter Fredette,
Goshen, MA

Makes 4–6 servings

Prep. Time: 10–15 minutes
Cooking Time: 4–5 hours
Ideal slow-cooker size: 4-qt.

½ of a 1.8-oz. pkg. dry beef-flavored soup mix
½ of a 1.8-oz. pkg. tomato-flavored soup mix
4 cups water
2 cups diced potatoes
3 cups chopped vegetables (celery, carrots, peppers, onions), or 1-lb. pkg. frozen mixed vegetables
leftover shredded pork

1. In slow cooker, blend powdered soup mix into water. Add vegetables.
2. Cover and cook on High 1 hour, and then on Low 3 hours, or until vegetables are tender.
3. One half hour before end of cooking time, stir in meat.

Barbecued Ham Steaks

Phyllis Good, Lancaster, PA

Makes 4–6 servings

Prep. Time: 15 minutes
Cooking Time: 3–4 hours
Ideal slow-cooker size: 6- or 7-qt. oval

1 small onion, chopped
7-oz. bottle 7up, Sprite, or ginger ale
¼ cup ketchup
1 tsp. dry mustard
1 tsp. salt
⅛ tsp. black pepper
4 whole cloves
3–4 lbs. ham steaks

1. Grease interior of slow-cooker crock.
2. Mix together chopped onion, soda, ketchup, mustard, salt, pepper, and whole cloves in crock.
3. Submerge steaks in sauce. Overlap steaks if you must, but as little as possible.
4. Cover. Cook on Low 3–4 hours, or until meat is heated through but not dry.
5. Fish out cloves and discard.
6. Cut each steak into smaller pieces and serve topped with barbecue sauce.

Macaroni and Cheese with Ham and Peas

Marcia S. Myer, Manheim, PA

Makes 6–8 servings

Prep. Time: 20 minutes
Cooking Time: 2–3 hours
Ideal slow-cooker size: 4- or 5-qt.

2 10¾-oz. cans cream of celery or mushroom soup
2 soup cans, or 2½ cups, milk
½ tsp. garlic powder
leftover ham, cubed
2 cups uncooked elbow macaroni
¼ lb. your favorite creamy cheese, cubed
1 cup frozen peas
2 Tbsp. (¼ stick) butter, melted
2 slices bread, torn

1. Grease interior of slow-cooker crock.
2. Whisk together soup and milk in crock until smooth. Stir in garlic powder, ham, uncooked macaroni, and cubed cheese.
3. Cover. Cook on Low 2–3 hours, or until macaroni are set and soft.
4. Twenty minutes before end of cooking time, stir in peas. Cover and continue cooking.
5. If you like a crusty top, or if water has gathered at the edges, uncover crock and cook on High another 15–20 minutes.
6. While macaroni are cooking, melt butter in skillet.
7. Whirl torn bread in food processor just until coarse crumbs form. Stir crumbs into melted butter and toast, stirring often, until browned.
8. Before serving macaroni and cheese, top with browned crumbs.

Potluck Baked Corn

Velma Stauffer, Akron, PA

Makes 10–12 servings

Prep. Time: 15 minutes
Cooking Time: 3–4 hours
Ideal slow-cooker size: 6-qt.

2 qts. frozen corn, thawed and drained
4 eggs, beaten
2 tsp. salt
1¾ cups 2% or whole milk
2 Tbsp. butter, melted
3 Tbsp. sugar
6 Tbsp. flour

1. Mix all ingredients in mixing bowl until well combined.

2. Pour into greased slow cooker.

3. Cover and cook on High 3–4 hours until set in the middle and lightly browned at edges.

Toffee Treasure Cake

Jeanne Allen, Los Alamos, NM

Makes 12–15 servings

Prep. Time: 30 minutes
Cooking Time: 2–4 hours
Ideal slow-cooker size: 6- or 7-qt. oval or round

1¼ cups sugar, *divided*
1 tsp. ground cinnamon
2 cups flour
1½ tsp. baking powder
1 tsp. baking soda
¼ tsp. salt
1 tsp. vanilla extract
8 oz. sour cream
1½ sticks butter, *divided*
2 eggs
¼ cup chopped nuts of your choice
6 5/8-oz. ("fun-sized") chocolate-toffee candy bars, coarsely crushed
confectioners' sugar, *optional*

1. Combine ¼ cup sugar and 1 tsp. cinnamon. Set aside.

2. Grease interior of slow-cooker crock, or a 9x5- or 8x4-inch loaf pan, or a baking dish that fits into your slow cooker.

3. Soften 1 stick butter. In a mixer bowl, combine flour, 1 cup sugar, baking powder, baking soda, salt, vanilla, sour cream, softened butter, and eggs.

4. Blend at low speed until moistened. Beat 3 minutes at medium speed, scraping bowl occasionally.

5. Spoon half of batter into greased crock, loaf pan, or baking dish.

6. Sprinkle with cinnamon-sugar mixture, then with nuts and crushed candy bars.

7. Top with remaining batter.

8. Melt remaining ½ stick of butter and pour over top.

9. Either suspend loaf pan from edges of slow-cooker crock or place loaf pan or baking dish on jar rings or small trivet in bottom of crock.

10. Prop slow-cooker lid open at one end with a wooden spoon handle or chopstick to allow steam to escape.

11. Cook on High 2–4 hours, or until tester inserted in middle of cake comes out clean.

12. Remove pan or dish from cooker and allow to cool.

13. Cut into slices or squares with a plastic or silicone knife. If you wish, dust with confectioners' sugar.

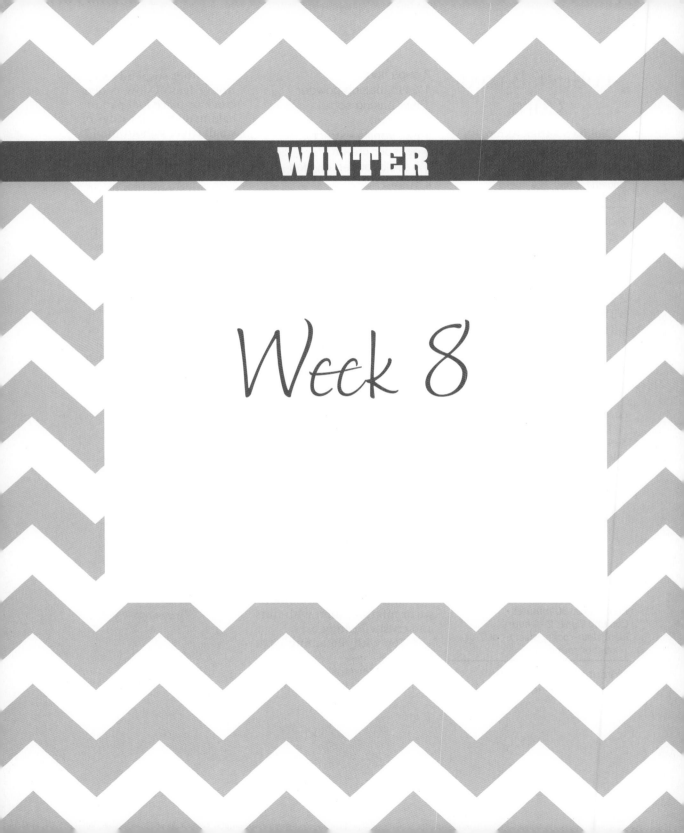

WINTER

Week 8

THIS WEEK'S
Menu

Sunday: Super Sausage Supper
Monday: Pasta Fagioli
Tuesday: Low-Fat Glazed Chicken
Wednesday: Low-Fat Chicken Cacciatore
Thursday: Slow-Cooker Shrimp Marinara
Friday: French Dip
Saturday: Barbecued Beef

Recommended Side Dish: Ethel's Calico Beans
Special Dessert: Self-Frosting Fudge Cake

Shopping List

PROTEIN

16 oz. hot or mild ground
  sausage
8 skinless chicken breast
  halves
1 lb. shrimp
2 lbs. beef top round roast
½ lb. ground beef
½ lb. bacon

FROZEN

16-oz. pkg. frozen mixed
  vegetables
6-oz. can frozen
  concentrated orange juice

DAIRY and REFRIGERATED

grated Parmesan cheese, for
  garnish
2 eggs

PRODUCE

1 cup chopped carrots
1 cup chopped zucchini
½ red onion
¼ lb. fresh mushrooms
½ bell pepper
1 small onion
2 medium onions
2 Tbsp. minced fresh
  parsley

CANNED/DRY GOODS

10¾-oz. can broccoli cheese
  soup
2 14¾-oz. cans diced
  tomatoes with garlic and
  onion
15-oz. can tomato sauce
6-oz. can low-sodium
  tomato sauce

Download this shopping list to your
smartphone!
(x.co/ShopList)

16-oz. can low-sodium chopped tomatoes

6-oz. can tomato paste

3 oz. low-sodium tomato paste

16-oz. can red kidney beans

14½-oz. can pork and beans

15-oz. can butter beans

18½-oz. pkg. chocolate fudge pudding cake mix

¼ cup dry red kidney beans

¼ cup dry great northern beans

¾ cups dry pasta of your choice

6 oz. dry spaghetti (yields 3 cups cooked)

¾ bottle barbecue sauce

½ 12-oz. bottle/can cream soda or root beer

rolls

buns

DO YOU HAVE THESE ON HAND?

garlic powder

onion powder

Italian seasoning

salt

pepper

dried marjoram

ground nutmeg

dried oregano

dried basil

seasoned salt

dried rosemary

dried thyme

bay leaf

whole peppercorns

1 clove garlic

oil of your choice

brown sugar

sugar

3 cups beef broth

cornstarch

1 cup light soy sauce

½ cup ketchup

apple cider vinegar

⅓ cup pecan halves

chocolate syrup

Super Sausage Supper

Anne Townsend,
Albuquerque, NM

Makes 3–4 servings

Prep. Time: 5 minutes
Cooking Time: 1–6 hours
Ideal slow-cooker size: 3-qt.

2 8-oz. pkgs. hot or mild
  ground sausage
16-oz. pkg. frozen mixed
  vegetables
10¾-oz. can broccoli cheese
  soup

1. Brown sausage in a pan. Reserve 8 oz. of it and place in the refrigerator for later this week. Place the remaining browned sausage in slow cooker.

2. Distribute frozen vegetables over the sausage.

3. Spread undiluted soup on top of the vegetables.

4. Cover and cook on High for 1 hour, or on Low 5–6 hours, or until meat is cooked and vegetables are tender.

Pasta Fagioli

Hope Comerford,
Clinton Township, MI

Makes 5–6 servings

Prep. Time: 20 minutes
Cooking Time: 8–10 hours
Ideal slow-cooker size: 7-qt.

leftover browned sausage
3 cups beef broth

2 14½-oz. cans diced
  tomatoes with garlic and
  onion
1 cups water
15-oz. can tomato sauce
¼ cup dry red kidney beans,
  soaked overnight, drained
  and rinsed

¼ cup dry great northern
  beans, soaked overnight,
  drained and rinsed
1 tsp. garlic powder
1 tsp. onion powder
1 tsp. Italian Seasoning
salt and pepper, to taste
1 cup chopped carrots

1 cups peeled and chopped zucchini
½ red onion, chopped
¾ cups dry pasta of your choice
Parmesan cheese, for garnish

1. Combine all ingredients (except the Parmesan) in the slow cooker and stir.
2. Cook on Low for 8–10 hours.
3. About 45 minutes before serving, add the pasta. Serve with a sprinkle of Parmesan cheese.

Low-Fat Glazed Chicken

Martha Hershey, Ronks, PA
Jean Butzer, Batavia, NY

Makes 6 servings

Prep. Time: 15–20 minutes
Cooking Time: 3¼–6¼ hours
Ideal slow-cooker size: 4-qt.

6-oz. can frozen concentrated orange juice, thawed
½ tsp. dried marjoram
¼ tsp. ground nutmeg
¼ tsp. garlic powder
8 skinless chicken breast halves
¼ cup water
2 Tbsp. cornstarch

1. Mix orange juice concentrate with marjoram, nutmeg, and garlic powder.
2. Dip chicken breasts in sauce. Place in slow cooker.
3. Pour remaining orange juice mixture over chicken.

4. Cover and cook on Low 6 hours or on High 3–4 hours.
5. Remove chicken from slow cooker and keep warm on a platter.
6. Pour remaining liquid in a saucepan.
7. Mix the cornstarch in water and pour into saucepan. Cook until thickened, stirring continually.
8. Pour sauce over the chicken.

Serving Suggestion: Serve with rice or noodles.

Low-Fat Chicken Cacciatore

Dawn Day, Westminster, CA

Makes 5 servings

Prep. Time: 20 minutes
Cooking Time: 5–6 hours
Ideal slow-cooker size: 3-qt.

¼ lb. fresh mushrooms
½ bell pepper, chopped
1 small onion, chopped
12-oz. can low-sodium chopped tomatoes
3-oz. low-sodium tomato paste
6-oz. can low-sodium tomato sauce
¼ tsp. dried oregano
¼ tsp. dried basil
¼ tsp. garlic powder
¼ tsp. salt
⅛ tsp. black pepper
leftover chicken, chopped

1. Combine all ingredients in slow cooker, except leftover chicken.
2. Cover. Cook on Low 5–6 hours. The last hour of cooking, stir in the leftover chicken.

Serving Suggestion: Serve over rice or whole wheat, or semolina, pasta.

Slow Cooker Shrimp Marinara

Judy Miles, Centreville, MD

Makes 6 servings

Prep. Time: 10–15 minutes
Cooking Time: 3¼–4¼ hours
Ideal slow-cooker size: 3½-qt.

16-oz. can low-sodium chopped tomatoes
2 Tbsp. minced fresh parsley
1 clove garlic, minced
½ tsp. dried basil
½ tsp. salt
¼ tsp. black pepper
1 tsp. dried oregano
6-oz. can tomato paste
½ tsp. seasoned salt
1 lb. shrimp, cooked and shelled
3 cups cooked spaghetti (about 6 oz. dry)
grated Parmesan cheese, for garnish

1. Combine tomatoes, parsley, garlic, basil, salt, pepper, oregano, tomato paste, and seasoned salt in slow cooker.

2. Cover. Cook on Low 3–4 hours.

3. Stir shrimp into sauce.

4. Cover. Cook on High 10–15 minutes.

5. Serve over cooked spaghetti. Top with Parmesan cheese.

French Dip

Loretta Weisz, Auburn, WA

Makes 12 servings

Prep. Time: 10 minutes
Cooking Time: 5–6 hours
Ideal slow-cooker size: 4- or 5-qt.

2-lb. beef top round roast, trimmed
3 cups water
1 cup light soy sauce
1 tsp. dried rosemary
1 tsp. dried thyme
1 tsp. garlic powder
1 bay leaf
3 whole peppercorns
rolls

1. Place roast in slow cooker. Add water, soy sauce, and seasonings.

2. Cover. Cook on Low 5–6 hours.

3. Remove meat from broth. Thinly slice or shred. Keep warm.

4. Strain broth and skim off fat. Pour broth into small cups for dipping.

5. Serve beef on rolls.

Barbecued Beef

Hope Comerford,
Clinton Township, MI

Makes 8 servings

Prep. Time: 5 minutes
Cooking Time: 3–4 hours
Ideal slow-cooker size: 3-qt.

1 medium onion, sliced into
   rings
¾ bottle barbecue sauce
½ 12 oz. bottle/can cream
   soda or root beer
leftover shredded beef
buns

1. Place all ingredients
except the shredded beef and
buns into the slow cooker.
2. Cook on Low for 3–4
hours.
3. Stir in the leftover beef
and cook for 1 more hour.
4. Serve on your favorite
kind of bun.

Ethel's Calico Beans

Ethel Mumaw, Berlin, OH

Makes 6–8 servings

Prep. Time: 15 minutes
Cooking Time: 8 hours
Ideal slow-cooker size: 4-qt.

½ lb. ground beef
1 medium onion, chopped
½ lb. bacon, diced
½ cup ketchup
2 Tbsp. apple cider vinegar
½ cup brown sugar, packed
16-oz. can red kidney beans,
   drained
14½-oz. can pork and beans,
   undrained

15-oz. can butter beans,
   drained

1. Brown ground beef,
onion, and bacon in skillet.
Drain.
2. Combine all ingredients
in slow cooker.
3. Cover. Cook on Low 8
hours.

Self-Frosting Fudge Cake

Mary Puterbaugh, Elwood, IN

Makes 8–10 servings

Prep. Time: 10 minutes
Cooking Time: 2–3 hours
Ideal slow-cooker size: 4- to 5-qt.

2½ cups of 18½-oz. pkg.
   chocolate fudge pudding
   cake mix

2 eggs
¾ cup water
3 Tbsp. oil of your choice
⅓ cup pecan halves
¼ cup chocolate syrup
¼ cup warm water
3 Tbsp. sugar

1. Combine cake mix,
eggs, ¾ cup water, and oil in
electric mixer bowl. Beat 2
minutes.
2. Pour into greased and
floured bread or cake pan
that will fit into your slow
cooker.
3. Sprinkle nuts over
mixture.
4. Blend together chocolate
syrup, ¼ cup water, and
sugar. Spoon over batter.
5. Cover. Bake on High 2–3
hours.

Week 9

THIS WEEK'S
Menu

Sunday: Minestra di Ceci
Monday: Turkey Fajitas
Tuesday: Turkey Fajita Soup
Wednesday: Sausage-Potato Slow-Cooker Dinner
Thursday: Swiss Steak
Friday: Rice and Beans—and Sausage
Saturday: Slow-Cooker Beef with Mushrooms

Recommended Side Dish: Artichokes
Special Dessert: Fruity Cake

Shopping List

PROTEIN

3 lbs. turkey tenderloins

2 lbs. sausage links

3-lb. round steak

DAIRY and REFRIGERATED

2½ cups shredded cheddar
  cheese

2¼ sticks butter

sour cream, for garnish

PRODUCE

1 sprig fresh rosemary

10 leaves fresh sage

4 ribs celery

5 medium onions

1 large onion, or 1 pkg. dry
  onion soup mix

1 cup chopped red onion

1 red bell pepper

1 yellow bell pepper

1 orange bell pepper

1 cup mushrooms

½ lb. mushrooms, or 2 4-oz.
  cans sliced mushrooms

4–6 artichokes

6 medium potatoes

lettuce, for garnish

chopped tomatoes, for
  garnish

CANNED/DRY GOODS

14½-oz. can diced tomatoes
  with green chilies

10¾-oz. can cream of
  mushroom soup

16-oz. can tomatoes

2 16-oz. cans kidney beans

1 or 2 21-oz. can(s) apple,
  blueberry, or peach pie
  filling

Download this shopping list to your
smartphone!
(x.co/ShopList)

18¼-oz. pkg. yellow cake mix	ground cumin
1 lb. dry garbanzo beans	cayenne pepper
1 cup uncooked small pasta	pepper
1¼-oz. envelope taco seasoning mix	cream of tartar
	dried oregano
8 7½-inch flour tortillas	dried thyme
rice	red pepper flakes
sliced olives, for garnish	paprika
1¾ cups tomato juice	3–4 cloves garlic
	flour
DO YOU HAVE THESE ON HAND?	Worcestershire sauce
	olive oil
salt	6 cups chicken broth
chili powder	½ cup beef stock
sea salt	1 cup lemon juice
garlic powder	⅓ cup chopped walnuts
onion powder	

Minestra di Ceci

Jeanette Oberholtzer,
Manheim, PA

Makes 4–6 servings

Prep. Time: 25 minutes
Soaking Time: 8 hours, or
overnight
Cooking Time: 5½–6 hours
Ideal slow-cooker size: 4-qt.

1 lb. dry garbanzo beans
1 sprig fresh rosemary
10 leaves fresh sage
2 Tbsp. salt
1–2 large cloves garlic,
  minced
olive oil
1 cup uncooked small pasta,
  your choice of shape, or
  uncooked penne

1. Wash beans. Place in slow cooker. Cover with water. Stir in rosemary, sage, and salt. Soak 8 hours, or overnight.
2. Drain water. Remove herbs.
3. Refill slow cooker with beans and fresh water to 1-inch above beans.
4. Cover. Cook on Low 5 hours.
5. Sauté garlic in olive oil in skillet until clear.
6. Puree half of garbanzo beans, along with several cups of broth from cooker, in blender. Return puree to slow cooker.
7. Add garlic and oil.
8. Boil pasta in saucepan until al dente, about 5 minutes. Drain. Add to beans.
9. Cover. Cook on High 30–60 minutes, or until pasta is tender and heated through, but not mushy.

Turkey Fajitas

Carol Ambrose,
McMinnville, OR

Makes 8 servings

Prep. Time: 10–15 minutes
Cooking Time: 3–4 hours
Ideal slow-cooker size: 2½-qt.

3 lbs. turkey tenderloins
1¼-oz. envelope taco
  seasoning mix
1 rib celery, chopped
1 medium onion, chopped
14½-oz. can diced tomatoes
  and green chilies, undrained
1 cup shredded cheddar
  cheese
8 7½-inch flour tortillas

Toppings:
lettuce
sour cream
sliced olives
chopped tomatoes

1. Cut turkey into 2½-inch-long strips. Place in zip-top plastic bag.

2. Add taco seasoning to bag. Seal and shake to coat meat.

3. Empty seasoned turkey into slow cooker. Add celery, onion, and tomatoes. Stir together gently.

4. Cover. Cook on High 3–4 hours, or just until turkey is cooked through and tender.

5. Stir in cheese.

6. Warm tortillas according to package directions. Spoon turkey mixture evenly into center of each tortilla, and roll up.

7. Serve with Toppings.

Turkey Fajita Soup

Hope Comerford, Clinton Township, MI

Makes 4–6 servings

Prep. Time: 10 minutes
Cooking Time: 3–5 hours
Ideal slow-cooker size: 4-qt.

1 cup chopped red onion
1 red bell pepper, chopped
1 yellow bell pepper, chopped
1 orange bell pepper, chopped
1 cup mushrooms, chopped
1 tsp. olive oil
1 tsp. chili powder
1 tsp. sea salt
1 tsp. garlic powder
1 tsp. onion powder
½ tsp. ground cumin
⅛ tsp. cayenne pepper

6 cups chicken broth
leftover turkey

1. Place all ingredients into the slow cooker except the leftover turkey.

2. Cover and cook on Low for 3–4 hours.

3. Add in the leftover turkey and cook an additional 30–60 minutes, or until the turkey is heated through.

Sausage-Potato Slow-Cooker Dinner

Deborah Swartz, Grottoes, VA

Makes 6–8 servings

Prep. Time: 25–30 minutes
Cooking Time: 3–9 hours
Ideal slow-cooker size: 4-qt.

1 cup water
½ tsp. cream of tartar
6 medium potatoes, thinly sliced, peeled or not, *divided*
2 lbs. sausage links, any kind you like, *divided*
1 medium onion, chopped, *divided*
¼ cup flour, *divided*
salt, to taste
pepper, to taste
1½ cups grated cheddar cheese, *divided*
2 Tbsp. butter
10¾-oz. can cream of mushroom soup

1. Combine water and cream of tartar in a good sized mixing bowl. Place potatoes in water as you slice them.

When finished slicing, toss potatoes in water to keep them from turning brown. Drain off water.

2. Layer half of potatoes, sausage, onion, flour, a sprinkling of salt and pepper, and half of cheddar cheese in slow cooker.

3. Repeat layers of potatoes, sausage, onion, flour, salt, and pepper until completely used.

4. Dot butter over top. Pour soup over all.

5. Cover. Cook on Low 7–9 hours or on High 3–4 hours, or until potatoes and onions are tender.

6. Sprinkle reserved cheese over top just before serving.

Swiss Steak

Marie Shank, Harrisonburg, VA

Makes 6–8 servings

Prep. Time: 5 minutes
Cooking Time: 3–10 hours
Ideal slow-cooker size: 4-qt.

3-lb. round steak, cut into serving pieces
1 tsp. salt
½ tsp. pepper
1 large onion, sliced, or 1 pkg. dry onion soup mix
16-oz. can tomatoes

1. Combine all ingredients in slow cooker.

2. Cover. Cook on Low 6–10 hours or on High 3–4 hours, just until meat is fork-tender.

Rice and Beans—and Sausage

Marcia S. Myer, Manheim, PA

Makes 8 servings

Prep. Time: 25 minutes
Cooking Time: 3–4 hours
Ideal slow-cooker size: 5-qt.

3 ribs celery, chopped
1 medium onion, chopped
2 cloves garlic, minced
1¾ cups tomato juice
2 16-oz. cans kidney beans, drained
¾ tsp. dried oregano
¾ tsp. dried thyme
¼ tsp. red pepper flakes
¼ tsp. pepper
leftover sausage

1. Combine all ingredients in slow cooker.
2. Cover. Cook on Low 3–4 hours.

Serving Suggestion: Serve over rice. Garnish with shredded cheese if you wish.

Slow Cooker Beef with Mushrooms

Grace W. Yoder, Harrisonburg, VA

Makes 6 servings

Prep. Time: 10 minutes
Cooking Time: 2–3 hours
Ideal slow-cooker size: 3-qt.

2 medium onions, thinly sliced

½ lb. mushrooms, sliced, or 2 4-oz. cans sliced mushrooms, drained
salt, to taste
pepper, to taste
1 Tbsp. Worcestershire sauce
1 Tbsp. oil of your choice
paprika, to taste
½ cup beef stock
leftover steak
rice

THIS WEEK'S
Menu

Sunday: Savory Chicken Meal #1
Monday: A-Touch-of-Asia Ribs
Tuesday: Savory Chicken Meal #2
Wednesday: Pork Thai Stew
Thursday: Walking Tacos
Friday: Upside-Down Pizza
Saturday: Beef Nachos

Recommended Side Dish: Chinese Vegetables
Special Dessert: Pears in Ginger Sauce

Shopping List

PROTEIN

4 boneless skinless chicken
  breast halves

4 skinless chicken quarters

6 lbs. country-style pork
  ribs

3 lbs. ground beef

FROZEN

16-oz. bag Asian stir-fry
  frozen vegetable mix

DAIRY and REFRIGERATED

1 cup grated mozzarella
  cheese

8 oz. shredded cheese of
  your choice

grated Parmesan cheese

shredded cheese of your
  choice, for garnish

3 eggs

1½ cups milk

sour cream or plain Greek
  yogurt, *optional*

guacamole, *optional*

PRODUCE

6 pears

¼ cup chopped sweet red
  bell pepper

2 cups sliced red peppers

½ medium green or red bell
  pepper

1 Tbsp. fresh chopped
  parsley, or 1 tsp. dried,
  optional

2 carrots

5 ribs celery

2 medium onions

2 small onions

½ cup chopped onion

6 green onions

Download this shopping list to your
smartphone!
(x.co/ShopList)

diced onions, for garnish
green onions, for garnish
¼ lb. fresh mushrooms,
  or 4-oz. can chopped
  mushrooms
1 cup sliced mushrooms
1 cup sliced green cabbage
2 cups bean sprouts
diced cucumbers, for garnish
diced tomatoes, for garnish
shredded lettuce, for garnish

CANNED/DRY GOODS

10¾-oz. can cream of
  chicken soup
27-oz. jar duck sauce
rice
individual-sized bags
  Doritos, Fritos, or other
  corn chips of your choice
tortilla chips
minced garlic
1 cup pizza or spaghetti
  sauce
¾ cup teriyaki sauce
¼ cup toasted coconut
salsa, *optional*

DO YOU HAVE THESE ON HAND?

dried parsley, or fresh
ground ginger
paprika
red pepper flakes
garlic powder
onion powder
ground cumin
chili powder
salt
dried oregano
dried basil
pepper
ground nutmeg
cornstarch
flour
sugar
baking soda
oil of your choice
soy sauce
rice vinegar
lemon juice
3 cloves garlic
creamy peanut butter
chopped peanuts, for
  garnish

SPIRITS

1 cup white wine

Savory Chicken Meal #1

Shari Mast, Harrisonburg, VA

Makes 8 servings

Prep. Time: 15 minutes
Cooking Time: 4–5 hours
Ideal slow-cooker size: 5-qt.

4 boneless, skinless chicken
  breast halves
4 skinless chicken quarters
10¾-oz. can cream of chicken
  soup
1 Tbsp. water
¼ cup chopped sweet red
  peppers
1 Tbsp. chopped fresh
  parsley, or 1 tsp. dried
  parsley, *optional*
1 Tbsp. lemon juice
½ tsp. paprika, *optional*

1. Layer chicken in slow
cooker.
2. Combine remaining
ingredients and pour over
chicken. Make sure all pieces
are covered with sauce.
3. Cover. Cook on High 4–5
hours.

A-Touch-of-Asia Ribs

Sharon Shank, Bridgewater, VA

Makes 8–10 servings

Prep. Time: 5–10 minutes
Cooking Time: 4–8 hours
Ideal slow-cooker size: 5- to 6-qt.

6 lbs. country-style pork ribs,
  cut into serving-size pieces
¼ cup teriyaki sauce

¼ cup cornstarch
27-oz. jar duck sauce
2 Tbsp. minced garlic,
  optional

1. Place ribs in the bottom
of your slow cooker.
2. In a large bowl, stir
together teriyaki sauce and
cornstarch. Blend in duck
sauce, and garlic if you wish.
3. Pour the sauce over the
ribs, making sure that each
layer is well covered.
4. Cover and cook on Low
8 hours, or on High 4–5
hours.

Savory Chicken Meal #2

Shari Mast, Harrisonburg, VA

Makes 3–4 servings

Prep. Time: 20 minutes
Cooking Time: 3¼–4¼ hours
Ideal slow-cooker size: 3-qt.

leftover chicken and broth
   from Savory Chicken Meal
   #1
2 carrots
1 rib celery
2 medium onions
2 Tbsp. flour, or cornstarch
¼ cup cold water

1. For a second Savory Chicken Meal, pick leftover chicken off bone. Set aside.

2. Return remaining broth to slow cooker and stir in thinly sliced carrots and celery, and onions cut up in chunks. Cook 3–4 hours on High.

3. In a separate bowl, mix flour or cornstarch with cold water. When smooth, stir into hot broth.

4. Stir in cut-up chicken. Heat 15–20 minutes, or until broth thickens and chicken is hot.

Serving Suggestion: Serve over rice or pasta.

Pork Thai Stew

Marilyn Mowry, Irving, TX

Makes 6 servings

Prep. Time: 15–30 minutes
Cooking Time: 2½–3 hours
Ideal slow-cooker size: 4-qt.

2 cloves garlic, sliced
2 cups sliced red bell pepper
¼ cup rice vinegar
½ cup teriyaki sauce
1–2 tsp. red pepper flakes,
   according to your taste
   preference
leftover rib meat
¼–½ cup creamy peanut
   butter
rice, cooked
chopped peanuts
chopped green onions

1. Place garlic, red bell pepper, rice vinegar, teriyaki sauce, red pepper flakes, and leftover rib meat into the slow cooker.

2. Cook 2–2½ hours on Low.

3. Stir in peanut butter. Continue cooking for 30 more minutes, until heated through.

4. Serve over cooked rice.

5. Pass bowls of chopped peanuts and sliced green onions for each diner to add as they wish.

Walking Tacos

Hope Comerford,
Clinton Township, MI

Makes 15–20 servings

Prep. Time: 5 minutes
Cooking Time: 6–7 hours
Ideal slow-cooker size: 3- to 4-qt.

2 tsp. garlic powder
2 tsp. onion powder
1 Tbsp. ground cumin
2 Tbsp. chili powder
1 tsp. salt
2 lbs. ground beef
1 small onion, minced
1 clove garlic, minced
½ tsp. dried oregano
½ tsp. red pepper flakes
Individual-sized bags of
   Doritos, Fritos, or other corn
   chips of your choice

Toppings:
shredded lettuce
shredded cheese
diced tomatoes
diced onions
diced cucumbers
salsa

1. Place all of the spices in a bowl and mix it up.

2. Crumble the raw ground beef into your crock.

3. Sprinkle the seasoning mix onto the beef and stir it up.

4. Cook on High for 1 hour to brown the beef a bit. Stir it and break it up a bit. Then, cook it on Low for 5–6 hours more.

5. To serve, give each person an individual-sized bag of Doritos, Fritos, or chip of their choice. Each person can then open it, crush the chips by squeezing the bottom of the bag, then add beef and the toppings of their choice.

Upside-Down Pizza

Julia Rohrer, Aaronsburg, PA

Makes 4–5 servings

Prep. Time: 30 minutes
Cooking Time: 5–6 hours
Ideal slow-cooker size: 6-qt.

1 lb. ground beef
1 small onion, chopped
½ medium red or green bell
    pepper, chopped
½ tsp. dried basil
½ tsp. dried oregano
1 cup pizza or spaghetti
    sauce
¼ lb. fresh mushrooms
    or 4-oz. can chopped
    mushrooms, drained
1 cup grated mozzarella
    cheese
sprinkling of dried oregano
sprinkling of grated Parmesan
    cheese

Batter:
3 eggs
1½ cups milk
1½ Tbsp. oil of your choice
½ tsp. salt
1 tsp. baking soda
1¾ cups flour

1. Grease interior of slow-cooker crock.
2. If you have time, brown beef, onion, and pepper together in a skillet. Using a slotted spoon, lift beef and veggies out of drippings and place in good-sized bowl. If you don't have time, place beef in bowl and use a sturdy spoon to break it up into small clumps. Mix in onion and chopped pepper.
3. Spoon beef and vegetables into crock.
4. Stir in herbs, sauce, and mushrooms.
5. Cover. Cook on Low 4 hours, or until hot in center.
6. Thirty minutes before end of cooking time, prepare batter by beating eggs, milk, and oil together in good-sized mixing bowl.
7. Add salt, baking soda, and flour, stirring just until mixed.
8. Uncover crock. Top beef and vegetables with grated mozzarella cheese.
9. Spoon batter over top, spreading it out evenly. Do not stir.
10. Sprinkle with oregano and Parmesan cheese.
11. Cover. Cook on High 1 hour, or until toothpick inserted in center of dough comes out clean.

Beef Nachos

Hope Comerford,
Clinton Township, MI

Makes 6 servings

Prep. Time: 8 minutes
Cooking Time: 10–15 minutes

leftover taco meat
tortilla chips
8 oz. shredded cheese,
    whatever kind you like
½ cup onions, chopped

Additional Toppings:
shredded lettuce
salsa
chopped tomatoes
diced cucumbers
sour cream or Greek yogurt
green onions, diced
guacamole

1. Preheat the oven to 400°F.

2. Spray your baking sheet with nonstick spray, then arrange as many chips as you wish across the baking sheet.

3. Top with the leftover taco meat, then evenly spread the oven across the chips. Cover all tortilla chips evenly with the shredded cheese.

4. Bake for 10–15 minutes, or until cheese is melted.

5. Top with any additional toppings you wish.

Chinese Vegetables

Rebecca Leichty,
Harrisonburg, VA

Makes 6 servings

Prep. Time: 20 minutes
Cooking Time: 3–4 hours
Ideal slow-cooker size: 5-qt.

4 ribs celery, sliced on the bias
6 green onions, sliced on the bias, *divided*
1 cup sliced fresh mushrooms
1 cup sliced green cabbage
16-oz. bag Asian stir-fry frozen vegetable mix
1 Tbsp. sugar
1 Tbsp. rice vinegar
3 Tbsp. soy sauce
¼ tsp. black pepper
2 Tbsp. water
1 Tbsp. cornstarch
2 cups bean sprouts

1. Combine celery, 4 sliced green onions, mushrooms, cabbage, and frozen vegetables in slow cooker.

2. Separately, whisk together sugar, vinegar, soy sauce, pepper, water, and cornstarch. Pour over vegetables, stirring gently to combine.

3. Cover and cook on Low for 2–3 hours, until vegetables are as tender as you like them and sauce is thickened.

4. Stir in sprouts and remaining 2 green onions. Cover and allow to rest for 15 minutes before serving.

Pears in Ginger Sauce

Sharon Timpe, Jackson, WI

Makes 6 servings

Prep. Time: 20 minutes
Cooking Time: 3–5 hours
Standing Time: 45 minutes
Ideal slow-cooker size: 6-qt.

6 fresh pears with stems

1 cup white wine
½ cup sugar
½ cup water
3 Tbsp. lemon juice
1 tsp. ground ginger
pinch ground nutmeg
pinch salt
¼ cup toasted coconut, for serving

1. Peel pears, leaving whole with stems intact.

2. Place pears in buttered slow cooker, upright, shaving bottoms slightly if necessary.

3. Combine wine, sugar, water, lemon juice, ginger, nutmeg, and salt. Pour evenly over pears.

4. Cover and cook on Low for 3–5 hours until pears are tender.

5. Allow pears and liquid to cool.

6. To serve, set a pear in a dessert dish, drizzle with sauce, and sprinkle with toasted coconut.

Week 11

THIS WEEK'S
Menu

Sunday: Honey-Baked Ham

Monday: Italian Sausage, Peppers, and Potatoes

Tuesday: Verenike (or Creamy Lasagna)

Wednesday: Sausage Town

Thursday: Black Bean Ham Soup

Friday: Salsa Chicken

Saturday: Salsa Chicken Salad

Recommended Side Dish: Au Gratin Green Beans

Special Dessert: Cookie Divine

Shopping List

PROTEIN
5-lb. fully cooked ham

2 lbs. sweet or hot Italian
  sausage

8 boneless, skinless chicken
  thighs

FROZEN
whipped topping, *optional*

DAIRY and REFRIGERATED
12 oz. cottage cheese

5 large eggs

1½ cups sour cream

2¼ cups shredded cheddar
  cheese

½ cup cubed Velveeta

3 sticks butter

⅔ cup cream

PRODUCE
½ cup pineapple chunks

½ cup cranberries

1 lb. small red potatoes

1 large onion

1 medium onion

1 cup chopped onion

½ cup diced onion

diced avocado, *optional*

2 red or yellow bell peppers

2 cups chopped carrots

1 cup chopped celery

1 head lettuce (romaine
  recommended)

chopped tomatoes, *optional*

CANNED/DRY GOODS
1¼ cups evaporated milk

Download this shopping list to your smartphone!
(x.co/ShopList)

2 15-oz. cans black beans
15-oz. can crushed tomatoes
2 14-oz. cans green beans
¾ cup dry lentils
4 14½-oz. cans chicken broth
2 14½-oz. cans vegetable or chicken broth
¾ cup uncooked long-grain brown rice
4–5 uncooked lasagna noodles
2¼ cups salsa
tortilla chips, crushed, optional

DO YOU HAVE THESE ON HAND?
black pepper
dried thyme
dried basil
dried oregano

dried sage
ground cumin
chili powder
sea salt, optional
salt
2 Tbsp. dry taco seasoning mix
4 cloves garlic
flour
baking soda
sugar
brown sugar
unsweetened cocoa powder
honey
2 vanilla beans or 2 Tbsp. vanilla extract
hot pepper sauce
Dijon mustard
sliced almonds, optional

SPIRITS
dry sherry

Honey-Baked Ham

Nicole Koloski,
East Sandwich, MA

Makes 6–7 servings

Prep. Time: 20 minutes
Cooking Time: 5¼ hours
Ideal slow-cooker size: 6- or 7-qt. oval

5-lb. fully cooked ham
½ cup brown sugar
¼ cup dry sherry
3 Tbsp. honey
3 Tbsp. Dijon mustard
¼ tsp. coarsely ground black pepper
½ cup pineapple chunks
½ cup fresh cranberries

1. Grease interior of slow-cooker crock.

2. Using a sharp knife, score surface of ham into diamond shapes, cutting about ¼-inch deep. Place ham in crock.

3. Cover cooker. Cook on Low 3 hours.

4. While ham is cooking, blend together brown sugar, sherry, honey, mustard, and black pepper.

5. Brush ham with glaze. Cover and continue cooking.

6. After ham has cooked 2 more hours (for a total of 5 hours), brush again with glaze.

7. Using toothpicks, decorate ham with pineapple chunks and cranberries, spreading pieces over ham evenly.

8. Cover and cook on High another 15 minutes.

9. When ham is heated through, remove from cooker with sturdy tongs and metal spatulas supporting. Slice meat.

10. Place slices on deep platter, covering them with glaze.

11. Put any remaining glaze, and any pineapples and cranberries that have fallen off, in a bowl to pass around the table for diners to add more to their individual plates.

Italian Sausage, Peppers, and Potatoes

Maryann Markano,
Wilmington, DE

Makes 4 servings

Prep. Time: 15–20 minutes
Cooking Time: 2–6 hours
Ideal slow-cooker size: 5-qt.

2 lbs. sweet or hot Italian sausage, cut on the diagonal in 1-inch lengths

1 lb. small red potatoes, each cut in half
1 large onion, cut into 12 wedges
2 red or yellow bell peppers, or 1 of each color, cut into strips

1. Grease interior of slow-cooker crock.
2. Put sausage, potatoes, and onion into crock. Stir together well.
3. Gently stir in bell pepper strips.
4. Cover. Cook on Low 4–6 hours, or on High 2–3 hours, or until sausage is cooked through and potatoes and onions are as tender as you like them.

Verenike (or Creamy Lasagna)

Jennifer Yoder Sommers, Harrisonburg, VA

Makes 4–5 servings

Prep. Time: 10–15 minutes
Cooking Time: 5–6 hours
Ideal slow-cooker size: 3-qt.

12 oz. cottage cheese
2 large eggs
½ tsp. salt
¼ tsp. pepper
½ cup sour cream
1 cup evaporated milk
1 cup leftover ham, cubed
4–5 uncooked lasagna noodles

1. Combine all ingredients except noodles in a good-sized mixing bowl.
2. Place half of creamy ham mixture in bottom of cooker.

3. Stack in uncooked noodles. Break them to fit if you need to.
4. Cover with remaining half of creamy ham sauce. Push noodles down so that they are fully submerged in the sauce.
5. Cover. Cook on Low 5–6 hours, or until noodles are tender but not mushy.

Sausage Town

Kathy Hertzler, Lancaster, PA

Makes 4–6 servings

Prep. Time: 15 minutes
Cooking Time: 9–10 hours
Ideal slow-cooker size: 5-qt.

1 cup chopped onion
¾ cup dry lentils, rinsed well and picked clean
¾ cup shredded cheddar cheese
2 cloves garlic, crushed
½ tsp. dried thyme
½ tsp. dried basil
½ tsp. dried oregano
⅛ tsp. dried sage
¼ tsp. salt
freshly ground black pepper, to taste
leftover sausage, cut into bite-sized pieces
4 14½-oz. cans chicken broth
¾ cup uncooked long-grain brown rice

1. Grease interior of slow-cooker crock.
2. Place onions, lentils, cheese, garlic, thyme, basil, oregano, sage, salt, black pepper, sausage, and chicken broth into crock. Stir together well.
3. Cover. Cook on Low 6–7 hours.

4. Stir in uncooked rice.
5. Cover. Continue cooking on Low another 3 hours, or until both rice and lentils are as tender as you like them.
6. If dish is juicier than you want, uncover during last 30 minutes of cooking and turn cooker to High.
7. Stir well and serve.

Black Bean Ham Soup

Colleen Heatwole, Burton, MI

Makes 8 servings

Prep. Time: 30 minutes
Cooking Time: 6–8 hours
Ideal slow-cooker size: 5-qt.

2 cups chopped carrots
1 cup chopped celery
2 cloves garlic, minced
1 medium onion, chopped
2 15-oz. cans black beans, undrained
2 14½-oz. cans chicken or vegetable broth
15-oz. can crushed tomatoes
1½ tsp. dried basil
½ tsp. dried oregano
½ tsp. ground cumin
½ tsp. chili powder
¼ tsp. hot pepper sauce
1 cup diced leftover ham

1. Combine all ingredients in slow cooker.
2. Cover and cook on Low 6–8 hours or until vegetables are tender.

Tip: Serve with hot cooked rice. Brown rice is more nutritious than white.

Salsa Chicken

Barbara Smith, Bedford, PA

Makes 6–8 servings

Prep. Time: 15 minutes
Cooking Time: 4 hours
Ideal slow-cooker size: 4- or 5-qt.

8 boneless, skinless chicken thighs
1½ cups salsa, your choice of heat
2 Tbsp. dry taco seasoning mix
1½ cups shredded cheddar cheese
¼ cup sour cream, *optional*

1. Grease interior of slow-cooker crock.
2. Lay thighs in slow cooker. If you need to create a second layer, stagger the pieces so they don't completely overlap each other.
3. Spoon salsa over each thigh, making sure not to miss the ones on the first layer that are partly covered by pieces above.
4. Sprinkle taco seasoning mix over each thigh, again, making sure not to miss the ones on the first layer.
5. Cover. Cook on Low for 4 hours, or until instant-read meat thermometer registers 160–165°F when stuck into the meat.
6. Thirty minutes before the end of the cooking time, scatter shredded cheese over each thigh, including those on the first layer that are partly covered.

7. Top each thigh with sour cream as you serve the chicken, if you wish.

Salsa Chicken Salad

Hope Comerford,
Clinton Township, MI

Makes 4 servings

Prep. Time: 5 minutes

leftover chicken, chopped
¾ cup salsa
¾ cup sour cream
1 head of lettuce of your choice, chopped (romaine would work great)

Additional Toppings:
crushed tortilla chips
diced avocado
chopped tomatoes

1. Warm the leftover chicken if you choose, or leave it cold.
2. Mix together the salsa and sour cream.
3. Place chopped lettuce in a bowl or dish, top with desired amount of leftover chicken and pour some of the salsa-sour cream mixture over the top.
4. Add any of the additional toppings you wish.

Au Gratin Green Beans

Donna Lantgen, Rapid City, SD

Makes 6 servings

Prep. Time: 10 minutes
Cooking Time: 3–4 hours
Ideal slow-cooker size: 2-qt.

2 14½-oz. cans green beans, drained
¼ cup diced onions
½ cup cubed Velveeta
¼ cup evaporated milk
1 tsp. flour
½ tsp. salt
dash of pepper
sliced almonds, *optional*

1. Combine all ingredients, except almonds, in slow cooker.
2. Cover. Cook on Low 3–4 hours.
3. Garnish with sliced almonds at serving time, if you wish.

Cookie Divine

Hope Comerford,
Clinton Township, MI

Makes 8–12 servings

Prep. Time: 20 minutes
Cooking Time: 3–5 hours
Ideal slow-cooker size: 6½- to 7-qt.

Cookie Ingredients:
2¼ cups all-purpose flour
1 tsp. baking soda
1 tsp. salt
2 sticks butter, softened
¾ cup granulated sugar
¾ cup packed brown sugar

Seeds scraped from 1 vanilla
bean (or 1 Tbsp. vanilla
extract)
2 large eggs

Brownie Ingredients:
⅔ cup flour
⅔ cup sugar
⅓ cup unsweetened cocoa
powder
¼ tsp. salt
⅔ cup cream
1 stick butter, melted
1 egg, slightly beaten

Seeds scraped from 1 vanilla
bean (or 1 Tbsp. vanilla
extract)
sea salt *optional*
whipped topping, *optional*

For the cookie batter:

1. In a bowl, mix together
the flour, baking soda and
salt.

2. In a separate bowl, mix
together the butter, sugar,
brown sugar, seeds from one
vanilla bean, and eggs.

3. Add your dry ingredients
slowly to your wet
ingredients until well mixed.

4. Spray the crock with
nonstick spray and spread the
cookie batter evenly in the
bottom of the crock.

For the brownie batter:

5. In a bowl, mix together
the flour, sugar, cocoa
powder, and salt.

6. In a separate bowl, mix
together the cream, butter,
egg, and seeds from of 1
vanilla bean.

7. Slowly add your dry
ingredients to your wet
ingredients.

8. Pour your brownie batter
on top of the cookie batter
that is already in your crock.

9. Take a knife and slowly
move the tip through the
batter in an S pattern,
dragging the batters through
each other to "marbleize"
your batter.

10. Cook on Low for 3–5
hours. Keep an eye on it;
when the middle is set, turn
it off.

11. Scoop it out into bowls
while warm and top with
a little bit of sea salt and a
dollop of whipped topping, or
let it cool and serve at room
temperature with a little bit of
sea salt.

Tip: This is also fantastic cold.
You can stick it in the fridge
and sprinkle a tiny bit of sea
salt on it before serving.

WINTER

Week 12

THIS WEEK'S

Menu

Sunday: Wine Tender Roast

Monday: Santa Fe Stew

Tuesday: Cranberry-Orange Turkey Breast

Wednesday: Fruited Turkey and Yams

Thursday: 10-Layer Slow-Cooker Dish

Friday: Hamburger Soup

Saturday: Company Seafood Pasta

Recommended Side Dish: Yummy Spinach

Special Dessert: Festive Applesauce

Shopping List

PROTEIN

4–5-lb. beef chuck roast

3–4-lb. turkey breast

2 lbs. ground beef

½ lb. crabmeat, or imitation
  flaked crabmeat

½ lb. bay scallops

1 lb. medium shrimp

FROZEN

½ cup frozen corn

3 10-oz. boxes frozen spinach

DAIRY and REFRIGERATED

½ cup orange juice

½ cup apple cider

2 cups sour cream

2 cups cottage cheese

3 eggs

1½ cups grated cheddar
  cheese

3 cups shredded Monterey
  Jack cheese

6 Tbsp. butter

PRODUCE

1 cup thinly sliced onions

1 large onion

1 cup chopped onion

1 medium onion

3 carrots

½ cup chopped carrots

3 zucchini squash

1 large yam, or sweet potato

3–4 medium potatoes

½ cup chopped celery

⅛ cup chopped fresh
  parsley

1 cup chopped apple

8 medium apples

5 pears

Download this shopping list to your smartphone!
(x.co/ShopList)

1 cup fresh cranberries, or
  frozen

1 lemon

2 tsp. orange zest

fresh ginger

CANNED/DRY GOODS

14½-oz. can diced tomatoes

14½-oz. can diced tomatoes

14½-oz. can green beans, or
  1 lb. frozen

14½-oz. can corn, or 1 lb.
  frozen

15-oz. can corn

15-oz. can peas

4-oz. can diced green chilies

14-oz. can whole berry
  cranberry sauce

8-oz. can tomato sauce

4 oz. tomato paste

10¾-oz. can fat-free,
  low-sodium cream of
  mushroom soup

½ cup chopped mixed dried
  fruit

½ cup orange marmalade

DO YOU HAVE THESE ON HAND?

salt

pepper

ground cumin

dried basil

garlic powder

onion powder

ground cinnamon

ground nutmeg

ground cloves

dried parsley flakes

8 cloves garlic

1 tsp. chopped garlic

2 beef bouillon cubes

3 cups beef broth

flour

dark brown sugar

SPIRITS

1½ cups red wine

Wine Tender Roast

Rose Hankins, Stevensville, MD

Makes 6–8 servings

Prep. Time: 10 minutes
Cooking Time: 6–8 hours
Ideal slow-cooker size: 4- or 5-qt.

4–5-lb. beef chuck roast
1 cup thinly sliced onion
1 cup chopped apple, peeled, or unpeeled
6 cloves garlic, chopped
1½ cups red wine
salt and pepper, to taste

1. Grease interior of slow-cooker crock.
2. Put roast in slow cooker. Layer onion, apple, and garlic on top of roast.
3. Carefully pour wine over roast without disturbing its toppings.
4. Sprinkle with salt and pepper.
5. Cover. Cook on Low 6–8 hours, or until instant-read meat thermometer registers 145°F when stuck into center of roast.
6. Remove meat from crock. Allow to stand for 10 minutes. Then slice or shred and serve.

Santa Fe Stew

Jeanne Allen, Rye, CO

Makes 6 servings

Prep. Time: 20 minutes
Cooking Time: 4–5 hours
Ideal slow-cooker size: 5-qt.

leftover roast meat, chopped
1 large onion, diced
2 cloves garlic, minced
1½ cups water
1 Tbsp. dried parsley flakes
2 beef bouillon cubes
1 tsp. ground cumin
½ tsp. salt
3 carrots, sliced
14½-oz. can diced tomatoes
14½-oz. can green beans, drained, or 1 lb. frozen green beans
14½-oz. can corn, drained, or 1 lb. frozen corn
4-oz. can diced green chilies
3 zucchini, diced, *optional*

1. Grease interior of slow-cooker crock.
2. Place all ingredients, except zucchini, into slow cooker.
3. Cover. Cook on Low 4–5 hours, or until meat is tender and vegetables are as tender as you like them.

4. One hour before end of cooking time, stir in diced zucchini, if you want to include it.

Cranberry-Orange Turkey Breast

Lee Ann Hazlett, Delavan, WI

Makes 9 servings

Prep. Time: 20 minutes
Cooking Time: 3½–8 hours
Ideal slow-cooker size: 6-qt.

½ cup orange marmalade
14-oz. can whole berry
  cranberry sauce
2 tsp. orange zest, grated
3–4-lb. turkey breast

1. Combine marmalade, cranberry sauce, and zest in a bowl.
2. Place turkey breast in slow cooker and pour half the orange-cranberry mixture over turkey.
3. Cover. Cook on Low 7–8 hours or on High 3½–4 hours, until turkey juices run clear.
4. Add remaining half of orange-cranberry mixture for last half hour of cooking.
5. Remove turkey to warm platter and allow to rest for 15 minutes before slicing.
6. Serve with orange-cranberry sauce.

Fruited Turkey and Yams

Jean M. Butzer, Batavia, NY

Makes 4 servings

Prep. Time: 30–40 minutes
Cooking Time: 3–8 hours
Ideal slow-cooker size: 5- or 6-qt.

1 large yam, or sweet potato, cut crosswise into ½-inch-thick slices
leftover turkey, chopped
½ cup chopped mixed dried fruit
1 tsp. chopped garlic
½ tsp. salt
¼ tsp. pepper
½ cup orange juice
⅛ cup chopped fresh parsley

1. Place yam slices in the slow cooker with leftover turkey on top.
2. Sprinkle with dried fruit, garlic, salt, and pepper.
3. Gently pour orange juice over top, being careful not to disturb fruit and seasonings.
4. Cover. Cook on Low 4–5 hours, or until the potatoes are cooked through.
5. Sprinkle with parsley before serving.

10-Layer Slow-Cooker Dish

Norma Saltzman, Shickley, NE

Makes 4–5 servings

Prep. Time: 25 minutes
Cooking Time: 3–6 hours
Ideal slow-cooker size: 5-qt.

2 lbs. ground beef, browned
3–4 medium potatoes, thinly
  sliced
1 medium onion, thinly sliced
½ tsp. salt
½ tsp. black pepper
15-oz. can corn, undrained
15-oz. can peas, undrained
¼ cup water
10¾-oz. can fat-free, low-
  sodium cream of mushroom
  soup

1. Brown ground beef in
nonstick skillet. Set aside
1 lb. in the refrigerator for
tomorrow's dinner. Then
create the following layers in
the slow cooker.
2. Layer 1: one-fourth of
potatoes, mixed with one-half
the onion, salt, and pepper.
3. Layer 2: half-can of corn.
4. Layer 3: one-fourth of
potatoes.
5. Layer 4: half-can of peas.
6. Layer 5: one-fourth of
potatoes, mixed with one-half
the onions, salt, and pepper.
7. Layer 6: remaining corn.
8. Layer 7: remaining
potatoes.
9. Layer 8: remaining peas
and water.
10. Layer 9: ground beef.
11. Layer 10: soup.
12. Cover. Cook on High
3–4 hours or on Low 6 hours.

Hamburger Soup

Hope Comerford,
Clinton Township, MI

Makes 4–6 servings

Prep. Time: 15 minutes
Cooking Time: 6–7 hours
Ideal slow-cooker size: 5-qt.

Leftover ground beef
3 cups beef broth
14½-oz. can diced tomatoes
8-oz. can tomato sauce
4 oz. tomato paste
1 cup chopped onion
½ cup chopped carrots
½ cup chopped celery
½ cup frozen corn
1 tsp. salt
1 tsp. dried basil
½ tsp. garlic powder
½ tsp. onion powder

1. Place all ingredients in
the slow cooker.
2. Cover and cook on Low
for 6–7 hours.

Company Seafood Pasta

Jennifer Yoder Sommers,
Harrisonburg, VA

Makes 4–6 servings

Prep. Time: 15 minutes
Cooking Time: 1–2 hours
Ideal slow-cooker size: 4-qt.

2 cups sour cream
3 cups shredded Monterey
  Jack cheese
2 Tbsp. butter, melted
½ lb. crabmeat, or imitation
  flaked crabmeat
⅛ tsp. pepper
½ lb. bay scallops, lightly
  cooked
1 lb. medium shrimp, cooked
  and peeled

1. Combine sour cream,
cheese, and butter in slow
cooker.
2. Stir in remaining
ingredients.
3. Cover. Cook on Low 1–2
hours.

Serving Suggestion: Serve
immediately over linguine.
Garnish with fresh parsley.

Yummy Spinach

Jeanette Oberholtzer,
Manheim, PA

Makes 8 servings

Prep. Time: 10 minutes
Cooking Time: 2½–3 hours
Standing Time: 15 minutes
Ideal slow-cooker size: 4-qt.

3 10-oz. boxes frozen
  spinach, thawed and
  squeezed dry
2 cups cottage cheese
1½ cups grated cheddar
  cheese
3 eggs
¼ cup flour
1 tsp. salt
4 Tbsp. butter, melted

1. Grease interior of slow-cooker crock.
2. Mix together all ingredients in the slow cooker.
3. Cover. Cook on Low 2½–3 hours, or until the dish sets up and is no longer jiggly in the center.
4. Let stand for 15 minutes so the cheeses can firm before cutting and serving.

Festive Applesauce

Dawn Day, Westminster, CA

Makes 12 servings

Prep. Time: 25 minutes
Cooking Time: 6 hours
Ideal slow-cooker size: 5-qt.

8 medium apples, mixed
  varieties, peeled and cubed
5 pears, peeled and cubed
1 cup fresh or frozen
  cranberries
1-inch piece fresh ginger root,
  minced
3 Tbsp. dark brown sugar
½ cup apple cider
3 tsp. ground cinnamon
¼ tsp. ground nutmeg
¼ tsp. ground cloves
pinch salt
juice and zest of 1 lemon

1. Grease interior of slow-cooker crock.
2. Combine all ingredients in slow cooker except lemon zest and juice.
3. Cover and cook on Low 6 hours, or until apples and pears are soft and falling apart.
4. Stir in lemon zest and juice. Serve hot, warm, or chilled.

WINTER

Week 13

THIS WEEK'S
Menu

Sunday: Corned Beef with Cabbage, Carrots, and Red Potatoes
Monday: Corned Beef Hash
Tuesday: Reuben in a Crock
Wednesday: Lamb Chops
Thursday: Lamb Stew
Friday: Shepherd's Pie
Saturday: Quick and Easy Spaghetti

Recommended Side Dish: Irish Soda Bread
Special Dessert: Harvey Wallbanger Cake

Shopping List

PROTEIN

6-lb. low-sodium corned
  beef brisket
4 lbs. loin lamb chops
1½ lbs. ground pork

DAIRY and REFRIGERATED

1 cup sour cream
2 cups shredded Swiss
  cheese
shredded cheese, for
  garnish
4 Tbsp. butter
1 tsp. margarine
¼ cup fat-free milk
4 eggs
1 cup plain yogurt
1⅓ cups orange juice

PRODUCE

1 head cabbage

3–4 large carrots
6–8 medium carrots
24 oz. baby red potatoes
1 lb. potatoes
3 large potatoes
3 medium potatoes
2 medium onions
5 small onions
1 cup diced onion
½ cup chopped bell pepper
4 ribs celery

CANNED/DRY GOODS

1 lb. sauerkraut
15-oz. can corn
½ of 26-oz. jar spaghetti
  sauce with mushrooms
10¾-oz. can tomato soup
14½-oz. can stewed
  tomatoes
4-oz. can mushrooms

Download this shopping list to your
smartphone!
(x.co/ShopList)

1½ cups Thousand Island
  dressing

12 slices dark rye bread

spaghetti

16-oz. pkg. pound cake mix

3-oz. pkg. vanilla instant
  pudding

**DO YOU HAVE THESE ON
HAND?**

salt

pepper

dried minced onion

dried oregano

dried thyme

garlic powder

cayenne pepper

paprika

chili powder

garlic salt

dried minced garlic

onion salt

Italian seasoning

ground cardamom

2 cloves garlic

2–3 cups chicken stock

flour

1 cup whole wheat flour

baking soda

honey

Worcestershire sauce

vinegar of your choice

oil of your choice

SPIRITS

¾ cup red wine

3 Tbsp. Galliano liqueur

Corned Beef with Cabbage, Carrots, and Red Potatoes

Hope Comerford,
Clinton Township, MI

Makes 8–10 servings

Prep. Time: 10 minutes
Cook Time: 9–10 hours
Ideal slow-cooker size: 7-qt.

6-lb. low-sodium corned beef brisket
1 head of cabbage
3–4 large carrots
24 oz. baby red potatoes
salt, to taste
pepper, to taste
water

1. Place the brisket in the bottom of the crock. It will come with a seasoning packet. Sprinkle the contents of that packet over your brisket.
2. Cover your brisket with water.
3. Place the veggies on and around your brisket.
4. Sprinkle your cabbage with salt and pepper to taste.
5. Cover and cook on Low for 9–10 hours.

Corned Beef Hash

Hope Comerford,
Clinton Township, MI

Makes 4–6 servings

Prep. Time: 10 minutes
Cooking Time: 7–8 hours
Ideal slow-cooker size: 4- to 5-qt.

1 lb. potatoes, peeled and diced
1½–2 cups diced leftover corned beef
1 cup diced onion
½ cup diced bell pepper (whatever color you like)
1 tsp. salt
⅛ tsp. pepper
2–3 cups chicken stock (just enough to cover your ingredients)

1. Place the potatoes, leftover corned beef, onion, bell pepper, salt, and pepper in your crock and stir.
2. Pour in the chicken stock, just until the mixture is just barely submerged.
3. Cook on Low for 7–8 hours.

Tip: If there is too much liquid left, leave the top off for a while and continue to cook, or add some gravy mix granules to thicken.

Reuben in a Crock

Joleen Albrecht, Gladstone, MI

Makes 8–10 servings

Prep. Time: 25–30 minutes
Cooking Time: 4 hours
Ideal slow-cooker size: 5- or 6-qt.

1½ cups Thousand Island salad dressing
1 cup sour cream
1 Tbsp. dried minced onion
12 slices dark rye bread, cubed, *divided*
1 lb. sauerkraut, drained
1½ cups leftover corned beef, cut thin
2 cups shredded Swiss cheese
½ stick (4 Tbsp.) butter, melted

1. Grease interior of slow-cooker crock.
2. In a bowl, mix together dressing, sour cream, and minced onion. Set aside.
3. Place half the bread cubes in crock.
4. Top with sauerkraut, spread out evenly over bread.
5. Add layer of corned beef, distributed evenly over sauerkraut.
6. Spread dressing mixture over corned beef.
7. Scatter shredded cheese over top.
8. Top with remaining bread cubes.
9. Drizzle with melted butter.
10. Cover and cook on Low 3½ hours, or until mixture is heated through.
11. Remove cover. Cook on Low 30 more minutes to allow moisture to escape.

Lamb Chops

Shirley Sears, Tiskilwa, IL

Makes 6–8 servings

Prep. Time: 10 minutes
Cooking Time: 4–6 hours
Ideal slow-cooker size: 5-qt.

1 medium onion, sliced
1 tsp. dried oregano
½ tsp. dried thyme
½ tsp. garlic powder
¼ tsp. salt
⅛ tsp. pepper
4 lbs. loin lamb chops
2 cloves garlic, minced
¼ cup water

1. Place onion in slow cooker.
2. In a small bowl, combine oregano, thyme, garlic powder, salt, and pepper. Rub over lamb chops. Place chops in slow cooker.
3. Top chops with garlic.
4. Pour water down alongside cooker, so as not to disturb rub and garlic on chops.
5. Cover. Cook on Low 4–6 hours, or until chops are tender but not dry.

Lamb Stew

Dottie Schmidt, Kansas City, MO

Makes 6 servings

Prep. Time: 15 minutes
Cooking Time: 7–8 hours
Ideal slow-cooker size: 5-qt.

2 tsp. salt
¼ tsp. pepper
¼ cup flour
2 cups water

¾ cup red wine
¼ tsp. garlic powder
2 tsp. Worcestershire sauce
6–8 medium carrots, sliced
4 small onions, quartered
4 ribs celery, sliced
3 medium potatoes, diced
leftover lamb, chopped

1. Place salt, pepper, and flour into slow cooker and briskly whisk in water and wine until smooth.
2. Add all remaining ingredients except the leftover lamb and stir until well mixed.
3. Cover. Cook on Low 7–8 hours, adding the lamb the last hour of cooking.

Shepherd's Pie

Melanie Thrower, McPherson, KS

Makes 6 servings

Prep. Time: 40 minutes
Cooking Time: 3–4 hours
Ideal slow-cooker size: 3- or 4-qt.

1½ lbs. ground pork
1 Tbsp. vinegar of your choice
¾ tsp. salt
¼ tsp. cayenne pepper
1 tsp. paprika
¼ tsp. dried oregano
¼ tsp. black pepper
1 tsp. chili powder
1 small onion, chopped
15-oz. can corn, drained

Topping:
3 large potatoes, unpeeled
¼ cup fat-free milk
1 tsp. margarine
¼ tsp. salt
dash of pepper
shredded cheese, for garnish

1. Brown the pork in a pan. Put away half of this for tomorrow's recipe.
2. Combine remaining pork, vinegar, salt, hot pepper, paprika, oregano, pepper, chili powder, and onion and spread it in the bottom of the crock.
2. Spread corn over meat.
3. Boil potatoes until soft. Mash with milk, butter, ¼ tsp. salt, and dash of pepper. Spread over meat and corn.
4. Cover. Cook on Low 3–4 hours. Sprinkle top with cheese a few minutes before serving.

Quick and Easy Spaghetti

Beverly Getz, Warriors Mark, PA

Makes 6–8 servings

Prep. Time: 30 minutes
Cooking Time: 3–4 hours
Ideal slow-cooker size: 4-qt.

Remaining browned ground pork
1 medium onion, chopped
½ 26-oz. jar spaghetti sauce with mushrooms
10¾-oz. can tomato soup
14½-oz. can stewed tomatoes
4-oz. can mushrooms, undrained
½ tsp. garlic powder
½ tsp. garlic salt
½ tsp. minced dried garlic
½ tsp. onion salt
½ tsp. Italian seasoning
spaghetti

1. Add all ingredients to the slow cooker and stir.
2. Cover. Cook on Low 3–4 hours.
3. Cook spaghetti according to package directions. Serve sauce over cooked pasta.

Irish Soda Bread

Phyllis Good, Lancaster, PA

Makes 8–10 servings

Prep. Time: 30 minutes
Cooking Time: 2–3 hours
Ideal slow-cooker size: 5-qt.

1 cup whole wheat flour
1 cup plus 1 Tbsp. all-purpose flour, *divided*
½ tsp. salt
1 tsp. baking soda
¼ tsp. ground cardamom
1 egg
1 Tbsp. honey
1 cup plain yogurt

1. In a mixing bowl, stir together whole wheat flour, 1 cup all-purpose flour, salt, baking soda, and cardamom.
2. In a small bowl, beat the egg well. Add honey and yogurt to the egg and beat again.
3. Pour egg mixture into dry ingredients. Stir with a large spoon.
4. Clean the dough off the spoon and get ready to knead! Knead the dough for a few minutes, until it becomes satiny.
5. Place a large piece of parchment paper on the counter— it needs to be large enough so you can grab the corners and lift the bread out of the slow cooker when it's done.
6. Shape the dough into a round, low loaf. Set it in the middle of the parchment paper.
7. Use a sharp knife to make a large, shallow cross on the top of the loaf. Sprinkle the top of the loaf especially in the cross indentation with the remaining 1 Tbsp. flour.
8. Lift up the parchment paper, carrying the loaf in it

like a sling, and place in slow cooker. Prop lid open at one end with a wooden spoon handle or chopstick.

9. Cook on High for 2–3 hours, until loaf is firm when tapped and tester comes out clean when inserted in the middle. Use the parchment paper to lift the finished loaf out of the cooker. Allow to cool 10 minutes or more before slicing. Best served warm, or toast it on day two.

Harvey Wallbanger Cake

Roseann Wilson,
Albuquerque, NM

Makes 8 servings

Prep. Time: 10 minutes
Cooking Time: 2½–3½ hours
Ideal slow-cooker size: 4- to 5-qt.

Cake:
16-oz. pkg. pound cake mix
⅓ cup vanilla instant pudding
   (reserve rest of pudding
   from 3-oz. pkg. for glaze)
¼ cup oil of your choice
3 eggs
2 Tbsp. Galliano liqueur
⅔ cup orange juice

Glaze:
remaining pudding mix
⅔ cup orange juice
1 Tbsp. Galliano liqueur

1. Mix together all ingredients for cake. Beat for 3 minutes. Pour batter into greased and floured bread or cake pan that will fit into your slow cooker. Cover pan.

2. Bake in covered slow cooker on High 2½–3½ hours.

3. Invert cake onto serving platter.

4. Mix together glaze ingredients. Spoon over cake.

Index

Index **435**

Index **439**